C000260578

THE INTELLIGENT ORGANISATION

The *Intelligent Organisation* proposes a radical way of designing organisations to capitalise on the potential offered by contemporary information capability. Integrated, coherent information is taken as a competitive advantage enabling synthesis of behaviour and processes in an organisation designed backwards from its customers to achieve desired outcomes. An Intelligent Organisation uses information to drive learning and adaptation at the level of individuals, tasks, processes and the whole organisation, to deliver transformational changes in business performance.

This fully updated second edition explores how to enable this change through systemic reinvention. Drawing on proven organisational applications exploiting data, information and management science, and grounded in tested theory, this book is not about incremental improvement but about fundamentally rethinking the whole. Building on the first edition, two chapters have been added to apply the ideas of the Intelligent Organisation to the individual as well as to the nation. Further discussion on the current issues around technology and ethics have been incorporated, as well as review questions and improved pedagogy. The text contains updated case studies throughout and is accompanied by a dedicated website, www.intelligentorganisation.com, with support materials for lecturers.

Uniquely bridging the gap between information systems and organisational behaviour, *The Intelligent Organisation* will be of particular significance to master's and undergraduate students of Information Systems, Knowledge Management and Organisational Theory.

John Beckford is a partner in Beckford Consulting and Visiting Professor both in the Department of Civil, Environmental and Geomatic Engineering at University College London, UK, and in the Centre for Information Management, School of Business and Economics, Loughborough University, UK.

If your aspiration as CEO is to capture and exploit as much value as you can from what your organisation knows but you are unsure how to achieve it, read Dr. Beckford's book. Based on practical experience but well-grounded in theory, these ideas will help you to achieve a more purposeful and valuable enterprise and to discover how being an intelligent organisation demands more than knowing what you know; it is about how to generate purposeful value by making good decisions and executing agile leadership.

Brian Collins *CB, FREng, Professor of Engineering Policy, Deputy Convenor of UKCRIC, Department of Civil, Environmental and Geomatic Engineering, UCL*

This is a challenging book: it calls for leaders to face the need to make their organisations "intelligent" – and in doing so engages with a crucial issue of our age: using data to create the information needed for decision-making while at the same time learning in such a way as to change the very organisation involved in creating the data. John Beckford illustrates his theses about how this can be done with examples from a wider range of examples and accepts the challenge of trying to apply the methodology to the individual (himself) and to the nation.

David Nussbaum, *Chief Executive Officer, The Elders Foundation, London*

Professor Beckford's revised and extended second edition of *The Intelligent Organisation* should be required reading for leaders at all levels in 21st-century businesses. He reiterates the central thesis of the need to think systemically about the way a business works in order to put information at the heart of providing value – both for customers and for the business. The text is accessible, with a balanced blend of theory and practical examples drawn from Beckford's eclectic consultancy work, and occasionally lightened with apposite comment, opinion and a certain black humour. More importantly the practical models, insights and guidance provide a series of clear approaches to the very challenging issues facing all businesses in today's rapidly changing environment.

Jim Johnson, *Director, Arup Digital Leader for UK, India, Middle East & Africa*

John Beckford's achievement here is threefold. First he makes systemic thinking accessible, while holding the reader to really consider systems in all their necessary complexity. Second he layers the work, interweaving a practical workbook of how we should do things with a philosophical exploration of why we should do them that way. I like particularly the way he emphasises the recursive nature of systems. Third he brings a sense of optimism and energy showing how, by thinking systemically and openly, we could do so much better.

Ronan Palmer, *Associate Director, E3G*

Professor Beckford's second edition of *The Intelligent Organisation* is substantially revised, adding two additional chapters and case reports including updates and progress on the cases from the first edition. The book gives an academic basis for the way of examining an organisation at all levels with practical application of the theory with real life examples both in the public and private sector. I particularly liked the emphasis on defining the core purpose of an organisation together with the customer focus being prevalent throughout all the chapters. These values are often neglected in the chaos that often occurs in a busy, ever-changing organisation. Today's politicians would be well advised to read the chapter on the Intelligent Nation! The chapter "The Individual as Intelligent Organisation" is a welcome addition. This book is well written and very accessible to the reader. This is essential reading for those who are serious about improving the way organisations perform.

Peter McDougall, *Honorary Clinical Professor,*
University of Melbourne and The Royal Children's Hospital,
Melbourne, Senior Clinical Advisor, Consultative Council,
Obstetric and Paediatric Mortality and Morbidity,
Department of Health and Human Services, Victoria

In the second edition of *Intelligent Organisation*, Beckford further crystallises the three principles of process, behaviour and information, providing a comprehensive understanding of how all three concepts are intertwined to form an intelligent organisation. He has again written an insightful study into organisations and provides the tools and methods to diagnose your business, rethink and then apply a systematic approach to addressing problems. Using vignettes and cases studies, a great addition, he brings the theory alive. This book certainly leaves you reflecting that in order to survive in an ever-changing world, you need to have courage to transform your business.

This is a must-read for any social entrepreneurs interested in embracing change and moving away from traditional ways of working!

Kuljit Sandhu, *CEO, Rise Mutual CIC*

The second edition of John's excellent book shows how, although we live in the "information age", we continue to run "machine age" organisations. In the book he gives plenty of ideas and advice on how to create an "intelligent organisation", through the individuals in it being able to learn and adapt, using a series of continuous learning cycles enable by value adding the use of information technology. Value, quite rightly, is a major theme – a big deal – throughout the book.

The book is well illustrated with case studies and vignettes from John's extensive and wide-ranging experience and research. And it is also well referenced.

John Oakland, *Emeritus Professor of Business Excellence and Quality,*
Leeds University Business School, Chairman, The Oakland Group

This second edition of John Beckford's masterful book *The Intelligent Organisation* adds new depth to what was already an exceptional work. Of primary relevance to consultants, academics and students of operations and information management, it is also of potential interest and use to anyone either working in or managing in an organisation in the 21st century (or indeed, and perhaps particularly so, for those managing their career in a self-employed capacity). Previous chapters have been reworked to make them more accessible to all, as well as to bring case studies fully up-to-date (and some important new cases have been added); in addition, there are new chapters on the Intelligent Nation and on the intelligent individual, and a new chapter section on the intelligent manager. These substantially broaden the relevance and remit of the book, enabling us to see not only how public administration and governance need to change, but how we as individuals can take mastery of our own futures.

Louise Cooke, *Professor of Information and*
Knowledge Management, School of Business and Economics,
Loughborough University

Provides great insight on how we can get far more value out of the information we have around us.

Jonathan Randall, *Civil Aerospace Finance – Business*
Planning & Forecasting Data Governance Lead, Rolls-Royce plc

THE INTELLIGENT ORGANISATION

Driving Systemic Change with Information

Second Edition

John Beckford

Routledge
Taylor & Francis Group

LONDON AND NEW YORK

Second edition published 2020
by Routledge
2 Park Square, Milton Park, Abingdon, Oxon, OX14 4RN

and by Routledge
52 Vanderbilt Avenue, New York, NY 10017

Routledge is an imprint of the Taylor & Francis Group, an informa business

First edition published by Routledge 2015

British Library Cataloguing-in-Publication Data
A catalogue record for this book is available from the British Library

Library of Congress Cataloging-in-Publication Data
Names: Beckford, John, 1958- author.
Title: The intelligent organisation : driving systemic change with information / John Beckford.
Description: Second edition. | Abingdon, Oxon ; New York, NY : Routledge, 2020. |
    Includes bibliographical references and index.
Identifiers: LCCN 2019024206 (print) | LCCN 2019024207 (ebook) |
    ISBN 9781138368484 (hbk) | ISBN 9781138368491 (pbk) | ISBN 9780429429200 (ebk)
Subjects: LCSH: Information technology—Management. | Knowledge management. |
    Organizational effectiveness.
Classification: LCC HD30.2 .B443 2020 (print) | LCC HD30.2 (ebook) |
    DDC 658.4/038—dc23
LC record available at https://lccn.loc.gov/2019024206
LC ebook record available at https://lccn.loc.gov/2019024207

ISBN: 978-1-138-36848-4 (hbk)
ISBN: 978-1-138-36849-1 (pbk)
ISBN: 978-0-429-42920-0 (ebk)

Typeset in Bembo
by Apex CoVantage, LLC

Printed and bound by CPI Group (UK) Ltd, Croydon, CR0 4YY

Intelligent:

Able to initiate or modify action in the light of ongoing events

Collins Paperback English Dictionary, 1992

CONTENTS

VIGNETTES

FIGURES

ACKNOWLEDGEMENTS

This book was inspired by three groups of people. First are those who have gone before; their insights and wisdom created the opportunity for a new question to be asked. Notable amongst these is Stafford Beer, whose work inspired my initial research and on whose foundations this work is built. Second are those in the many organisations who have allowed me the privilege of working with them, testing theory in practice on them and their organisations, helping me to understand what appears to work and why. Third are the clients, consultants and academics on whose support and friendship I have drawn to test practice in theory, to understand how the practical pursuit of increasing effectiveness can be embedded in our theoretical understanding of organisations.

In updating and changing the case studies I have drawn upon the support of a number of individuals who have worked with me in the development and application of the ideas. Many of the case studies have been written in partnership with individuals involved in and affected by them, and I am grateful to

- Richard Berry, Assistant Chief Constable, NPCC Lead for the Investigatory Powers Act Capabilities
- Mark Chadwick, Director of Business Services, Fusion21
- Andy Champness, CEO, Office of the Police and Crime Commissioner for West Mercia
- Dr. Tom Dolan, Senior Research Associate, UKCRIC Coordination Node & University College London
- Rev. Keith Elford, Director, Elford Consulting
- Dr. Charles House, Medical Director, University College Hospitals NHS Foundation Trust
- Catherine Lawes

- Richard Parry, CEO, Canal and River Trust
- James Robbins, Chief Customer Officer and Chief Information Officer, ArrowXL

for their great contributions both to those studies and for their comments on and contributions to certain chapters.

Mary Pounder took on the task of making sense of and drawing all of the diagrams.

A diverse group of friendly but demanding critics reviewed the proposal and offered support and challenge in equal measure. The work is much better for their contributions. The mistakes, errors and omissions are all mine.

Finally, as always, my thanks to Sara, Paul and Matthew, whose unending task it is to keep me grounded.

PREFACE TO THE FIRST EDITION

Living in the information age, we continue to run machine age organisations. For all our advances in technology we still focus inward on making the machine work instead of outward on the value exchange with the customer. The result? We waste lots of money pursuing nugatory improvements. As Eliot (1934) asks in *The Rock*, "Where is the wisdom we have lost in knowledge, where is the knowledge we have lost in information?" We have been in thrall to technology since the early 1960s. Technology has delivered significant gains in performance, but those gains have been constrained by our adherence to a conventional form of organisation. We have at our disposal the technological means to transform our organisations, but without radical change in the way we comprehend information we will remain trapped in machine age thinking. Einstein (1946) suggests (in at least one version) that "You cannot solve a problem from the same consciousness that created it. You must see the world anew". Machine age organisations are doomed to failure in a rapidly changing world. An intelligent organisation exploits the value of information and releases the capability of its people.

We need to invest ourselves in a new way of thinking, to understand the flaws in current practices and to clearly see the unrealised value. There is a compelling business case for change; simply appreciating the latent value of information will allow us to realise potential for people and organisations. We continually tinker with our machine age organisations to keep them running. How much better would it be if we designed them so that they modify themselves? If we built in capability for adaptation rather than bolting it on?

The machine age organisation is functionally arranged and siloed. The Intelligent Organisation is systemic. It is made up of four interacting, interdependent parts, and those interactions generate emergent properties, properties which belong only to the whole not to the parts. Those four parts are a value-generating system, a value-enabling system, an identity system (for maintaining a shared purpose) synthesised through the fourth part, an information system. That allows a trialogue (a conversation in three parts) ensuring that the organisation communicates with itself and its environment and enables it to do three things simultaneously:

- manage its present (efficiently carry out value-generating activity);
- create its future (enable new value by anticipating, influencing and responding to changing needs);
- nurture its identity (maintain alignment of its purpose, people and processes).

Every organisation exists for a reason. It is purposeful in pursuing its own sustainability and in fulfilling the needs of its customers. It fulfils that purpose through interactions with its customers which deliver value to both them and itself: the relationship is dynamic and reciprocal, potentially symbiotic. Each organisation must understand what it does that provides value to its customers, what need it fulfils, what outcomes it seeks to achieve and focus on them and, as Wiener (1948) suggests, "the importance of information and communication as mechanisms of organisation proceeds beyond the individual into the community".

Designed backwards from the customer, the value-generating system is comprised of the end-to-end processes (together with their embedded tasks and procedures) that deliver goods and services. It is self-regulating, self-aware at the level of its processes, using information about its performance to control and improve itself in a known environment. This self-regulating structure is called a "homeostat" and is a core idea in the transformation. Its job is to ensure that we do things right.

The value-generating system is the customer of the value-enabling system which provides resources to support and enable it. It does this by understanding, anticipating and influencing both the organisation itself and what is happening in the world outside it. It enables its adaptation to ensure survival. The value-enabling system renders the whole organisation self-regulating and self-aware. It uses information about the performance of all the value-generating activities and about the unknown or problematic environment of the organisation to steer it towards the future. Custodian of strategy, its job is to ensure that we do right things.

These distinct functions combine to constitute a logical hierarchy based on information rather than positional or functional power. The whole is unified through the shared purpose, a common sense of identity amongst the human actors which needs to be nurtured and through which people's different perspectives and understanding can be reconciled. That whole is synthesised through an information system which has both hard and soft dimensions. The hard dimension is quantitative, addressing objective characteristics. The soft dimension is qualitative, addressing cultural and social characteristics.

In a logical hierarchy based on information, we also need to address the question of autonomy. Control is distributed throughout the organisation; decisions are made where the information is available, and, to enable responsiveness, that needs to be close to the customer. The information available to the value-generating system is constrained (it can only see its own part), whereas that available to the value-enabling system provides a view of the whole. It is therefore essential to design appropriate autonomy into the organisation so that freedom to do things right is preserved at the process level whilst the prerogative to do right things is exercised at the whole organisational level in a manner consistent with the shared purpose and values.

Now, if all that has been said so far is going to work then we need to provide accurate, timely information in an appropriate format to the human actors in the organisation. As the Joseph Rowntree Reform Trust (2009) suggested, "If you think IT is the solution to your problems, then you don't understand IT and you don't understand your problem either". The information system must itself be designed backwards from the (highly distributed) decisions that need to be made through-out the organisation so that it does not generate a costly and inefficient internal "reporting" industry. At the operational level it must filter and segregate data to provide only that information which is required at each decision point, while at the strategic level it must aggregate, collate and interpret data to enable longer term decisions. Only in this way can the information system and the people have requisite variety to make useful decisions. In essence the Intelligent Organisation is defined by the way it uses information, and the organisation and information architecture need to be isomorphic images of each other.

In developing the organisational architecture, applying the notion of the home-ostat, distributing decisions and creating an information system that supports all of that, we have to a large extent embedded in the organisation the essentials of performance management. It is self-regulating, aware of its "self" in relation to its environment and has capability for adaptation built in throughout. Nonetheless, there remains a need to explore how we should manage the performance of the whole. This is a paradox: we have built autonomy into the architecture, and now we need to control it. That requires a deeper understanding of what we mean by performance, a richer understanding of how information can help us to understand and trace the roots of under- or overperformance and how we need to engage peo-ple in decision-making. We also need to reconcile the short- and long-term aspects of performance from which may arise tension.

All that has been said up to this point can be addressed to any organisation from the ultra-large conglomerate to the individual (people are organisations too). The public sector, however, requires some additional consideration. Challenged as they are in most countries with the demand to "do more for less", public sector organi-sations operate under different constraints and conditions to organisations in the private sector, and those affect both how we can think about them and how the challenges can be addressed.

All that thinking is fine, but the point of thinking about organisations, the pur-pose of this book, is to enable us to address their challenges. So, having started by understanding the information challenge and explored how very differently we can think about organisations, we finish by exploring how we might take action to change them, to realise the Intelligent Organisation.

Mature economies struggle to deliver growth (increase in the total value of the economy), and mature organisations fight to increase productivity (increase in the efficiency of use of all types of resources). Meanwhile developing economies and developing organisations are mimicking the behaviour of both. Rather than proposing and developing a new way of doing things, they are replicating established practices with success often enabled by lower cost labour rather than substantial innovation.

If, as is often attributed to Einstein, "insanity means doing the same thing over and over again and expecting different results", then perhaps many of us are trapped in an insanity of tradition − following well-trodden paths, seeking and finding marginal, incremental improvements but remaining closed to the possibility of real innovation. Finding it easier to remain within "what is" and complain about it, we perhaps lack the insight or the courage to consider "what could be" and embrace it.

The Intelligent Organisation is offered as a way out of this trap.

PREFACE TO THE SECOND EDITION

Opening the first edition of *The Intelligent Organisation*, I wrote, "Living in the information age, we continue to run machine age organisations". That line was variously accepted, rejected, repudiated and repeated depending on the experience of the reader. In the intervening years, I have worked with a range of clients in the private, public and third sectors embracing infrastructure, healthcare, social care, policing, education, housing, energy, logistics, asset management and transport. I have worked with chief executives and machine operators, accountants and delivery drivers, planners and mechanics, data scientists, information systems developers and information technologists. My conclusion? That opening line still holds true.

There are numerous organisations whose conversion of data into information for decisions is excellent, where synthesis of people, process and information into a coherent whole underpins great performance. Yet for every organisation that considers itself engaged in "4IR", the Fourth Industrial Revolution (Schwab, 2017) at the cutting edge of so-called big data analytics and leading the advancement of the "Internet of Things" (Greengard, 2015), machine learning (Alpaydin, 2016) and artificial intelligence (Warwick, 2012), there are several others mired in the treacle of unstructured data, failing end-of-life systems and in some cases failing beginning-of-life systems – those which fail on technical grounds or, more commonly, whose costs outweigh their benefits.

Perhaps, constrained by lack of appreciation of the opportunities, by lack of funds for investment or by ignorance or denial of the world changing around them, their approach to management, to data, to information and reporting has not grasped the potential gains from new thinking and emerging technologies. Unless these organisations recognise, comprehend and take action on the information challenge, their efficiency and effectiveness are compromised, their continued existence under severe threat. Doubtful? Consider the impact on global high streets seemingly arising from Internet shopping. Accountants PWC, looking only at retail chains with more than five shops, reported a net reduction of 1123 shops in Britain during the first six months of 2018. [Webref1] It is not just retailing that is changing; the ways that data can be captured, verified, codified and monetised are transforming everything from construction to manufacturing to healthcare.

In parallel, many public service organisations, often under continued financial pressure, are unable or unwilling to invest in information systems and, when they do, are constrained (or perhaps constrain themselves) to opt for "safe" solutions, a slightly better version of what they already have, rather than embracing the radical and innovative. In one day, while writing this, I have had contact with three such organisations.

- The first (healthcare) called to say "our data is wrong", the consequence of poor data capture and reporting design;
- The second (civil administration) sent a report that contained fundamental logic flaws in the relationships between the numbers, which rendered the beautifully presented content meaningless and valueless;
- The third (security) had bought a supposed artificial intelligence application called a "chat bot", which was simply an electronic version of a decision tree yet was probably not as useful.

These cases have arisen because the organisations have disconnected data from the processes that generate and use it, have disconnected the activity of reporting (administration) from the activity of decision-making (management) and have failed to recognise where and how they need to innovate. There is a difference between the competence to present data in a spreadsheet and the competence to construct a meaningful decision model in which the gap between actual and desired performance provides the basis for corrective action. Many organisations and their people are falling behind 4IR at a dramatic rate; the survival of those organisations and the jobs of their employees are threatened.

However, there is a need for individuals and organisations to be intelligent in their acquiescence in the 4IR thinking. Not all new technology adds more value than it does cost, nor is all of it as new as may be claimed, and not all data should be collected, shared or monetised. As much as we collectively need to capitalise on the capabilities being proffered, we need to be wise buyers, sceptical of the claimed benefits and alert to the risks to our privacy and security and that of our customers. As I revise this book just prior to submission, Apple, Google and Facebook are all in the news over data privacy while TSB, a UK high-street bank, has reported substantial losses arising from a problematic investment in technology, causing widespread failures and impairments to its customers.

The traditional yet illusory certainties of centralised command and control structures can no longer suffice. In a world of technology-enabled distributed control, whether through different working practices or distributed ledgers (Tapscott & Tapscott, 2018), with freedom for action at the nearest point of the organisation to its customer, perhaps it is customer activity that drives the management of organisations. Perhaps the wider outcomes achieved for customers outweigh the outputs delivered.

If your organisation and your work are going to survive and thrive in this continuing maelstrom of change, then you must individually and corporately create capacity for rapid adaptation and learning. In a rapidly changing world it must be sufficient to know enough, rather than expect to know everything, and to accept and manage uncertainty and risk in new ways.

In revising the book for this second edition, I have tried to take account of the comments and suggestions arising from readers of the first. Two chapters are added, one applies the ideas of the Intelligent Organisation to the individual and explores how that might help you to be more effective in achieving your aims; the other considers how the ideas might be applied at the level of the nation. The chapter on methodology has been substantially revised; other sections have been moved to improve the flow and reader comprehension. Elsewhere throughout the text the changes have been made for the sake of clarity or explanation, but the substance of the ideas remains the same.

The book uses vignettes and case studies to bring the theory to life, to help explore the challenges and dilemmas and to provide a systemic approach to resolving them. New case studies have been introduced embracing healthcare (University College London Hospital), asset ownership and entertainment (Canal and River Trust), public services (Policing, Public Sector Procurement), energy production, distribution logistics (Arrow XL) and national infrastructure research (UKCRIC).

The Intelligent Organisation synthesises the organisation through the lenses of process, behaviour and information in parallel, giving primacy to none but seeking the optimal balance of the three for each circumstance. It deals with information systems from a business not a technological perspective, recognising that the function of the information system is to provide information for decisions. It emphasises the value of information in pursuit of viability as the primary driver for decisions about all aspects of the information system. This systemic perspective is underpinned by the comprehension that information systems are not themselves purposeful but are enablers of the achievement of organisational objectives. For the Intelligent Organisation, its information systems act as a "nervous system" distributed throughout and aiming to deliver the right information, in the right form, at the right time to the people who need it.

The job of this book is to address two challenges simultaneously. First is to share ideas about how to better enable an organisation to adapt and the individuals within it to learn. Second is to enable generation of increased value from the money spent on information technology. The essence is to think of all organisational and human activity as embedded in a series of connected virtuous learning cycles.

I do not claim to be the first with all of these ideas; I will let you see who and where they stem from. I am able to show you how to make them work!

1

THE INFORMATION CHALLENGE

Introduction

The tsunami of big data flooding through organisations is overwhelming us. Organisations, processes and decision-making commonly adhere to norms developed when instant messaging meant sending a telegram and the telephone was a rare and exotic instrument. We are beyond the once seemingly impossible idea of the paperless office (rarely realised) and are heading towards a world of blockchain (Tapscott, 2018): distributed systems under no single ownership, with data stored securely and anonymously (or so it is claimed). Emerging generations of technology will exacerbate the organisational, informational, practical, legal and moral challenges we face both in sustaining organisations and in preserving some semblance of privacy for the individual. We cannot continue as we are and expect a good outcome.

The revolution in our organisations since the 1940s has been technological, not informational. The development of data processing machines from Colossus in 1943, the first digital programmable computer, to powerful and highly portable devices, contemporary communications capability and emerging fifth generation wireless has been astounding. Jackson (2015), citing Forrester Research, highlighted how the growth in our ability to process, retrieve, store and transmit data is stupendous, while our collective ability to make effective use of it lags far behind: "90% of data stored within a company is not available for analysis".

While, as Kaplan suggests (2015), we are seeing the emergence of "a new generation of systems that rival or exceed human capabilities" for a significant proportion of organisations, the old rules are still being applied. They continue to capture and store data in unstructured, difficult-to-search formats and to file or archive using, let us be gentle for now in what we call them, "flexible" approaches and methods that, in some cases, render the data irretrievable for practical purposes. Such approaches make it ever more difficult for organisations to extract value from the data that they hold let alone claim compliance with legislation such as the Data Protection Act 2018 (UK), the EU GDPR (General Data Protection Regulations) and other privacy requirements that underpin them.[Webref 2]

Pagnamenta, writing in *The Daily Telegraph* (2018), meanwhile speculated on the death of email and its replacement by messaging systems. He stated that 269 billion emails are posted every day, many generated by machines, damaging productivity and with many unanswered. While he reports an average of 121 emails per worker per day, 48% being spam and only a few actually warranting a reply, he also cites a colleague claiming an unread total of over 100,000. To even attempt to read or process that volume of data would be pointless.

Data, as Silver (2012) suggests, is just that. We have too much data when what we need is information, although even an excess of information has been cautioned against in the psychology literature on risk. Information is data which has been filtered, integrated, assimilated, aggregated and contextualised. Critically, data enables confusion, but information enables decisions.

Thinking inside the box?

Technology and technologists are very good data providers; organisations and managers must become very good data converters, interpreters and users. For many people and purposes the delivery technology is often quite irrelevant. What is relevant is the information. It is information that allows us to comprehend things, to understand them, to decide what to do. We need both thinking tools and intelligent organisations to do this with; the "T" in information technology (IT) is predominantly the means of capturing then conveying the valuable thing, the information. Value is what is derived from what we, people, do with the data and information, that is, the thinking, the processes, problem-solving and analytical tools that we apply to and with information. There is vastly more potential information available to us and our organisations than ever before, and that availability will increase, possibly exponentially, in the coming years. It seems to me, though, that we are ill equipped to exploit this potential, either through the software tools of business intelligence (BI) or our human skills and ability in interpreting and understanding it. Collectively we seem to neither appreciate the value of information nor design our organisations to generate value from it.

Relative to the potential offered by information many of our organisations are deeply dysfunctional. Their operating models are rooted in the idea of command and control, the mechanistic, bureaucratic, functional, centralising structures and managers who, frequently, secure decisions through bureaucratic means asserting positional power: "It's my decision. I am in charge". While they are mainly kidding themselves in that respect, for such organisations, much of the money spent on IT has been wasted. Structured and organised in line with "traditional models of organisation" (Beckford, 2017), they are not able to exploit their investment in technologies. Both the hardware and software work; the machines operate with extremely high levels of reliability (greater than six sigma uptime – 99.999%); parts and components are exchangeable, hot-swappable; data is backed-up, mirrored and replicated; millions of messages are transmitted and received with almost no losses.

So, if that is all right, where is the failure?

IT has been attempting to deliver organisational value since the 1960s with the implementation of computerised accounting. Some substantial progress has been made, but, typically, the IT has been retrofitted to the established organisations and structures, not used to create a new organisational paradigm. Technology has commonly been applied to automate tasks previously carried out by people, tasks which can be represented in machine logic (an algorithm or programme) as routine, logical, methodical, number crunching and, relatively, unchanging. Those tasks are not characterised as needing "ideation, creativity and innovation" (Brynjolfsson & McAfee, 2014). Computers can, so far, only work inside the box.

Automation has delivered substantial efficiency gains but has often deliberately and, even more often, unconsciously removed discretion from people in the organisation, particularly those who directly deal with customers. Decision-making travels further up the hierarchy as technology makes more data more available and more rapidly to decision makers. This does not always lead to better decisions being taken but to more decisions being taken further away from the customer, problem source or need. Many organisations are developing IT-enabled, dysfunctionally over-centralised structures, not through intent, desire or need but simply because the information systems enable it. No one notices it happening or thinks to stop it. Collectively we have not re-examined the notion of what it means to "control" an organisation. We have not grasped that, particularly for service organisations, performance is subjective, an interpretation of events. When the service is created and consumed on the fly, the quality of the service rests in the human interaction not in the machine process. That cannot be controlled by an automaton, it requires people and judgement. Revising my position from the previous edition, I suggest performance is, ultimately, perhaps *more* a function of the customer than it is a function of the organisation.

Beynon-Davies (2013) determined that 67% of UK organisations have suffered at least one "systems" project that has failed to deliver expected benefits or experienced time and cost overruns, while Gartner [webref 3] state that 80% of SAP clients are disappointed in benefits realised, the measurability of those benefits and the competency of system users. They argue that 90% of IT projects do not return real benefit to the organisation and that 40% fail completely. Meanwhile, McKinsey are reputed to have stated that, historically, two-thirds of chief information officers have not had to defend their budgets; because nobody else knew enough of the arcane language of IT to ask them the right questions. Morgan Stanley [webref 4] estimated that even as long ago now as 2002 companies threw away billions of dollars of their IT capital expenditure on "shelfware" (software licences and systems never used), a situation that has certainly deteriorated in the intervening years. I regularly encounter CIOs proudly boasting of the number of software licences they have cancelled, never apologising for having acquired them in the first place! In 2003 Reichheld and Markey in *Harvard Business Review* suggested that "IT doesn't matter". *HBR* did not see IT as a source of strategic advantage; in this new age of data science, online retailers and other information-intensive organisations might not agree. Universities meanwhile continue to produce computer science graduates who rely on "geek speak" (*Times Higher Education*, 14th August 2014), not having the communication or business skills to render themselves useful to organisations. If all this is true then somebody, somewhere must be doing something wrong – or maybe we are collectively valuing and focusing on the wrong things.

The continuing convention in commissioning an information system or information technology project is to identify a problem to be solved, to identify a technological means of addressing it, estimate the potential payback and measure the cost of solving it, (that is the hardware, software, configuration, customisation, training, backfilling and business disruption). The cost is capitalised; because such projects have a value over time, the accountants can depreciate the investment. The payback is then measured through productivity gains estimated through reduced headcount, increased system availability, better compliance with regulators, improved reporting, reduced "clicks" to use the system, improved appearance and better toys. Still, most organisations hold nobody properly accountable for any difference. Instead they consider IT as a necessary evil, an infrastructure cost to be minimised rather than a productivity-enabling tool to be, at least, optimised. Organisations are often seduced into IT projects with the prospect of better technology, more data and information which is faster rather than more valuable, failing to appreciate the difference. This mentality drives underinvestment in what really matters, the information derived from the system.

The epiphenomena of an IT system are its gadgets: artefacts connected in the "Internet of Things", "home hubs" and other digital personal assistant devices, mobile devices, smartphones and all the other physical, commoditised ephemera. Software houses have modified their licensing models, lowering the initial cost while, often, increasing the cost of support, configuration and upgrades – the total life cost of the product increasing overall. The business opportunity to monetise client data, dressed up as "reducing the capital required for new investment", has accelerated the trend towards "cloud-based" approaches, "software as a service", and "online everything". While this approach can undoubtedly offer some benefit, it introduces a new set of challenges, dependencies, interdependencies and risks which many organisations fail to adequately comprehend and address.

I'm going to pick up my email

An organisation with a highly distributed network of locations, many in rural areas with no access to high speed broadband services, decided to implement an "online" suite of workplace applications. In a number of locations, employees requiring access to those applications would leave the workplace several times each day to drive to a location with good mobile connectivity to send and receive emails and access other systems. Whatever financial performance gains were achieved at the centre of the organisation, they were more than offset by losses in the distributed locations.

Many "upgrades" add little value; of themselves they often do not make the user more productive, efficient or effective in their role. They do not, in general, "serve the customer better", and they do not make individuals better at their jobs. Often the result is a faster, more efficient way of making the same mistakes. Individually each mistake is cheaper and faster – is that an increase in productivity we want to celebrate when the total cost of all the mistakes is often greater than it was before?

The various integrated "enterprise wide" software packages in widespread use throughout the world still largely reflect the traditional, functional and siloed structures of the organisations that use them. This is partly a reflection of the preferences of the individual buyers – "I need a better finance package" – and partly a reflection of the challenges of developing applications that are truly comprehensive. It would be fatuous to deny the challenge of creating completely comprehensive programmes that "do everything". The proliferation of functional applications and the need (and it is a need) to use the same data in more than one functional silo often leads to replication of data across those silos. This generates a requirement to synchronise the data and maintain its integrity. However, not only is data often shared through unstable, insecure transfer and integration methods and taken from a context in which it has meaning to one in which that meaning is lost, but in being duplicated or replicated many times, it loses its integrity, definition and meaning. Integrity becomes almost impossible when even minor changes are applied to the arrangement or order of data or where it is merged with other data. Even where there is good intent it is difficult to sustain a data maintenance routine, and, anyway, "it won't have changed much. Let's use last month's data". Organisations have accumulated more and more applications with more and more versions of the data so that it becomes nigh on impossible to determine which data set contains the "truth". Each (whether accurately maintained or not) is applied to a particular, often functionally partial or siloed decision. Meanwhile reliance is placed on often unverified, untested data. In one organisation there were more than 30 different versions of a particular "truth" with consequently inadequate decision-making and many arguments about which was "right". Of course, in this situation none were absolutely wrong or right; rightness (or not) depended upon the underlying assumptions and the question to be answered.

The challenges of integration arise because

- there is no agreed information architecture;
- there is inadequate understanding of the desired or needed outcome;
- the organisational and behavioural implications have not been addressed;
- system design is poor;
- project control is inadequate;
- the business benefits are not properly invested in; or
- things are done with haste to meet arbitrary, usually budgetary, deadlines.

These inadequacies compromise the integrity of the system, the data and, ultimately the organisation itself because it is relying on inadequate information to make customer- and business-critical decisions. This reflects a weak understanding of the value of information.

Multifold replication of data carries with it the likelihood of error. When we couple to that the absolute logical precision of algorithms, we discover potential for further amplification of those errors. When somebody, anybody, searches for stored data on the Internet or the corporate intranet they find, and here I am simplifying massively from MacCormick (2012), all the possible data related to the question they asked, ranked in order of the number of connected pages and the number of links to that page. The question they ask will probably not use the precise words or have the same precise meaning (to them) as the person, people or machines that populated the data sources being searched. The "Internet of data" is a global data proliferation engine, massively increasing its data storage requirements every day and, very often, doing so by storing even more copies of things that are already there – and, as yet, it doesn't forget.

Perhaps the Internet is a Borgesian Library (Borges, 1962), a repository of wrong answers to poor questions? The simplicity and ease of use of web browsers and other search tools, coupled to the inadequacy of the ways that data is stored and archived, attenuate our ability to ask good questions – if we let them.

Data has cost but is the raw material of information. We can use it many times. Information has value; we derive it from data, calculate it, present it, use it, exploit it. However, our poor discipline in the management of data, coupled to multiple applications and devices, compounded by the use of the Internet (especially for "cloud" data storage), fuels this highly effective data proliferation engine. We capture and store ever more copies of, approximately, the same data but have less and less useful information to make decisions with. This leads us, to Beckford's Law of Data, which is, as revised, "Information availability is inversely proportional to data availability". Data proliferation is exponential in two dimensions, volume and frequency; information declines in proportion. Because of the rate of data proliferation we probably have more potential information in absolute terms, but the rate of growth of information is much smaller than that of data. But we need information to make decisions – *not* data – while data proliferates as a function of

the number of users
times the number of devices
times the number of applications
times the number of backups
times the ease of transmission (the propagation rate)

Information availability decreases accordingly.

This is because generating information relies on our ability to source correct data, to structure, interpret and present it to convey meaning to a recipient. If we cannot rely on the data, we cannot meaningfully communicate.

If data were treated, in accounting terms, as a "material good", it would be acquired, stored, compiled, applied, used in a manner that respected its cost and value just like a washer, nut, press or other physical element. It would be regarded as part of the assets of the business. Failure to do this (and I am not suggesting it is easy) undervalues those businesses whose stock in trade is data and which make their living from information provision. All organisations, whether they recognise it or not, draw on data all the time to inform their decisions and do so with only a limited sense of its value and unstated, or unknown, assumptions about accuracy.

We don't recognise the value of data because it is often invisible and because the cost of data capture and storage is hidden, embedded in other things. If we consider the stock of data in the same way we consider the stock of raw materials or work in progress then we should be horrified at the mess in the data warehouse and its inefficiency. I have tried this with more than one business – they were.

The ready availability and apparent cheapness of both hardware and software have enabled a situation in which data is overwhelming us but real information is scarce. Rooted in a partial or functional understanding of a particular problem rather than a holistic understanding of the information needs of the organisation, information solutions often exacerbate the data handling challenge. The consequence is fruitless discussions and arguments in which the protagonists are unable to resolve their problems because, since they are working with different data, their arguments are all right. A frustrated and frustrating dialogue of the deaf ensues in which the participants are unable to understand the perspective of the others because "that's what my data tells me".

The challenge of inconsistent data needs to be resolved. While sound methods exist for addressing this, such as Master Data Management, the expansion of data across multiple devices and cloud-type solutions exacerbate it. The cost of growth in data capture and the benefit to the organisation of useful information must be articulated; the value of solving it must be demonstrated. The many sceptics in the organisation must be challenged and encouraged towards a new way of thinking.

With each new generation of technology it appears increasingly difficult to generate substantial payback on fresh investment. We have reached a plateau in our ability to improve operational efficiency within the existing structures and norms. Doing more of the same is not and will not deliver benefits; we struggle to realise gains from previous investment and, once a cost has been saved, we cannot claim the saving again (although many try). Fortunately, as both managers and technologists consider the situation, there is an increasing recognition of and demand for new, innovative thinking about the situation. If the old solution is not delivering benefits, what might a new solution look like?

The key is this: information is more important and valuable than technology.

The Intelligent Organisation: dissolving the information challenge

The information challenge is to escape the thrall of technology and to design whole organisations as adaptive systems embedding distributed control through the use of information. A new organisational form, an adaptive organisation, is needed, coupled to a fresh appreciation of the roles of managers and of the meaning of systemic efficiency and effectiveness. In this new model the information system (in its broadest sense) is not simply an attribute of the organisation, it *is* the organisation.

Since their inception, our technological information systems have been thought of as adjunct artefacts, bolted on to the core of the organisation but not integral to it. Early systems were often associated with telecommunications: extensions of the telephone system, sharing some of their technology, a faster means of moving data and calculating results. Others were associated with finance, the early accounting systems automating the work of bookkeepers and clerks. These systems have supplemented and sometimes replaced more traditional means of transmission or accounting, but the focus has been on the devices and the software not the information content. Today, it is information flow that defines the true structure of the organisation and enables the integration of process with behaviour and skills, so perhaps our organisational arrangements should reflect the information flow?

Our organograms, job descriptions and reporting structures are, for the most part, refined evolutions of control mechanisms developed in societies long before the sort of formal organisations now seen. Many organisations continue to employ a somewhat militaristic command and control structure with decision power concentrated in the hands of a small number of people, perhaps increasingly so with flatter organisations and more task automation. While armies and religious orders have followed the same essential form for more than two millennia, large scale civil enterprises have only really developed since the 1700s. The Industrial Revolution in the United Kingdom, powered by Newcomen's steam engine and its successors, enabled, perhaps demanded, a progressive urbanisation of the population as people moved to work in factories which depended upon command and control in order to function. With low levels of automation, the whole depended upon the conformance of the individual to the requirements of their task. The evolution of organisations, their success and the increasing "wealth of nations" (Smith, 1776) are coupled to that of social norms, values and expectations including the emergence of a managerial class: people who are neither direct owners of the means of production nor directly productive workers but whose task is to be the control system of the organisation, quite literally the middle class.

The late Victorian era through to the Great War of 1914–1918 saw the emergence of formalised ways of thinking about managing. Henry Ford, inspired by mechanisation in abattoirs, developed the moving production line; Frederick Taylor (1911) developed the notion of "scientific management", thinking of the organisation as a "machine"; and Henri Fayol (1916) built on this with his proposals for the duties of managers, especially "unity of command "clearly defined duties". Max Weber's Bureaucracy Theory (1924) reinforced this, considering the legitimacy of authority in organisations and suggesting that a bureaucratic approach was indispensable to the survival of organisations. Thinking developed through the work of researchers such as Mayo, Roethlisberger and Dickson (1949) with the Hawthorne experiments, emphasising the critical role of human behaviour in organisational success. Hertzberg (1959) and Maslow (1970) developed theories of motivation, emphasising the role of people and challenging the notion that any organisation can be treated, simply, as a machine, their view being more oriented to the notion of an organism. In the second half of the 20th century thinking about organisations as "socio-technical" systems developed, building on the early work of the cyberneticians Wiener (1948) and Beer (1959, 1979, 1981, 1985), while the human, soft systems perspective was heavily influenced by Ackoff (1981) and Checkland (1981). Each of these thinkers developed perspectives which addressed the systemic nature of organisations, but each emphasised a particular "weltanschaaungen" (a world view or set of assumptions about the world), political, behavioural, structural. Notwithstanding all of these ideas and experiments, most organisational management is conducted with some blend of the "machine" and "organism" models, while the systemic perspective is becoming more visible, more prevalent.

If we are to tackle all of the challenges of contemporary, increasingly complex organisations we need a new approach, the Intelligent Organisation, shown in Figure 1.1.

The Intelligent Organisation synthesises fulfilment of purpose with generating and enabling value all through the production and use of information. It recognises

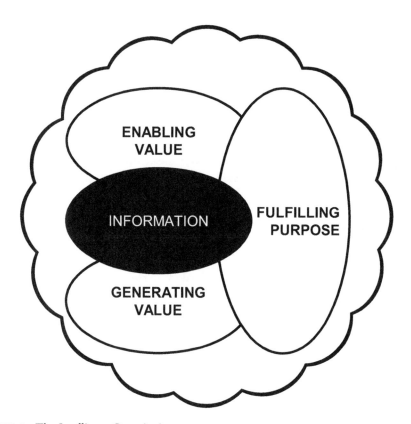

FIGURE 1.1 The Intelligent Organisation

and embraces the complexity inherent in contemporary organisations at a requisite level which matches that of the organisation's environment. It deals with the irreducible complexity so that the claimed benefits of information investment can be realised. Information must deliver value; that value must become obvious. This makes the business case for continuing sometimes discontinuous change. While both costs and benefits need to be explored in monetary terms, they also need to be considered in terms of the impact on the people in the organisation. The Intelligent Organisation redefines the role of the manager as enabling allostasis; they keep things the same (achievement of outcome) by making them different (adaptation). An entire industry which functionally separates "change management" needs to be challenged. In an organisation run on information, which seeks dynamic ultra-stability through self-regulation, continuing adaptation and learning, managing change (the adaptation) is not an addition to the day job, it *is* the day job.

Value cannot solely relate to the monetary measure; behaviours (the ways individuals express their values and beliefs) and skills (the competences applied to the conduct of any particular task) inform and are informed by available information. Behavioural coherence and consistency in the organisation (how we do things) are driven by the alignment of the decisions made (what things we do), with achievement of purpose and the organisational goals (why we do things). Any mismatch between those dimensions will have psychological and monetary consequences. Those consequences will not necessarily be explicit or obvious but will be realised in hidden costs through inefficiency, low staff retention, high staff turnover rates, and very commonly, sickness and absence rates. Ultimately, all these things are expressible in monetary terms and are important to profit maximisation in commercial organisations, to cost minimisation in public services and to surplus generation in the third sector. Whilst the focus and purpose in each sector may be different and the benefits of effective information use realised in differing ways, the value proposition is the same for all.

Understanding the value of information creates the business case for adaptation and realising that value becomes the imperative to ensure sustainability. This is particularly important in the light of the challenge of mature markets and economic, social and technological change. The idea of Intelligent Organisation, inspired by Beer (1981, 1985) and developed through theoretical and applied work since the early 90s, is essential to think about its philosophy and design principles; how it can be structured and developed, how information needs can be identified, how autonomy and empowerment can be embedded to address the continuously shifting balance of control, empowering individuals, increasing responsiveness and immediacy in dealing with clients.

The Intelligent Manager

Intelligent organisations will need intelligent managers, capable of managing the nuanced conversation between people and technology.

In the Little Britain vignettes of modern life, a customer would ask a perfectly reasonable question, and the service agent, following a tap-tap-tapping on the keyboard, would reply, "Computer says no". Although this is perhaps an extreme version of a world dominated by computer algorithms, set scripts and the processes and procedures to make our complex world function, there was always just enough truth in each sketch.

The Intelligent Manager has to operate in the real-world version of this environment. Granting a precondition that organisations abide by legal and regulatory obligations, let's assume the following.

- They operate to standard processes, with a dispute resolution mechanism.

  - The processes and procedures established for commercial or government activities such as online shopping, telephone or web-based helplines serve the same purpose: to provide order, clarity, consistency, efficiency and effectiveness to "what we do" in responding to myriad situations, often complicated by special circumstances and individual preferences.

- They have constraints on the types of failure they are willing and able to address.

  - The frequency and cause of issues range from genuine one-offs and rare events to common/uncommon and systemic/non-systemic problems. There is even the simplicity of a poorly designed standard process.

- They have constraints on what they are both willing and able to do when they address any issues.

  - These will be influenced by the consequences of not properly resolving issues.

The "willing" element of the last two is limited by the expectations and consequent response of the customers. Both the organisation and its customer prioritise and balance possible outcomes, and those will be determined by a range of factors such as cost/benefit, quality, convenience, great customer service, legal constraints, reputational and financial damage and so on.

Finally, technology and data can provide information more quickly and more accessibly than paper and manual searches; it can store the same data cut in a number of different ways, but what it can't do is determine how well that data and information are used. That, and the helpfulness of the response, involves a human judgement.

Where, then, does the Intelligent Manager fit in this semi-automated world? Why do we need them? If our systems and processes are perfect, our customers' needs homogenous and the outcomes consistent, then technology solves nearly everything except where personal service is the USP. However, this world demonstrably doesn't exist, or there wouldn't be complaint procedures or regulatory complaint panels. A glance at any newspaper complaints page bears this out. Given that the vast majority of actions and transactions conform to the standard process and are solvable within the constraints of standard methods, the remaining issues fall within the remit of the Intelligent Manager. That manager would consider these questions:

- What is the issue?
- Is it addressable?
- Do we and the customer want it to be addressed?
- What is the impact of not addressing it properly?
- Can/should the issue be fixed at source?
- Can we redesign the process to prevent recurrence?

This vignette looks at the Intelligent Manager's value to the internal workings of an organisation from a technical and process perspective.

Procurement: outstanding payments

An organisation introduced a new procurement module covering the raising of purchase orders, automatic invoice to order matching and a "manual" process to cover a small amount of non-purchase order activity. Invoices once approved moved into the organisations standard payment system. The module generally worked well, the standard procedure included an inbuilt procedure, which resolved the majority of the queries. However, on occasion the process didn't work, and the complainant would try to resolve the issue through phone calls. Some of these calls related to the one-offs, but others were about recurring problems (shown by the volume of feedback). The business approved a supplier invoice in the appropriate manner. The invoice was one of several annual invoices raised by the supplier on the business and the other invoices had been approved and paid. This invoice was not paid.

The initial explanation was that the vendor account had been "blocked" for payment, apparently pending a bank verification check. Three months later nothing had changed. A second investigation suggested that the invoice had been applied to the wrong vendor number (it was the same supplier) and that the correct procedure was to allocate the invoice to the standard vendor number, which would release the payment. The solution had been identified. However, it was not clear why the account had been blocked in the first place nor by whom and how that action had been approved. The Intelligent Manager recognised that it wasn't enough just to sort out the specific invoice and that the organisation needed to understand why the account had been blocked for payment, whether the account should continue to be used and that the procedure for blocking or rendering inactive supplier vendor numbers needed clarifying and amending. Although only responsible for part of the overall process, the IM determined to get to the root of the problem and put in place a permanent fix.

Without a willingness to get to the root and fix a not uncommon and systemic problem, people in the business would waste hours of time solving the same basic problem again. Sometimes it is just not enough to only correct the mistake.

Intelligent autonomy

A much-loved grandfather died, and the family ordered his favourite wine for the funeral. When it was delivered several days later the supplier had sent the wrong wine. The family called the supplier, who checked the order, confirmed the mistake and agreed to replace it with the right wine, in line with its standard process. So far, so good. Unfortunately, the funeral was the next day. A computer-says-no approach would say, "Standard delivery three days, have to pay for next-day delivery with delivery confirmed by 1 p.m." (too late!). However, the supplier process clearly allowed for supervisor/managerial discretion, and the Intelligent Manager recognised the critical and fraught nature of the problem. So what happened? The correct wine was organised and sent 70 miles by taxi, arriving a few hours after the original complaint. This is great customer service, with a very human recognition that funerals are emotional events. This approach is still remembered by the family as a bright spot in a difficult time. Result for the business? They have been used for subsequent events (not just funerals) because the customer is confident that any problem will be resolved, dealt with, fixed.

Here the procedures and processes of the organisation clearly allowed managerial discretion, effective autonomy. However, knowing that you are allowed discretion and actually using it effectively are two different things. In this example, the Intelligent Manager used the procedures and their discretion to bring about a satisfactory outcome for both the organisation/supplier and the customer.

The Intelligent Manager will work in and abide by the systems and processes while their effectiveness will depend on the quality of the processes, openness to constructive feedback and the willingness to amend processes to both fix the problem and prevent a recurrence if possible. On a personal level, it is about the attitude, behaviour and skills of the individual, the knowledge to understand the rules, to make use of the available technology but not be driven by it and to have the judgement and courage to know when to apply discretion. In other words, it is a synthesis of good processes, appropriate managerial discretion and the genuine desire to be helpful and provide a great service. The computer may say "No", but the Intelligent Manager says to both the organisation and customer, "Let me see what I can do".

Summary

Radical though they may seem, the ideas explored in this book have a long history. The ideas are rooted in the concepts and ideas of managerial cybernetics which have developed from Plato's steersman (390 BC approx.) through the work of Weiner (1948, 1954) and the formal conception of a "neuro-cybernetic" organisation created by Stafford Beer from the 1950s and Clemson's "psycho-cybernetics" in 1984. Weiner (1948) defined cybernetics as "control and communication in the animal and the machine" while Beer defined managerial cybernetics as "the science of effective organisation" (1985). Thinking about the Intelligent Organisation builds on those foundations to draw on thinking about and applying the ideas over the last 25 years or so.

The established organisational models are descriptive and prescriptive with organisation charts described by Beer (1985) as "frozen out of history", they tell us who to sack when things go wrong but nothing of how the organisation actually works. Beer (1985) asserts: "The cybernetics of any situation will assert themselves so that ALL organisations necessarily answer to the 'laws' of cybernetics". If rather than allowing them to "assert themselves" we design the cybernetics in, then we can make them work for us. Before we start to design the Intelligent Organisation, we need to understand the value of information. Currently costs and payback are typically measured in terms of hardware, software and reduced headcount while the benefits are in the information. We don't measure the value of that. Perhaps it's time we did.

2

THE VALUE OF INFORMATION

Introduction

Information is valuable in its own right to organisations. It is a resource that must be captured, managed, retrieved and invested in for the benefit of the whole. Its value is realised when it allows us to make decisions which enhance the effectiveness of the organisation in fulfilling its purpose. However, while we talk about the "information system" and invest in infrastructure, software and hardware, we rarely think about the information itself and how we exploit it for value.

Accounting for information

An organisation operating a continuous production process has around 200 software applications, invests annually about £25m capital and spends more than £20m of revenue on information systems.

The value of the information provided to the organisation? Unknown. No one is held to account for it; the basis of investment is "best endeavours", and, bizarrely, they don't have the information to make good decisions about investing in information.

Many organisations conform to this example. They don't seem to know why they buy what they buy; they don't really know why they use what they use. Many have no real idea what the information systems cost to buy or run and cannot even estimate what value is generated. If the mantra that "what gets measured gets managed" holds true, then organisations need to get serious about benefits realisation from investment in information. They have much latent information in the form of data but do not use it in an intelligent manner, and many of the true costs of information systems are, in one way or another, lost in the budgets of other parts of the organisation.

Feeding the monster

A sweet manufacturer installed a "state-of-the-art" enterprise resource planning (ERP) system to improve production and financial control and to reduce costs. Production staff, working within local budgets, all upgraded local PCs and spreadsheet software to generate the data to "feed" the ERP. The costs of these upgrades were in the production budget, not the IS budget. Savings were claimed while costs went up.

Often a system change in one part of a business does not remove a cost so much as displace it to another so that while one manager is receiving a bonus for improved performance and reduced costs, another is negotiating for an increased budget whilst being criticised for overspending. The particular case mentioned above is from around 2004, and I was concerned about its continued relevance – until told in May 2014 of another organisation experiencing exactly the same thing, and in 2018 I came across several further examples.

All this happens for several reasons:

- Organisations (and budgets) are managed functionally rather than as integrated whole systems.
- Interdependencies between parts of the organisation and between data sets are not understood, observed or respected.
- The wider organisational implications of proposed changes are not recognised.
- Costs are often exported to other silos, displaced rather than reduced.
- It is difficult to generate a clear business case when we do not, or cannot, articulate the value of the information to be provided – because we have not thought about that aspect.
- Investments are driven by technology change rather than information need.

What's IT worth?

Organisations often spend money on technology and systems (sometimes driven by the end of life of existing systems) when they should be investing in information to enable intelligent decisions. They need to measure the value of the information provided and off-set that against the cost of information systems provision just like any other business case, but it is the information that needs to be valued, *not* just simple headcount-based efficiency measures.

That is a fundamental shift, a challenge to the conventional way of thinking, but is relatively easy to express in terms that should make sense for the organisation and its customers. To support that challenge let us think about how much the effective use of information could

- improve response times to customers (external and internal);
- enable recognition of and response to opportunities;
- enable better decisions, closer to the customer;
- reduce time on data collection and enable more effective analysis;

- reduce product development time and time to market for new products;
- enable effective recognition of and response to threats and adverse events;
- enable the organisation to exploit data for value.

Answers to all of these questions can be expressed in terms of the critical success factors of any particular organisation. These might include profit, volume, customer satisfaction, social and societal outcomes. Measuring the value of information not only allows for it to be both understood and realised; it also allows for more conventional questions to be tackled:

- How much easier is the system to use?
- How much duplication has been eradicated?
- How much more authoritative for decision-making is the information?
- How much more efficient are we?
- How much more effective are we?
- How can what we know about our organisation, ourselves, our clients, be monetised?

Value rests in our ability to deliver information to generate strategic or operational insights. That allows us to use it to deliver sustainable improvements in customer service, competitive position, costs and revenues.

That suggests that some further important questions need to be addressed:

- How much is a happy customer worth?
- What is the value of time in the market?
- What is the true cost of error or failure?
- How productive are we?
- What is our data worth in the marketplace?

The value of a happy customer

A happy customer offers two potential sources of value, one easily measurable, the other more difficult. In the first case it is reasonable to assume that a happy customer will be a repeat customer, and that makes for a simple equation:

Net Profit per Item ★ *Number of Repeat Purchases* $= \pounds V(\copyright C)$

This value is then amplified by the number of repeat customers.

However, in order to solve the sum (to provide the information as opposed to the data) we cannot work in silos. We need data from different parts of the organisation:

- Finance need to be able to state the net profit per individual item sold;
- Commercial need to provide the repeat cycle frequency;
- Marketing need to be able to state the number of repeat customers.

No functional silo can solve this apparently simple problem alone.

The second potential source of value is the number of other people the happy customer tells who then go on to become customers. The data to calculate this is not easily available in the organisations' systems. It might be obtained through effective customer surveys, in particular through the idea of the "net promoter score" (Reichheld & Markey, 2011), which calculates the proportion of your customers who would recommend you to somebody else. It is equally important to recognise that the inverse question is also valid: "What is the cost of an unhappy customer?" Here the negative amplifying effect of telling others is often held to be greater than the positive cycle: "If I am happy with the service then I will shop there again; if I am not happy with the service I will tell everybody I know". And social media (another IT-enabled activity) means that a lot of people can be told very quickly.

Happy customers are not produced by sales, finance or marketing alone. They result from all of the interactions of the customer with the organisation, its collective ability to understand and inform the customer, to meet their expectations and needs. While the impact can be measured at the customers, it is the alignment of the organisation towards them that generates the value.

The value of time in the market

The value of time in the market is vitally important when there are finite limits to the product or service life. These include shelf life for perishables, patent life for pharmaceuticals and other protected goods and services, or "first to market" advantages for technology-based products. Again, the equation is simple:

*Net Profit per Item * Volume per Day * Number of Days Advantage = Value of Time in the Market*

For a pharmaceutical company, with strict time limits on a patent before generic competitors can enter the market, being faster is potentially worth billions in additional revenues. At the other end of the scale, fresh produce that does not hit the market immediately is valueless, generating cost but no revenue. That can mean not just profit or loss but survival of the business for a low-margin producer. While the particular specification of information arrangements will necessarily differ widely between these situations, nobody likes a day-old doughnut.

Let's turn first to the pharmaceutical company. Information flows from opportunities for therapeutic treatments in a global market, through research and development, testing and regulatory compliance, marketing, production, "detailing" to clinicians and, finally, prescription. The process may take around seven to eight years to be fully worked through to the first prescription, at which point the company has perhaps only six or seven protected years to exploit its product. The commercial benefit of being six months faster to the market for a product likely to generate billions in revenue is huge. The need for effective conversion of data into information across the whole process is evident, the challenge substantial, the benefits massive.

While the holder of a pharmaceutical patent has a legal advantage against competitors, the same does not apply, at least not as much, to innovators in technology markets. Whilst particular technical components might be protectable by patent, there is nothing to prevent a competitor marketing a product with similar or even identical functionality, and, often, functionality can be replicated quickly. In this case, time to market needs to be complemented by rapid client acquisition; it is vital to be both first and fast. Information about the market and the customers is key to both, and its value can be expressed in terms of products, market penetration and revenue. Every day the product is in the market without competition the revenue opportunity against competitors increases.

The true cost of error or failure

Fresh goods production generates some particular challenges for information; there is a limited market for stale bread.

For the producer of perishable goods working with very short timescales, intelligent use of information is critical. Market demand and responses to changes in that demand, time to market, delivery times, prices (which are often dynamic) and current consumption rates are key. Producing too much generates unrecoverable costs; producing too little misses profit opportunities.

Mushroom management

Working with a mushroom grower, primarily a supplier to the major supermarket chains, we determined that there was a major process issue that might be solved by information. At best, mushrooms have a 48-hour shelf life before they are unsaleable. The presenting issue was that the final order from the supermarkets was received at 7 a.m. for shipping by noon. This shipping deadline was enforced to meet the "just-in-time" delivery schedule for distribution centres and shop deliveries. An order not delivered to the distribution centre on time would most probably be returned and the product scrapped.

While the supermarkets provided "indicative" purchase plans a year ahead, updated quarterly, monthly and weekly, they only committed to the product on the day. Actual order volumes varied to reflect unsold stock on the supermarket shelf from the previous day and changes in the weather; any sudden change in temperature or precipitation could trigger an immediate change in both the volume of mushrooms produced and the demand in the market, but these were often not consistent with each other.

The picking, packing and despatch process had a maximum five-hour window and assumed availability of sufficient product in the growing sheds.

A mushroom, under the right conditions, doubles in size every 24 hours. In broad terms the crop (combined volume and weight) is fixed by the combination and composition of components — compost, casing material, spores — and the growing conditions — temperature, moisture, draught. They can be flexed to give a +/- 24-hour change in crop readiness. Because of the overall growing time, the production volume decision is taken 42 days before the first cropping day and the decision about volume of compost is taken five to seven days before that. The producer is therefore cropping on any given day a volume and weight of mushrooms determined 42–49 days beforehand against an order received that day. Every order not met is a lost revenue opportunity; every mushroom not sold is an unrecoverable cost.

Value of time in the market can be comprehended in this case by effective estimation 42–49 days ahead of the likely market demand and by accurate forecasting of the volume of mushrooms available from a given weight of materials under anticipated weather conditions. It is well known that weather forecasts are rarely accurate any more than three days ahead.

This is a substantial probabilistic challenge. Almost nothing can be known to a certainty. Realising value lies in eliminating as much uncertainty as possible while making defensible assumptions about the rest. The whole then needs to be brought together in a decision model, its accuracy enhanced by learning from experience such that, over time, the mean gap between volume produced and volume sold is reduced: a form of optimisation.

Critically in this instance the organisation needs to use data at two levels. The first level deals with the prediction of production and demand; an operational cycle. The second level uses data about the accuracy of the first level predictions to improve the utility of the model itself. This requires consistent, considered use of multiple data sets over time, not an attribute of most organisations or their information systems. The tradition of the organisation was "judgement", a best guess based on experience. Whilst useful – experienced people are very good at making judgements – this had its limitations.

An information model was developed that brought the disparate elements together in a systemic whole. The impact of this robust information model over time was to reduce the mean gap in value terms by around £1m per year taking account of the cost of lost opportunity and the cost of scrappage. For a business with a turnover of around £20m and a net bottom line of £1m, that was a significant gain.

Street traders in many tourist destinations provide a good example of market responsiveness. In the few minutes that it takes to observe an imminent change in the weather they shift from selling parasols to selling umbrellas, or mini-copters, buckets and spades or caps, and back again.

Success, for either an individual or a large corporate, rests in the ability to process and respond to changes in internal and external information at the same rate as the rate of change of the data. This is a truly dynamic requirement that will not be fulfilled through the traditional approaches of reporting, discussing and deciding. Adaptation must be done in something approaching real time, and when the organisation is really smart it can adapt in anticipation; it can be intelligent.

How productive are we?

Assessment of productivity has been a key concern for organisations for hundreds of years and is of increasing importance in sustaining performance. Such assessment brings together a number of interacting factors:

*   capacity of plant and machinery,
*   reliability and "downtime",

- resilience of infrastructure,
- process and job design,
- application of skill,
- attitudes and behaviours,
- supervision and management and
- use of information as an enabler of decisions.

These things are not always brought together to optimum effect.

The benefit of understanding interdependency

A manufacturer was fighting in a dynamic market to increase value to customers by increasing volume while holding their cost base static. Increased product availability had immediate sales benefit and every additional tonne of sales generated revenue of around £350. Daily production volume was erratic and appeared unpredictable; the annual production and sales targets, around 300,000t, were constantly missed.

A model, a computer simulation of the plant, was built which analysed the production capacity of the whole and identified potential production volume both for each stage and the whole interacting process. This showed an opportunity to generate budgeted volume plus 30% if run effectively. Multiple simulations were explored with the management team to find optimum performance. One finding was that the yield losses between the first two stages of the process were stable at about 3%, i.e. to obtain 1 tonne of product after stage two required 1.03 tonnes of product after stage one. However, the budgets (negotiated in silo fashion) required stage two to produce 10% more than stage one. This had a bizarre consequence: stage one could only succeed by making stage two fail, and stage two could only succeed if stage one failed. In establishing the production plan, notice had been taken of the capacity of each phase but not their interactions.

A plan was devised to balance the throughput across the process and manage the plant to increase output to meet market demand. Within 12 months the plant was producing at the 400,000t level and all output was sold. The value of information? 100,000t * £350/t = £35m additional revenue in a full year.

The simulation in this instance initially considered only the relationships between the physical artefacts of the system and their interactions. However, in addition to the "simple" identification of the performance characteristics of the interacting machines (volumes, flow rates, downtime and reliability) the creation of the simulation tool depended on engagement with the people who actually did the work, the operational stakeholders. Sharing information about the relationships and interdependency of the whole system stimulated reflection on the design of operational jobs, limitations and constraints applied by "management", the maintenance regime, construction of budgets and a host of other matters. All of these impacted, and usually impaired, the achievement of the full potential of the plant. Revealing "new" information to the stakeholders about overall plant performance and their part in it led to significant shifts in their thinking about what was possible. It was those shifts which delivered the change. This shows that we can, must, use information as the link between processes and structures, skills and behaviours. Neither will change without impacting on the other.

When we shift focus to service organisations the challenge becomes harder. Services, like manufacturing, rely on good process, but the emphasis of service delivery is on human interaction (Beckford, 2017). Unlike manufacturing, service productivity cannot easily be measured to a highly precise level. A high level of certainty can be obtained in a manufacturing process using quantitative metrics and appropriately frequent measurement. Services rely for their completion on the application of the necessary "skills" to carry out the relevant task in conjunction with the appropriate "behaviours" (of both service provider and customer). Whilst there are tangible aspects to this which lend themselves to measurement, there are significant intangibles which do not. Did the right things happen? How did it feel?

The assessment of intangible aspects has a great degree of probabilism associated with it. It cannot be modelled or represented in the same way as a manufacturing activity. Key elements of service are ephemeral: they exist only in the moment of the transaction itself and cannot be captured, monitored and measured quantitatively. In these cases measurement may be obtained through a variety of qualitative tools which, appropriately applied, can give statistically reliable indicators of performance.

Uncertainty can be reduced in relationship-based transactions by investment in the development of both skills and behaviours. The first of these relies on training operators in the skills relevant to the task, the "what" of the transaction. The second requires a behavioural focus, the "how". This is a sophisticated need. It means that the individual must choose to adhere to the values and norms of the organisation, the "why". They must also, in so far as it is possible (Wilson, 2002), understand their own behaviour (and its impact on others) and the behaviour of others (and its impact on them).

Modification of skills and behaviours relies upon effective communication of information between the organisation and its employees. This technical information explains how to carry out the process while behavioural information is about how to interact with customers, and it concerns values, why those things are done. Measurement of a particular instance of a service transaction will always be problematic and to some extent subjective. It relies on human interpretation of what happened, what was said, what was meant and what was understood. Such transactions are highly amenable to quantitative analysis in the aggregate and on an understanding of the systemic rather than point impact of success or failure.

Service provision in a call centre (which is a very common means of providing customer service) is often measured, expressed and incentivised in terms of

- number of calls handled and
- length of call.

The incentive mechanism, an expression of information about what is really important to the organisation, encourages a particular type of behaviour; that is, the call receiver is encouraged to terminate calls quickly in order to get to the next caller.

If, as is often the case, the customer need is not satisfied during the first call then a second call is received from that person. The call centre appears to be succeeding; lots of calls are being handled very quickly; the customer is increasingly irate.

Observation suggests that each subsequent call roughly doubles in length. The customer has to explain that they have called before, still have the problem and repeat the explanation of the problem. Because the call receiver is now failing (the call is taking longer), it is likely either to be escalated ("Your call is being held in a queue for . . .") or to receive a promise for action in order to clear the line. The call operator can then get back to the original queue. The information about performance (and the incentive) given to the call receiver is driving precisely the wrong behaviour. The costs of service are increasing because the number of calls is driven up. The organisation risks losing the customer to a competitor, another cost.

Now, if your call really was important to them? The call centre performance would be measured on "first-time resolution". The operator would be incentivised to stay on the call longer, fix or immediately escalate the problem and satisfy the customer. The measurement of productivity would not be about how many calls were handled (efficiency – an internal measure) but about how many customers were satisfied (effectiveness – an external measure). The Intelligent Organisation would capture useful data about the content of the calls, to understand what drives the volume, and use that information to modify behaviours and processes in other parts of the organisation. This "feedback" of information would drive overall performance improvement.

Exploiting data for customer value

In May 2018 major changes, negotiated and agreed with Network Rail, the infrastructure provider, were implemented in the timetable for a number of train operating companies in the UK. It was reported by The House of Commons Select Transport Committee (CST) as "a shambles". Their report (webref5) *indicated an expected 42300 individual service changes affecting 46% of services; the size and scope of the change must not be underestimated.*

The changes led to such a large proportion (11%–12% according to the CST) of service failures (missing trains, missing crews, driver shortages, service clashes) that the CST commented:

> *The statistics cannot do justice to the severe effects on people's lives. The disruption cost passengers money, with working people forced to pay for taxis and additional childcare costs, for example. Businesses and local economies suffered. Children were late for school. Anxiety about getting to and from work put a considerable strain on people's mental health. Confusion resulting from last minute cancellations and platform changes subjected passengers to "uncontrolled risks" in over-crowded stations. Effective communication broke down. The situation was chaotic.*

Train operators introduced emergency and interim timetables in order to restore stability.

> *It is not immediately apparent from the ORR main report* (webref6) *that any mean-ingful estimate of the costs to individuals, companies, train operators or the country as a whole is available. The ITV News website* (webref7) *estimated, though, a direct cost of £38m to businesses affected by just one of the franchises.*
>
> *The government, industry and regulators set up inquiries* (webref8) *in order to deter-mine what had gone wrong and to make recommendations for improvement.*
>
> *Among the recommendations is:*
>
> *Clearer scope for industry boards to oversee major network change. This will ensure greater scrutiny of the interdependencies involving new timetables, infrastructure, rolling stock and franchises.*
>
> *Now, the critical part of this is "scrutiny of the interdependencies". The report says nothing of how that should be done, however the other recommendations point to "system-wide advice and auditing" and addressing "optimism bias" by learning from others.*

None of that, it seems to me, will really help with solving what is a large, compli-cated but ultimately limited problem. Given contemporary computing capabilities and because the industry has available to it all of the necessary data, such as

- the planned timetable,
- the realised timetable (the history of what has happened in the past),
- the network capacity,
- the network constraints and rules (e.g. only one train on one piece of track at a time!),
- the signalling and control system,
- the rail vehicles and sets required for each service,
- the rail vehicles and sets available for each service,
- the crew requirements (drivers, guards, on board services),
- the crew availability,
- the passenger capacity and
- the likely passenger demand (for services and numbers of seats),

it would have been possible for the industry as a whole to build and run a simula-tion of the current and proposed timetables. From that they would have been able to identify

- potential failure points (no train, no crew) and
- potential delay points (that train will be late because *this* train is occupying the track).

The application of a learning algorithm to the structured data, focused on opti-mising one (or satisficing several) performance characteristics, could have then generated a "best" solution and resolved many, if not all, of the challenges before the plan was implemented.

In this case, utilisation of the already available data has a value of no less than £38m *plus* all of the human/social benefits!

Summary

This chapter has shown how we commonly fail to realise the value of the information already held by organisations and how we might come to understand what that value is. We have seen how the functional orientation of our structures, systems, processes and behaviours acts to inhibit effective use of that information.

The Intelligent Organisation is a dynamic, self-reflective, adaptive system understanding both the cost of information and the value generated from it, and in the next chapter we shall see how it can overcome the limitations of our current models.

3

GENERATING VALUE

Introduction

We have established that the key to organisational survival, for Intelligent Organisation, is the integration of information to enable the realisation of its value. That requires us to conceive an organisational architecture for the information age capable of synthesising people, behaviours, skills and processes enabled by shared information. That new architecture must transcend the traditional forms, processes and behaviours that inhibit adaptation and build a customer-centric value-generating engine to drive the organisation. The Intelligent Organisation is cybernetic in design, using information about its performance to regulate that performance.

Thinking about Intelligent Organisation

Traditional command and control structures inhibit the ability of an organisation to match the rate of change in the data (volume, frequency and content) that flow around it. Decisions are made based on the problem we had (a structural assumption that nothing has changed), not the one we have now. The frequency of shocks to the organisation is greater than the frequency of response; it is still trying to deal with the last problem while being hit by the next! The "mean time between perturbations of the system" (Beer, 1974) is shorter than the time it takes the organisation to respond. The goalposts are necessarily moving; the players cannot keep up.

Typically, information systems reflect the functional, siloed structures of the organisation, making it difficult to bring data together in coherent ways to inform decisions. Not only do data definitions vary widely, but the same expression may, in any one organisation, have different meanings for different people. Seemingly the same data may be differently defined in different functional silos. Even in a process-oriented organisation the partiality of decision-making within the silos embedded in the process inhibits the development of true customer orientation. The allocation of budgetary responsibilities and authorities, the "holding to account" for local performance and the frequent requirement to refer to a higher authority all inhibit effectiveness in value generation.

Because structures are siloed, data, information, decisions are ineffectively distributed and we end up with a "perpetually failing problem-solving engine" (see figure 3.1, adapted from Beckford, 1993).

Figure 3.1 demonstrates the cycle simply.

1   At T1 a problem is identified and modelled, M1, leading to a proposed solution, P1.
2   A change process ensues.
3   Meanwhile, the situation has evolved to M2, and the P1 solution is no longer suitable.
4   At T2 a fresh look is taken, M2, and a further solution, P2, is developed.
5   The evolution continues so that at T3 the situation is different again and the P2 proposal no longer holds.

To resolve this cycle and ensure that the organisation can respond effectively to necessary change, it must, through use of information, respond to the Conant-Ashby Theorem (1970): "Every competent regulator of a system must be a model of the system". This proposes (Conant and Ashby did the mathematics, so I needn't) that for an organisation to be effective in self-regulation it requires an internal "model of self" (MoS), i.e. an abstraction or representation of its ideal or desired

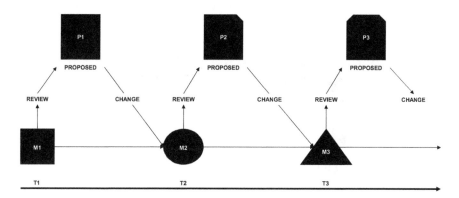

KEY
P = PROCESS
M = MEASUREMENT
T = TIME

FIGURE 3.1   The perpetually failing problem-solving engine

Source: Adapted from Beckford (1993)

state against which current performance can be measured and which provides the basis for change. The organisation must see itself; it must be self-aware. Information is generated through the MoS which tells us the gap between where we are and where we want to be and tells us much about how we should design our organisation, measure its performance *and* represent that performance in information that directs us towards the actions required to deliver our desired outcome. This use of information becomes an embedded capability to deliver continuing change as part of business as usual rather than as a separate programme. The very simplest representation is the Plan, Do, Check, Act cycle so prominent in the literature on "quality" (see Beckford, 2017).

In this cycle the intent and parameters of success (Plan) is established and executed (Do), the outcome verified and tested (Check), the process managed (Action) – this last element being the embedment of the change and the modification of the plan for the next cycle. This, considered as an embedded improvement cycle fundamental to the continued survival of the organisation, can also be found in any human learning process. Cycles of adaptation, improvements in process performance (behaviour, action, information) which bring us closer to our intended outcomes, are the basis of adaptation, of Intelligent Organisation. They are integral to its existence, belonging to the people who constitute the organisation.

To manage our world we need a model of the organisation including those characteristics of itself and its external world, its environment, that are of significance to its performance. To be a competent manager (regulator) we need to ensure that our model (process, behaviour, information) is sufficiently rich to reflect those aspects that we are trying to control and that our information flow is sufficiently rich (and rapid) for us to know whether our objectives are being achieved. Deficiency in either respect will mean failure; management is closing the gap between the two.

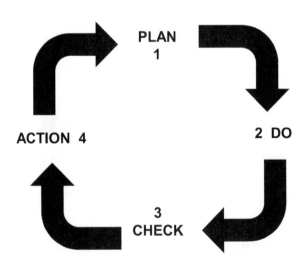

FIGURE 3.2 PDCA cycle

In order to act intelligently the organisation must create an informational model of itself which is much richer than the traditional financial "budget". It must be able to change its processes, behaviours and systems to become better at being itself and to do that at least as fast as the situation is changing – preferably faster so that it can anticipate rather than simply respond to change in its situation. To become truly adaptive it must maintain an internal model of its environment (that is, all those market, technical, social, political and environmental issues that affect its viability) and use that to adapt itself to the environment and adapt the environment to itself.

Intelligent organisations, capable of survival in a changing environment, must be conceived as purposeful, adaptive, self-aware and dynamical systems. Traditional or conventional organograms are unhelpful. They tell us who to fire when things go wrong but say nothing of how the organisation actually functions, the processes, tasks and procedures, the skills we bring to bear or the values that underpin our behaviour. The organogram tells us who reports to whom, who is (at least notionally) responsible for what, but tells us nothing of how the organisation becomes bound into a purposeful entity. However, an organisation is of necessity "organised"; without structure and some form of hierarchy arising in its internal and external relationships, it will be chaotic, perhaps anarchic, each part struggling to interact meaningfully with others, maybe attempting to create rules and impose them on the other parts. Neither the organogram nor anarchy appears particularly useful.

An organisational philosophy is essential: a way of thinking about the possibility of whole organisations as being self-regulating, adaptive, self-aware and dynamical. To be

- self-regulating means able to manage itself towards its goal;
- adaptive means that change capability must be designed in, not added as an afterthought, an initiative or a strategy;
- self-aware means the organisation must be able to see "itself" as a whole nested in its environment of customers, market, competitors, economy and a societal and political context;
- dynamical means it must have embedded capability to interpret the ongoing evolution of its environment and change itself in relation to it.

The organisation, its customers and its environment must co-evolve.

To be co-evolutionary the organisation must have the ability to adapt locally in its immediate interactions with its customers. This demands a significant level of autonomy for customer-facing individuals; it cannot adapt at a very local level without it. To be customer-centric it may need to offer different products or services in different markets or segments or offer the same products and services through different delivery mechanisms. A one-size-fits-all procedure cannot offer a solution to this. It doesn't matter how long we make the procedure chart; it will never quite reach the customer whose needs will nearly always fall between two possible outcomes. That demand for autonomy causes tension; while adapting itself to the needs of individual customers the organisation needs consistency and coherence around its processes in order to *be* an organisation. The Intelligent Organisation must achieve a dynamic level of autonomy in its operation that is best described as tight-loose control. It must tightly constrain those things which define it as itself and nothing else, while at the same time exercising only loose control on other factors, creating conditions under which individuals can empower themselves. This is not an invitation to anarchy. A logical hierarchy will emerge from the design, a hierarchy based on information, the need for both constraint and autonomy and a more adequate definition of what "management" means.

The Intelligent Organisation – overview

In the Intelligent Organisation, effectiveness (figure 3.3), that is the fulfilment of purpose, is a function of the interactions of processes, structures, people, (the values, skills and behaviours they apply to the processes and structures) and information. These are integrated to provide three perspectives:

- What: the "hard", quantitative processes, structure, numbers.
- How: the "soft", qualitative, skills and behaviours.
- Why: "purpose", the expression of personal and organisational values.

Effectiveness is given meaning in the interaction of these perspectives and should be thought of as a measure of the extent to which the organisation fulfils its purpose.

Effectiveness is not a measure of financial performance or profitability but a measure of how well the organisation is able to fulfil its purpose, meet the expectations of its customers and of its capability to survive. Financial performance is subsumed into this richer understanding. We shall return to performance measurement later on. For now let it suffice that, within the legal and financial conventions adopted in most economies, *all* organisations are constrained, over time, to generate

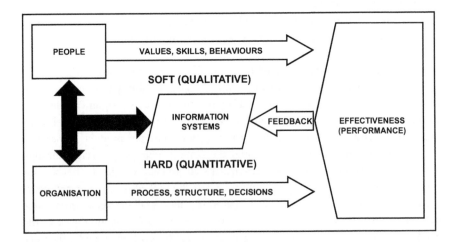

FIGURE 3.3 Organisational effectiveness

at least as much revenue as cost. Financial performance is best thought of as one in a basketful of measures and is just as important to public and third-sector organisations as it is to commercial enterprises.

To comprehend the need for designing integration in, from the outset we need to recognise the interconnectedness and interdependence of modern organisations. Traditional hierarchies lead, inevitably, towards silos of influence and control, a situation in which each manager is charged with improving the performance of the part for which they are responsible. The interests and performance of the whole organisation are only visible to those at the peak of the hierarchy. Any attempt to improve the performance of the whole by improving only the parts is doomed. Real improvement is only possible through enhancing the interactions (Ackoff, 1981), for which no one appears responsible. Figure 3.4 indicates the extent of internal interdependence for any organisation.

If you are not familiar with process diagrams this looks a bit daunting, so try this:

1   Find the heavily outlined box at the centre of the figure.
2   For some reason (it matters not what) there is to be a change in process, skills requirements or standards. Now follow the arrows.
3   Assuming first a process change follows the vertical arrow upwards to "Any Process", you will find that has three exit arrows – follow each of them in turn to follow the impact around the organisation.
4   Done that? Now assume a skills change and follow the horizontal arrow going towards the "competencies" box and again follow the subsequent arrows.
5   Nearly there. . . . Assume a change in standards.

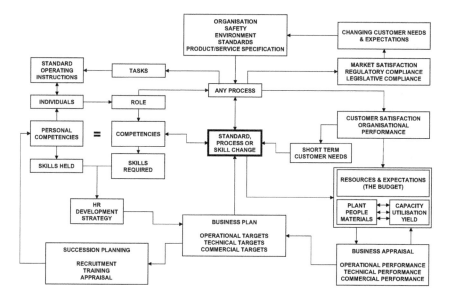

FIGURE 3.4   The interdependence of organisations

That's interesting: we can't get to the "standards" box from the "change" box without considering first the consequences for process or skills. The ability to meet a standard will be a function of change in process or skill or both! Change in one implies change in the other two.

Now that you have pursued the interdependencies from one fixed start point, see what happens if you start in any other box. Eventually you will find that regardless of your starting point, you will work your way through every box. The point? It is simply not possible to change one aspect of an organisation without affecting many others. These interdependencies can best be conceived as information flows, a change in one relying on information being conveyed to another to activate the appropriate response, perhaps analogous to gene activation in cells.

While we must deal with the organisation as a whole, we do need to break up the story into manageable parts; it is not a linear discussion. In the rest of this chapter we deal with the value-generating parts of the organisation. They interact directly with customers; they fulfil the fundamental purpose of the organisation.

Generating value: the fundamental activity

Designed backwards from the customer, the Intelligent Organisation is process based, and the customer is the ultimate beneficiary of the process, however many steps there may be. Core processes, and there is usually more than one, are company-wide (Feigenbaum, 1986) connected and dependent chains of activities (tasks and procedures) that integrate to produce goods and/or services that meet the desired customer and organisational outcomes (figure 3.5). The purpose of the core process(es) is to generate value for the customer and the organisation. To simplify writing, the word "customer" has been chosen to embrace both clients and users.

Represented generically here for the purpose of explanation, a core process converts inputs into outputs that meet desired outcomes. Outcomes are the things that are actually valued by the customer, hence they are value generating; profit, earning more than is spent over time, is a constraint upon continued existence (Beer, 1985), while value embraces both financial and non-financial measures.

The process design must be rooted in understanding the needs and desires of customer(s) (who may be internal or external), the extent to which the organisation

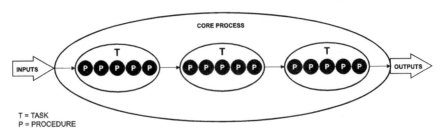

FIGURE 3.5 Core process

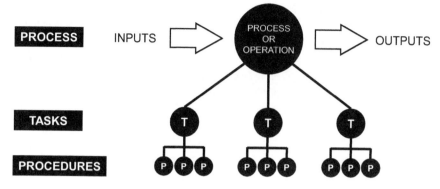

FIGURE 3.6 Processes, tasks and procedures

is willing to fulfil them and the determination of what activities and inputs are required to meet them. Outputs include not only the products and services required by the customer but also by-products: residual materials, cash, waste, data and experience which should be utilised in the next iteration of the process. The input-process-output is shown for convenience at this stage as a single line; don't worry – it will get more complicated soon.

Looking at the core process we find that it is broken down into a series of tasks or sub-processes, and those tasks are further broken down into detailed procedures. Figure 3.6 teases these apart vertically.

A helpful starting point for identifying core processes is to understand what constitutes value for the customer and note the connected stream of activities that generate it.

What is a core process?

A water and sewerage company's customer expects potable water from the tap and the removal of dirty water via the drains. This suggests a minimum of two core processes for the company: one which collects, cleans and delivers water and one which removes used water, treats it and disposes of it. The process for potable water, then, can be considered as a series of tasks, working from the beginning of the process as the following:

Collect Water – Treat Water – Distribute Water

The sewerage process tasks can be considered as:

Collect "Used" Water – Treat Water – Dispose of Water

The water company probably needs to add to that a customer service process for repair and invoicing. It will have a lot of assets connected to create its network (a highly distributed water factory) and it can be argued that maintenance of that "water factory" is also a core process. Alternatively it can be argued either that maintenance is a task within the production processes or that it is an "enabling" process (see Chapters 5 and 6). The "right" answer, to some extent, depends upon how we choose to interpret the organisation and how responsibility and accountability for performance are to be managed. In essence a choice needs to be made about whether the activity is understood and managed as value generating or value enabling.

For a motor car manufacturer, the thing that the customer values is perhaps the car, so the overall core process tasks can be considered as

Design Car – Manufacture Car – Distribute Car

An interesting argument, here, is about what is valuable. For the motor manufacturer it might be the sale of the car, in which case they would optimise the manufacturing and distribution processes. It might, though, be that what is of value to them is the revenue generated by the finance provided to the customer to acquire the car (or the right to use it). The finance may well be more valuable to the manufacturer than the car itself, in which case they would seek to optimise that aspect.

However, while the customer may value the car, they may instead value the journeys that it lets them make, the car itself being a useful but distress purchase element ("Because of where I live, I can't complete the journey without the car"). The manufacturer sets a price for the car; that is what they value. The customer may well value something else. The optimisation, or maximisation, of processes needs to grasp this difference.

In the UK the greater part of the new car market is for leased company vehicles while in the private market a significant proportion are acquired on personal contract plans or hire-purchase. The focus for all these sales is on periodic cost rather than outright purchase price. The manufacturer receives the capital at once via the dealer or the finance company, whilst the user is paying for the vehicle over time. It may be that each party is valuing different aspects of the transaction. It is important to understand the perspectives of both the customer and the organisation in establishing the purpose of any process.

The solution rests in understanding the purpose of the organisation from the perspective of the customer: the need or opportunity it exists to fulfil.

In the service context the outcome does not sustain as it does in manufacturing. It is largely created and consumed in the momentary interaction of the individual operator and customer. The same essential logic applies, however. The output of a dental practice might be considered as "completed dental treatments". While the process which produces that has both curative and preventative characteristics, the outcome is patients with healthy teeth. The greater part of the output rests in the application of professional knowledge, skill and judgement; it relies more on skills and behaviours than on pure process but nonetheless relies on a simple statement of the process steps:

Receive Patient – Assess Patient – Treat Patient

These are, of necessity, massive simplifications. Processes must focus on delivering the purpose of the organisation, the reason it exists, and, ultimately, their performance defines its effectiveness. However, as the following case shows whilst the process is critical, it is not the whole but one part of the essential "triple" of what, how and why.

Visiting the dentist

While considering the effectiveness of a dental practice, the dentist was asked to define the detailed tasks and procedures that underpin the high-level process description. The detail of "Receive Patient" was quite short and simple, essentially the verification of identity and appointment. The detail of "Assess Patient" took a dozen pages of written description just to get the patient into the chair. It required the dentist to assess everything from the mood and demeanour of the patient (determining in what manner they should be dealt with) to the clinical requirements (the overall apparent health of the patient to the specific condition of every individual tooth). Thereafter "Treat Patient" consisted in over 180 different things that might be done for every individual tooth. It was neither useful nor practical to attempt to document in procedural terms every possibility. That was best left to the judgement and skill of the dentist. That is rooted (pardon the pun) in extensive initial training, continuing professional development and experience.

Understanding organisational purpose is fundamental to adequately addressing the challenge of identifying core processes. Public services (whether directly provided or through an agency or NGO) often have multiple parties who might be considered as the customer. Is it the funder? The beneficiary? Both? Does one core process satisfy all needs? In healthcare, especially with commissioning of services, is the process focused on patient benefit? Provider benefit? Referrer benefit? Funder benefit?

If the role of the police in the UK is to "preserve the Queen's peace", who is their customer? The individual citizen? The victim of crime? The criminal? The Home Office? The Police and Crime Commissioner (as representative of the citizen)? Society at large? It might be argued that the police have two core processes. First might be the prevention of harm and crime, second the detection and arrest of criminals – the final output of which is a "prosecution-ready" case file, because the prosecution itself is undertaken by a separate service. The answer chosen has implications for both design and management of the core process and for understanding performance. If "harm and crime prevention" and "crime detection and arrest" are treated as the core processes, then complete success on the first (zero crime) renders the second redundant, whereas complete failure on the first will (probably) mean that the second is overloaded.

There is a need to achieve the most appropriate (under the varying circumstances) definition of "purpose" and clarity of process. In a knowledge economy we must understand how to balance the constraints necessary for process standardisation and compliance with the freedom necessary to allow professional judgement to be exercised.

It is critically important that design for an intelligent organisation starts with the customer-oriented process(es), the fundamental activity flow. Once the core processes have been defined, they can then be disaggregated into the discrete tasks and contained procedures required for their completion. Note that the start point is rather different to a conventional approach, which would build from the bottom up. Disaggregation ensures that the sense of purpose is always embedded. It ensures that all of the activities of the organisation at this level are focused on the customer and that improvement at either the task or procedure level is measured in terms of contribution to process performance. This avoids the risk, so commonly experienced, of an improvement that answers to Hutber's Law (1973), "improvement means deterioration", so we don't simply do the wrong thing better.

The homeostat: the logical emergence of hierarchy

The process so far described will produce only the outputs it has been designed for. It will be autonomic: as long as it is supplied with energy (whatever form that may take) it will keep doing what it does. However, as with any system, left to itself the process will change and, most likely, decay. Materials, people, skills and data all change over time. The customer perception of the value of the service or product and the social, economic, political and environmental circumstances all evolve. Left to itself the process will tend towards either chaos or crystallisation. For the physicists, this answers to the Second Law of Thermodynamics, which states, roughly, that the amount of free energy in a closed system will decrease over time. In our case, the free energy (usually money) will be wasted sustaining a chaotic system (anarchy) or consumed in an inflexible way of working (bureaucracy). The latter arises when the organisation does not adapt to the environment, the former when the attempts at adaptation are individually arbitrary. Either way it dies. There is therefore a logical need to regulate the process. This ensures local self-regulation (how well are we doing what we said we would do?), adaptation and moderation to ensure that the process remains aligned with its environment and continues to be efficient. This mechanism of self-regulation is called a "homeostat" (Ashby, 1952). The output from the process that enables this is information which is used to make decisions (figure 3.7).

In figure 3.7 the manager as regulator (the divided oval) is shown as receiving feedback (measurement of output) from the end of the process. The manager compares what was achieved (actual) with what was desired (capability) and acts to close the gap between them by changing one or more of the inputs (i.e. materials, energy, cash, skills, behaviours, data). The regulator, the logically necessary activity of management, is essential to keep the process aligned with the customer and organisational expectations. If done right then, on the next iteration of the process cycle the gap between actual and desired gets smaller. The manager is using feedback about the process, embedding self-correction. This same reflective cycle approach is also applied to the contained tasks and procedures. In this way all the elements of the core process are both self-regulating and adapting, improving through experience.

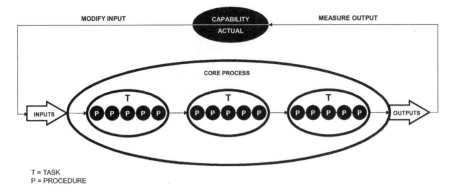

FIGURE 3.7 The emergence of hierarchy

Management is the name we give to the activities of those responsible for "regu-lating" our organisations. It consists in closing the gap between things as they are (actual) and things as we desire them to be (capability) and is logically necessary. How that management is exercised is not yet considered. (We are not yet explor-ing the "how" of management, simply the "what"). Readers will be very familiar with simple regulators, they exist in heating and cooling systems (thermostats for regulating temperature), lighting systems (rheostats for regulating light levels) and in motor vehicles (cruise control systems and anti-lock braking systems). These examples are very simple, typically operating with a single externally generated goal and an on/off response. In the organisation the regulator needs to be more sophisticated, it needs to deal with a range of possible goals and a range of possible responses. This needs judgement and that needs people.

Figure 3.8 shows the regulators in place at the task level and how the process constrains both tasks and procedures. These and their regulation may all be con-ducted by a single individual (self-management is entirely legitimate and highly desirable) or may involve hundreds of people in a large organisation. For now, it is the principle of this integration of process and regulation that is important.

Figure 3.9 opens up the regulator so that the management task can be seen. It shows that the input to the management process, at this level of consideration, is the output performance metrics of the operational process.

The explicit task of management (a process running backwards from the output to the input) is to compare actual with desired output and modify the inputs to close the gap. It is important to appreciate that management is limited in the things it can modify:

- the process itself (the "what") – tasks, procedures, materials;
- the skills and behaviours to be applied (the "how" and "why");
- the desired output (standard) – perhaps in response to a change in customer requirements or market conditions or even the internal capability of the pro-cess itself.

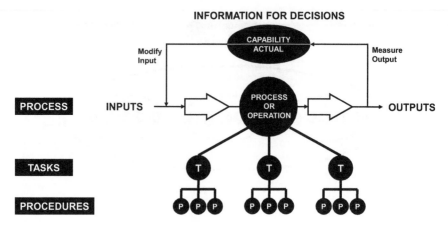

FIGURE 3.8 Process and task regulation

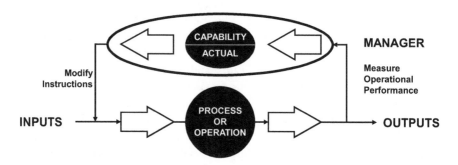

FIGURE 3.9 The process of management

Management does this through the use of information. Implicit in this regulation of process is the need to capture and report data about process performance, applied skills and behaviours and customer requirements. This demands an "information system" comprised of both hard and soft elements that must operate at least at the same cyclic rate as the process itself in order that "self-regulation" can be effective. Shingo's quality idea of Poka-Yoke (Beckford, 2017) embraces this cybernetic concept; the mechanism for self-regulation uses feedback about process performance to maintain that performance within target parameters and acts to minimise use of resources in achieving it, stopping the process if it is failing.

The management of any particular process is relying on feedback from the process output. It is unimportant whether the output of each cycle is a single unit, a batch of products or a continuous stream. It is only important that the output is measured in a consistent and coherent manner and that the measurement(s) is useful to the manager (regulator) in modifying the input to the next cycle. A well-designed process will embed data generation, as one of its outputs, to support timely information flows rather than being a separate activity of reporting. Measurement must be built into the work, not added on, and should impart minimal ongoing cost. The process then generates the information to support its own management, and the management process (the act of regulation) generates information to support related processes (figure 3.10). It exchanges information with its embedded tasks and procedures, with prior or subsequent process(es) and, very importantly, with its boss, that is the higher order process within which it is contained.

For the rest of the book to make sense, it is important that you have really understood the homeostat as the essential core structure of Intelligent Organisation. If you are unsure about your understanding, then read this section again. When you have done that, close the book, lean back, stare at the ceiling for a while and think how different it is to convention. When I was first working with these concepts, I called my PhD supervisor and said, "This is really hard," to which he replied, "Yes, it is," and put the phone down.

Now, take some time out from reading and attempt to map your organisation into the model.

- What outcomes does it seek to achieve?
  - What do the customers or users value?
- What are its outputs?
  - What goods or services are produced?
- What are the core processes?
  - What are the core sets of activities that produce the goods or services?
  - What are the task steps that make up the processes?
  - What procedures underpin the task?

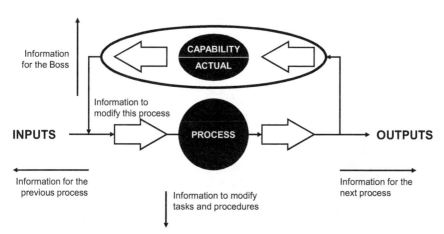

FIGURE 3.10   Information dissemination

- How is information used to manage them?

  - What are the performance standards?
  - How is performance measured?
  - What are the managerial actions that arise from that information?

Requisite complexity

The homeostat is regarded as the fundamental unit of organisation. It replaces the functional hierarchy to which we have become inured with an information-based hierarchy rooted in managing (improving) process performance. Subject to the already discussed notion of "tight-loose control", it is "permeable", closed enough to allow it to be self-regulating. As long as it is provided with appropriate forms of energy, it will keep on doing whatever you designed it to do in the first place. It must also be open enough to exchange information with its environment of managers, subordinates, customers, and predecessor and successor processes. It contains sub-processes (tasks and procedures) with which it exchanges information, and it is, itself, a sub-process of a higher order regulator (it exchanges information with its boss). The homeostat is informationally permeable, and so its information exchanges need to be structured. It needs information, not data, with which to inform managerial decisions.

The understanding developed so far is good but not rich enough. The homeostat so far presented has but a single arrow, implying perhaps a single channel for information flow. This has been a convenience to help with the writing. In any real situation the homeostat must have requisite complexity to deal with variety, the range of possible conditions or states it can be in, thrown up by the whole process. The process is productive through the interaction between all the elements of production. I have arbitrarily chosen six factors of production to represent the general case of a process in an extended homeostat (figure 3.11). I know that we are all different – everybody is a "special case" – but every actual process will be a particular case of this generic one.

The manager is receiving information (aggregated and contextualised data) about all the outputs of the process expressed as measures of operational performance and is understanding the performance gap, usually referred to as efficiency

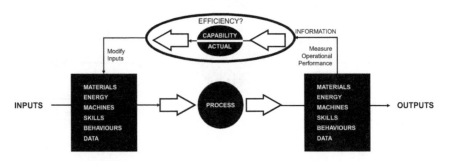

FIGURE 3.11 The expanded homeostat

or productivity. We ask how well did we utilise the various inputs compared with the desired or target level of utilisation? When there is an actionable gap (utilisation will rarely be 100%) the appropriate managerial response is to consider which of the inputs to modify for the next cycle of the process in order to close the gap. This is *not* about punishment or retribution for past performance; it is about error prevention in the next cycle. The manager needs both to receive information and to respond to it sufficiently quickly to achieve this. It is critical to remember interdependency at this point. Changing any one input may have consequences for the others. It is inadequate management to change one parameter ("use less materials") without understanding the impact that may have on others ("apply a higher level of skill" or "use more energy").

Working through this systemic understanding, we can now make effective use of all of the conventional tools and techniques of operations management (Slack et al, 1995). It may be appropriate to apply the tools of statistical process control (Oakland, 2019), business process improvement (Tucker, 1996), business process re-engineering (Hammer & Champy, 1993), lean manufacturing (Ohno, 1988) or lean administration (Seddon, 2005, 2008). If considering skills and behaviours, you may desire to apply ideas around organisational learning (Senge, 1993), knowledge management (Hislop, 2013) and organisational psychology (Schein, 1998) and to draw on the established work concerning motivation and performance, such as that of Herzberg (1959); Mayo (1949); and Maslow (1970). The works of the quality gurus (Beckford, 2017) collectively offer a range of tools and techniques many of which would be useful with this challenge.

The management of management

Adding further complexity, now that we have one homeostat, we can imagine that in any sort of process or organisation there will always be more than one. We need then to think about how they combine. Each is, in and of itself, relatively simple; however, when we connect homeostats through information flows, they interact and become interdependent. Like flocking birds or swarming bees, their collective interactions exhibit apparently complex behaviour. What we have is lots of (relatively) simple things, each doing (relatively) simple things but all joined together and activated by information. In physical terms, each might be thought of as a single cell which joins together with other simple cells collectively acting in ways which display apparently complex, even emergent, behaviours.

It is unlikely that an organisation of any significance (even an individual) will have only one process. There are likely to be two or more divided on some basis.

Looking at figure 3.12, the homeostats might represent

- four identical processes operating in different geographical markets, e.g. USA, Europe, Middle East, Asia-Pacific;
- four different processes in the same market (e.g. a utility company providing power, gas, telecommunications and water);

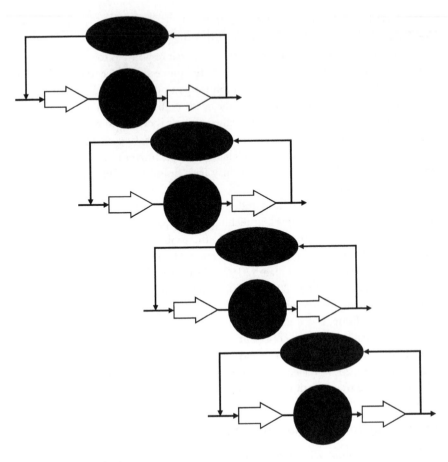

FIGURE 3.12 Multiple processes

- four different market segments in a common geographical domain, e.g. the division of banking customers into mass-market personal, high-net worth personal, small business, corporate.

In each case it is essential to recognise that because of the size of the organisation or the nature of its environment (or commonly both) it is necessary to find useful ways of discriminating segments of the environment and developing processes which are focused into those segments. This division stimulates the need for a next higher level of management, a regulator that regulates the regulators (figure 3.13), that is, the management of managers.

If the role of the manager at the process level is to maintain performance and ensure local adaptation, within constraints, to changes in the environment then the role of senior management is to maintain and improve the management process. That is to say that higher management should not, indeed must not, intervene in the management of the process itself. Rather, senior management should observe

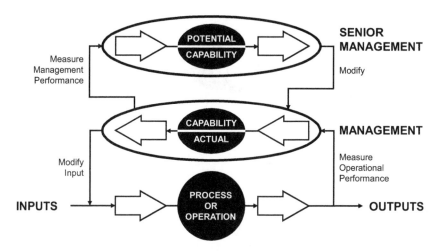

FIGURE 3.13   The management of management

the effect of managerial action on process performance and take action to modify the management process. Note how in figure 3.14 the flows to higher management are linked to the information flow, not the process flow.

Thus, no doubt to the surprise of many, there *is* a useful, twofold role for senior management: first to manage the process(es) of management, second to manage across multiple processes in order to balance and optimise performance for the benefit of the whole organisation. This higher order management manages the present of the organisation, managing the delivery of current products and services to current markets in a known environment.

The hierarchical "superiority" of management can now be seen for what it is. It is

- logically necessary to sustain the coherence of the whole system and
- able to make decisions *not* because it is more "politically" powerful but because it has more appropriate information.

This information is available because senior management, the higher order homeostat, has an overview of the entirety of the processes and is the guardian of established standards and goals. In the Intelligent Organisation, information truly is power.

That does not make senior management omniscient nor all-powerful. For the organisation to be survival worthy, power must be devolved to those who deal with the customers, otherwise the capability for local adaptation is lost. The Intelligent Organisation needs to maintain capacity for operational adaptation, the things that it does that interact with customers and the market. At the same time, it is constrained to do only those things which are legitimate in fulfilling its defined purpose and to use only those resources (data, materials, skills etc.) which belong

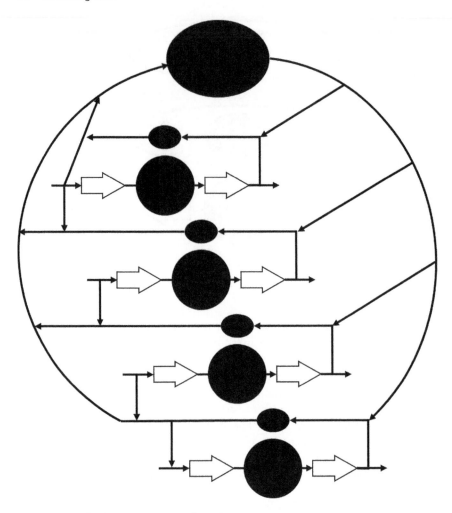

FIGURE 3.14 Senior management observing management

to it. There is then tension. The requirement for local adaptation is in conflict with the constraints of consistency and coherence, whilst power will have a tendency to centralise simply through the operation of the organisation.

Autonomy is not accidental: it needs to be structured and managed, built in to the design of the organisation, embedded in its operational processes and its meta-processes, enshrining the capability for local adaptation. Whilst the operation of the organisation necessarily constrains, there is at the same time a need to maintain freedom. No manager or management system, however powerful, wonderful or enlightened, can empower an individual. What we must do is create the conditions under which individuals can empower themselves within the constraints of belonging.

A fuller discussion on the notion of autonomy is pursued in later chapters.

Summary

This chapter has started to build the whole of the Intelligent Organisation around the central idea of the homeostat, the device using feedback about performance to enable self-regulation. It has introduced the idea of both an organisational form and the logical necessity of a hierarchical decision structure based on information. You should perhaps spend a little more time now thinking about the implications of what you have just read before you look at the examples in the next chapter.

4

GENERATING VALUE

Cases

Introduction

As I introduced a way of thinking holistically about organisations that challenges the traditional approach so radically, it seemed important to lay out the whole value-generating system in a single flow rather than in a fragmented way. Hopefully you have taken a few minutes to think about your own organisation before we put theory into practice by considering three case studies:

- Fusion21: a third-sector procurement and training business;
- The Canal and River Trust: a health and well-being charity;
- Southern Mill: a paper maker.

Profits into people, not into pockets: Fusion21

Fusion21 is a social enterprise that promotes efficient public procurement as a means to generate social value and reduce costs. Originally established on Merseyside, it aims to create demand led training and employment. It achieves this by offering an intelligent procurement service to its clients, reducing their costs by operating cost-effective procurement frameworks and by training unemployed people in relevant skills, placing them in work with the contractors and suppliers fulfilling the contracts. A pleasing, circular outcome: the more the members spend through the frameworks, the more people in their own communities are able to find work. Fusion21 sets itself the goal of being the market leader in procurement efficiency and social value with the business objectives being

- maintain and support existing clients,
- attract and retain new clients,
- undertake research and development in improving products and services and
- fitness for purpose.

Achieving the first two of these objectives is the focus of this study, and Fusion21 works towards them through their

- procurement services,
- training and employment services and
- consultancy services.

Fusion21 looked at through a conventional organogram is represented in figure 4.1.

As we have already established, that tells us remarkably little of how the organisation works and how it generates value for its stakeholders. How much more helpful might it be to consider the organisation through the processes (figure 4.2) it engages in to generate value?

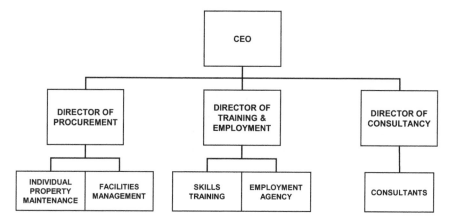

FIGURE 4.1   Fusion21: conventional hierarchy

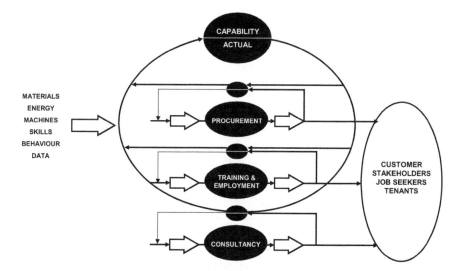

FIGURE 4.2   Fusion21: process perspective

This shows us how each of the individual homeostats (the core processes) is focused on the environment in which Fusion21 seeks to do business. While each has a unique process, they draw on a shared pool of organisational resources for their completion. They share data (about customers, contractors, suppliers, tenants and jobseekers), they have shared beliefs and behaviours (the culture of the organisation), but they require different skills for each process. At least some of the skills required for delivering an efficient procurement process are different from those required for training or consultancy. Each process can be locally managed whilst there is a view of the whole (senior management) attempting to balance performance, the demand for resources and so on.

It is critical to recognise the legitimacy and necessity of shared data in this context. Remember the "circular outcome": the environment of the organisation (the social and economic context in which it undertakes its business) is common to all processes. Sharing of data enables a situation in which the procurement process generates a surplus. That surplus is invested in the training of jobseekers who can be offered work in the delivery of the project; in some cases Fusion21 has employed the individual rather than placing them with a contractor. The "training and employment" process needs to be aware *both* of the opportunity, the "procurement" of a contract, *and* of the availability of an individual with appropriate skills so that they can close the circle and place the jobseeker. That demands information sharing; an intelligent organisation shares data rather than duplicating it in different silos.

It was established in the previous chapter that these overall processes are themselves made up of embedded homeostats (the tasks and procedures), so we shall now explore the next two levels of organisation in the procurement process (picking the biggest one of the three).

Figure 4.3 shows that the process of procurement breaks down into a series of tasks:

- recognise the opportunity,
- invite tenders from suppliers/contractors,
- evaluate the tenders,
- appoint supplier and contractor and
- monitor delivery.

Each of these tasks is itself constituted as a homeostat which receives "inputs" from the previous step, is self-regulating and generates "outputs" in a progress accumulating flow to achieve the overall output desired. The process homeostat (the higher level) monitors the achievement of this. Tasks may be undertaken by one individual or by a series of individuals who may be made up into teams. The job of "monitoring", the local supervision or management of each task step may be carried out by self-managing individuals, a team leader, supervisor or manager depending perhaps on the volume of activity and the skills of the individuals.

Meanwhile, the tasks themselves are broken down into procedures. I have chosen here, for reasons of simplicity and space, to investigate only one of the embedded

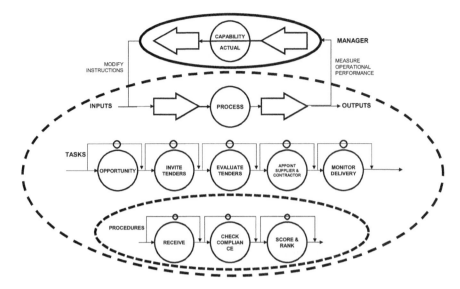

FIGURE 4.3   Fusion21: embedded tasks and procedures

procedures, "evaluate tenders". Figure 4.3 shows that it breaks down into three procedural steps:

- receive tender,
- check compliance and
- score and rank.

The output of these procedures is the prospective appointment of suppliers and contractors to deliver the contract. The conduct of these procedures will most likely be self-managed, the individual operators will manage themselves, and against standards and norms for throughput, accuracy, response times embedded in the process, i.e. they will know what is expected of them and manage themselves to achieve it.

The whole systemic assemblage of procedures embedded in tasks embedded in a process depends on appropriate information being provided to appropriately skilled and knowledgeable individuals. The process itself is relatively simple but its desired output provides the "why" which informs the "what" and "how" for the tasks and procedures.

This process flow was determined with the Fusion21 procurement team as being the most appropriate overall flow with a number of the tasks and procedures being required to demonstrate a legally compliant process. The design was not determined by technology but by the professional skills and knowledge of the individuals involved.

Each task could be broken down as has been done for "evaluate tenders", revealing the possibility of further choices being made. Fusion21 objectives require that they both "maintain and support existing clients" and "attract and retain new clients". The "opportunity" task, therefore, might be broken down to recognise that split and the procedures for those different groups of clients may vary. There are additional procedural steps for new clients compared with existing ones, and the ways of engaging with them to stimulate opportunities require different skills. Similarly, figure 4.3 treats the environment of the organisation as a homogeneous whole while Fusion21 operates in multiple markets, differentiated by type of customer, geography and types of procurement activity. The procurement process therefore has separate workstreams which deal with three distinct sets of activities:

- planned maintenance,
- retrofit and
- facilities management.

The overall process for each of these is as represented in figure 4.3, while at the task and procedural level there are significant differences. This workstream breakdown is shown in figure 4.4.

In designing the Intelligent Organisation, we must grasp the needs of the particular situation and understand how to build requisite complexity into the design to address it appropriately whilst at the same time developing a consistent representation.

In the case of Fusion21 a key determinant of the design is the recognition of the particular skills and knowledge required to fulfil the process. We shall return to Fusion21 in later chapters as we continue building the whole organisation. In the meanwhile we look at a case where the technology is the principal determinant of the organisation design.

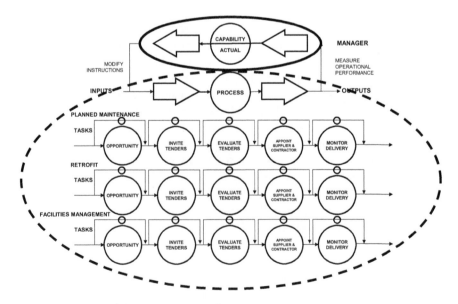

FIGURE 4.4 Fusion21: procurement workstreams

Fusion21: five years on

Since the original case study, Fusion21 has spent time considering how best to achieve both commercial *and* social purposes. The original case study explored how the procurement function was effectively managed (using the homeostat) and how this was used to enable "social value" to be generated from the procurement activity (i.e. getting people into jobs). As you would expect, the procurement part of the business has not stood still and has developed over the years, but the homeostat still remains recognisable from the one in the case study.

New "categories" have been established that sit above the workstreams and provide a higher order management structure. This has been supported by a conscious decision to develop and enhance the knowledge and skills of the team via an emphasis on improving both the procurement and category-specific technical skills. The products (frameworks/workstreams) have also evolved to continue to meet the needs of the customers using them (an approach that is heavily based on customer-led research).

The homeostat provided a consistent mechanism to understand the processes and tasks needed to service the requirements of the customer. This consistency has helped to retain the existing customers and attract new ones to the offer. It has also provided a mechanism to introduce improvements to the processes in response to the changing markets and customer demands.

Cost saving is still an important part of the offer, but the focus is centred on delivering "value for money", which can mean different things to different customers (efficiency, cost management, quality, social value, SME and localism engagement) and the products (and associated processes have had to incorporate this flexibility). Social value is still an integral part of the offer, with more flexibility built into how this can be delivered, which has been managed through the processes and task-based approach of the homeostat.

Having this approach embedded within the organisation has allowed the organisation to focus on higher order challenges. This included the development of the notion that that "profits into people" can be achieved in two ways: by empowering other organisations (including social businesses) to deliver the desired social impact, and by a specialist charitable arm of the business whose sole purpose is to channel the "profits" into social investments in charities and social business to help achieve the social purpose.

Social value is also derived from the planning system as well as procurement, which demonstrates how the approach outlined in the original case study has been used to continue to meet the commercial and social purposes and has provided a structure to support the transformation required to achieve this.

Fusion21 has a firm belief that in order to be an organisation that creates sustainable social impact it must have a strong (and viable) commercial business model in place. The dual-purpose concept only fully works when the organisation is correctly aligned to work toward both goals. All the changes outlined above still have (and need) the basic structure of the homeostat in order to deliver their stated objective. This has permitted greater clarity over how both the commercial and social purposes of the organisation can be achieved.

The Canal and River Trust

The Canal and River Trust is a charity established in 2012 in succession to the state-owned British Waterways Board to take on the task of sustaining much of the canal and river network in England and Wales. The Trust has a turnover of around £200m, is responsible for about 2000 miles of waterway including about 5000 major structures (bridges, tunnels, culverts, locks and buildings) and has a substantial investment estate, the revenues from which help to sustain it (Canal and River Trust, 2018).

The initial engagement with the Trust was to explore operational performance, including how it was being measured, and to consider how the prevailing central oversight and control arrangements might be contributing to or inhibiting the achievement of operational objectives, i.e. to understand what might have been getting in the way of operational performance. The work was undertaken through a series of semi-structured interviews with key individuals, a desktop review of organisation charts, budgets and performance reports and reflective discussions with the commissioners of the work. It rapidly became apparent to all that any change at the operating level would need to be consistent with an emerging strategic change, a shift from the traditional focus on the protection and stewardship of the network, and its necessary asset maintenance, to a wider external focus on the user experience and benefit and the role that these post-industrial waterway networks can play in enriching people's lives in the communities around them. A number of structural, behavioural and informational challenges became apparent.

- A high number of operational units generated a reporting and control challenge;
- Contrarily, local autonomy was low;
- Objectives were not always clear;
- Performance information was financially focused, lacked direct connection to activity levels and outputs and did not guide on improving efficiency and effectiveness;
- Reports were sometimes hard to comprehend and lacked an action focus;
- Skills and behaviours of management were often aligned to historic rather than current need (though a programme was in course to address this);
- Maintenance activity could sometimes focus on the inputs – the capacity and the schedule for delivery – rather than linking to strategic outputs.

Initial thinking, using the ideas of Intelligent Organisation, suggested that the Trust might function better with accountability more devolved, with fewer managers each carrying out bigger roles. That would of course require clarity about purpose and objectives, as well as investment in people and information systems, coupled to a drive to enhance processes and reduce or eliminate unnecessary or non-value-adding work.

To ensure that the strategic direction of the Trust was reflected in any changes arising, the dialogue was rapidly extended to engage the whole of the executive team plus a number of other managers responsible for key functions (asset planning, management accounting, information technology). Again, from semi-structured interviews and analysis of a range of information, there emerged general agreement that there was scope for – and recognition of the need for – change. The prevailing structure was recognised as being fragmented, perhaps unmanageable, with numerous boundaries and hand-offs. Partly structural, partly behavioural, too many decisions were taken too far from the problems and challenges they were intended to address, both imposing delays on their resolution and reducing autonomy at the local level. Critically it was very evident that information management was greatly separated from the work itself and that a significant number of people were required both to construct reports and to support managers in their interpretation. The predecessor organisation, in effect a civil service entity, had not significantly invested in information, and the Trust was still catching up.

The functionally organised structure gave primacy to the internal needs of the organisation. Meanwhile, the strategic direction of the Trust was to shift its attention to meeting the needs and desires of the waterway users and customers, to develop the organisation to deliver social value as well as to become self-sustaining. A virtuous circle had been devised under which it was believed that the virtuous cycle shown in figure 4.5 would be realised.

It had been determined that the identity of the Trust, the expression of its purpose, should be about enabling societal health and well-being. To that end, the Trust identified six strategic domains to which it aims to contribute.

- Health, well-being, happiness: embracing both physical and mental health and well-being.
- Engaged people, cohesive communities: embracing community engagement, broadening opportunities and inclusivity.
- Learning and enhanced skills: embracing education, skills, lifelong learning.
- Prosperous and connected places: embracing economic growth, regeneration and development.

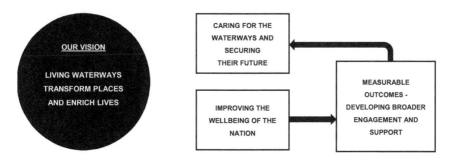

FIGURE 4.5 The canal and river trust: the virtuous circle

- Green and blue futures: embracing sustainable transport, renewable energy, water resourcing.
- Cultural and environmental assets: embracing culture and heritage, biodiversity and environmental stewardship.

The structure of the organisation and specifically its information management was no longer fit for purpose; it could not deliver the desired outcomes. Observation of the organisation, coupled to the discussions with the executive, allowed a shared model to arise, an understanding that fulfilment of the purpose of the Trust meant, at the corporate level, it should be organised around three essential core processes.

- Customer service and engagement: improving the day-to-day experience for waterway users and visitors and attracting the public at large.
- Asset management and delivery: maintaining the waterway assets in a sustainable long-term condition.
- Income and investment: guardianship of the endowment and exploiting other revenue-raising opportunities.

These were to some extent aligned with the traditional role of the organisation, albeit in need of improvement in process and information.

The first of these represents a significant shift towards recognising that the value of the waterways does not rest solely in the engineered assets but also in the wider utilisation and impact of those assets on lives today. It is also very important to note the dependency on the success of the core functions; without a well-maintained and safe canal and towpath network, the wider benefits could not be realised. There was significant discussion about whether they, and the rest of the organisation, should be defined as a single process or as two. The decision taken to cast it as two reflected a pragmatic approach to optimising the use of skills and behaviours and to balancing workload, but it is important to note that the immediate customer of maintenance activity is internal to the organisation (as the service delivery teams in effect depend upon those undertaking their long-term care). If the first process is about encouraging the use of the waterways and their surroundings and the second is, essentially, about keeping the water in the waterway, the third is about ensuring that there is money available to support the other two. Guardianship of the endowment describes the investment activity undertaken by the Trust which must both financially support the day to day operations and sustain the value of the endowment itself by generating a profit on investments. So, again, the customer of investment management is the Trust itself. The value-generating elements of the Canal and River Trust can be represented as shown in figure 4.6.

In addition, the Trust recognised it had three new areas of focus that would be essential for its long-term future:

- Wellbeing, delivering outcomes to people and communities.
- Brand, influence and support – raising awareness of the Trust and converting the millions of local users into supporters.
- Changing the organisation to become more agile and lean, fit for the future in the third sector.

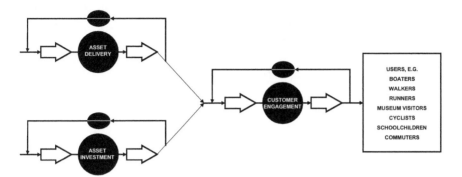

FIGURE 4.6   Canal and river trust: the process chain

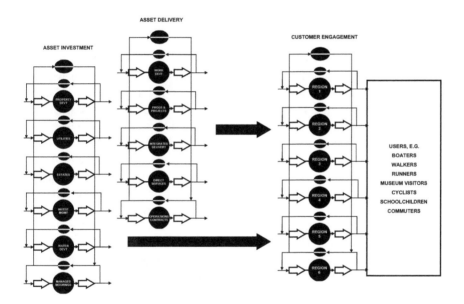

FIGURE 4.7   Canal and river trust: processes with embedded tasks

Further elaboration of the organisation structure followed (with agreement from the trustees), and a negotiated process of change saw the Trust adopt that over-all architecture for value generation. Each of the three core processes was then examined to understand what the embedded sub-processes or tasks should be. The breakdown is provided in figure 4.7.

This shows that "customer service and engagement" activity is divided into six geographic regions rather than the ten under the previous structure. "Asset deliv-ery" has been primarily divided into areas of technical competence and task size with geography secondary. "Income and investment" was divided to reflect the differing types of investments being made (and income streams created), reflect-ing the technical expertise required to be effective. Within the overall common architecture each element has been composed in a way that suits the particular need, the principles are common, the execution unique.

Of course, simply reorganising the structure is only one of several steps to which the Trust needed to commit to deliver a different future. In concert with that, a number of other actions were taken:

- Creation of a delivery group to see through the change;
- Redesigning processes and behaviours to be agile, lean and engaged;
- Recognising information needs and redesigning information systems to fulfil them.

We shall return to this case in later chapters as we continue to build our comprehension of the Intelligent Organisation.

Southern Mill: "a good tonne"

Southern Mill is small by the standards of the paper industry, capable of producing 50k gross tonnes per annum. The business recycles waste paper into new paper and places it in the market in over 3000 sizes, colours and shapes from full reels to customised and packaged small quantities. When first encountered, Southern Mill was struggling organisationally and financially. It had experienced a number of changes of key personnel in a short period of time and a fall in demand (blamed on the global recession), and it was not an investment priority for its parent company.

The business was functionally organised around sales, production, conversion, warehousing and despatch with representative "head office" functions. The site General Manager, also responsible for another larger business some miles away, explained that sales were down, production poor, stocks excessive and, despite all that, on-time in full (OTIF) deliveries were running at only around 70%. Clearly something was amiss. The functional organisation chart is provided as figure 4.8.

The existing situation was unsustainable; the business was under threat of sale or closure by its parent if improvement was not delivered.

A detailed review of performance highlighted that the functional management of the business coupled to inadequate information systems had generated a situation in which processes were suboptimal and none of the key functions had the right information to support their decisions. Each was making decisions to optimise its own performance while potentially being damaging to the overall output.

The production function was charged with producing "100 good tonnes per day", and for themselves, had defined "good" as being paper of merchantable quality. If a particular paper was running well on the paper machine, they would keep making it in order to reach target even though they had exceeded the amount of that paper required by the plan and despite the delay to fulfil other orders. Stock was rising because unsold paper was accumulating in the warehouse while orders were left unmet.

Meanwhile, the sales team were pushing volume, offering increasing ranges of colours, weights and sizes and offering discount for bulk orders whilst having no

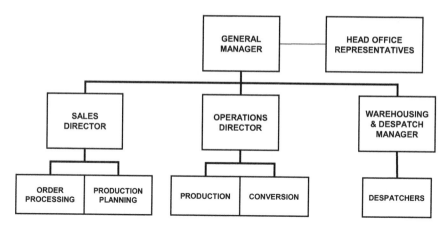

FIGURE 4.8 Southern mill: organisation chart

clear picture of the production cost or profitability of any given line. A "quick and dirty" early analysis showed that, for at least some products, they would have been better off sending the order back with a £50 note attached to it than actually providing the product.

Customers were taking advantage of discounts by placing orders for large quantities to be called off, and then not calling them off. The increasing range of colours, weights and sizes being offered by sales was exacerbating the production challenge. A complete cycle through all of the colours and weights stretched to 16 weeks while the supposed delivery cycle was 4 weeks. This ensured that OTIF would continue to deteriorate.

Every significant change of product on the paper machine required a "change off" period which would cause at least one hour of lost production (about four good tonnes lost) and the conversion activity (splitting reels into sheets) was very labour intensive further increasing costs. Customers, relying on just-in-time deliveries to keep their own plants running, would contact Southern Mill and demand order fulfilment. The production team would interrupt the flow, insert an urgent order, disrupt the cycle, lose more good tonnes and further delay output. If a significant colour change was required then the mill might experience two change offs, losing two hours production (eight tonnes), for order quantities commonly less than five tonnes. The cost of the change-offs (or lost production) was not factored into the price of the inserted product, and more paper was being made for "waste" than for the customer.

The conversion activity was some distance from the mill, as was the despatch and warehousing operation, making both difficult to manage. Meanwhile, missing and inaccurate information about stock levels meant that the sales staff were re-ordering items already in stock. Lack of accurate information meant that despatch and warehousing staff, unable to identify the existence or whereabouts of stock, would either despatch incomplete orders or newly produced paper. Meanwhile existing stock aged and deteriorated.

It was clear that the challenges of Southern Mill could not be addressed in a linear fashion but needed to be tackled through a process which recognised its dynamics and adopt both process control and appropriate information to dissolve the problems. Figure 4.9 shows how integrated the organisational processes were and how inappropriate was their attempt, in this particular case, to manage it from a functional perspective.

For those unfamiliar with process flow:

- Sales activity stimulates customer orders.
- Customer orders goes to the fulfilment plan.
- Fulfilment plan checks warehouse stock and,

  - if stock is available, generates a despatch order directly to the warehouse, but
  - if stock is not available, generates a requirement for the production plan.

- The production plan informs preparation, which allocates fibre stock and other raw materials to the paper machine.
- The paper machine produces reels of paper which are split with three channels for output:

  - reel direct to warehouse (increasing stock),
  - reel to conversion (cutting the paper into sheets and packing it) and
  - broke (paper damaged during production and reel trim offcuts).

- Warehouse stock goes to fulfil customer deliveries.

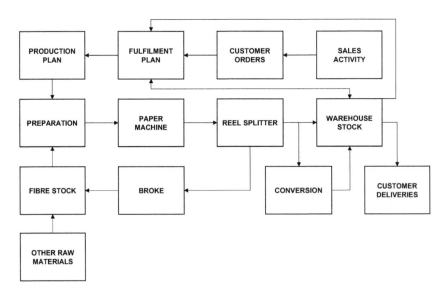

FIGURE 4.9 Southern mill: the process view

It should be clear that this overall process of "meeting customer orders" needs to be managed as an integrated whole.

With the manufacturing processes essentially fixed by the nature of the technology (the paper machine only makes paper one way; what can be varied is the machine speed, paper weight, width and colour) we had to consider effective process control (the natural activity of the homeostat) and accurate, useful information as the basis of improvement. While there were three distinct key processes (figure 4.10) their interdependence and interrelationship meant that any attempt to manage them within the functional silos was doomed to failure. At the same time, attempting to fully integrate them and manage them as a single process was not appropriate; they were too large, too diverse and too physically separate.

The interrelationship needed to be fully articulated, accepted by the business, and a mechanism needed to be established for information sharing to enable better decisions. The cycles could then be synchronised, using information effectively to optimise the whole. The best performance of the weakest link will always act as the bottleneck.

A number of critical steps were taken. A model of the whole process was developed, shared, tested and agreed with the management staff to both confirm understanding of the overall situation and allow discussion of the challenges. It was agreed that the purpose of the business was to fulfil customer demand for speciality papers. That could only be done if the business itself was financially, organisationally and informationally sustainable. This generated a flurry of activity:

- Development of a formal, mathematical, statement of the capacity of the whole process from end to end (a demand-driven process perspective);
- Development of costing and pricing models replicating the structure of the process model but in the "language" of money;

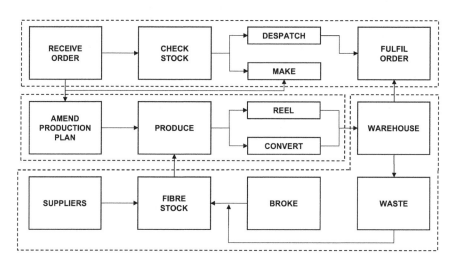

FIGURE 4.10 Southern mill: key processes

- A stock audit, by product and age and updating of the stock records. This was accompanied by the placing into raw materials deteriorated stock and a change to the stock management process;
- Despatching ordered but "uncalled" product and removal from the production plan of any items now known to be held;
- A change in the "check stock" process, with a lock step, so that, using now reliable stock data, an order could not be placed to "make" if the product was already in stock;
- Redefinition of a "good tonne" for production to become "a tonne of paper of merchantable quality for which there is a customer order", i.e. no longer "making for stock" or "keep it going because it is running well".

All of this was accomplished through the establishment of a daily operations meeting at which representatives of each of the key processes (not functional "heads") met to populate a "dashboard" (figure 4.11) which compared actual daily performance against the plan. This regular sharing of information allowed the teams to make the cycles synchronous and ensured that all decisions, overseen by the Operations Director, were taken for the benefit of the whole organisation.

Over a period of about eight months stocks were reduced, bringing substantial cash into the business (destocking generates cash). OTIF increased to 96% compared with only 70% at the outset, and product complexity was reduced through negotiation with customers. Accurate costing allowed the sales team to have fact, based discussions with customers about the price of certain products.

DAILY DASHBOARD: SOUTHERN MILL										
PRODUCTION			CONVERSION				SALES			
PLAN	ACTUAL	DIFF TO PLAN	PRODUCT	PLAN	ACTUAL	DIFF TO PLAN		PLAN	ACTUAL	DIFF TO PLAN
132	138	6	Sheeted	4	3	-1	Stock	600	630	30
Net Tonnes			Laminate	3	4	1	>180	0	45	45
Planned	Actual	Diff to Plan	Coated	2	2	0	>365	0	0	0
80	100	20	Colour	1	1	0	Despatch	104	100	-4
Hold	Over-make	Broke	Coiled	1	1	0	OTIF	98%	96%	-2%
20	50	5	Coiled SS	2	3	1	Orders	100	105	5
Shut			Collated	3	2	-1	Rev	£90000	£94500	£4500
Plan	Unplan	Diff to Plan	Guillotine	5	5	0	Credits	£0	£3000	£3000
48	56	8	BPOP	6	6	0	Unplan £	0	£500	£500
			Packed FP	4	4	0	Complaints	0	1	1
			Packed BP	5	5	0	Accidents (LT)	0	1	1

FIGURE 4.11 Southern mill: daily dashboard

The production cycle time was brought down to six weeks and was progressing towards four.

All of this was brought about by the effective use of information.

Summary

We shall return to these case studies and introduce others later in the book. The intention of this chapter has been to encourage you to think about how you might apply the ideas outlined in the previous chapter to your own organisation. I hope you had some success.

Everything covered in the last two chapters has essentially been concerned with the operation and management of the Intelligent Organisation; it has been focused on managing the present. In the next chapter we shall focus on how the Intelligent Organisation can create its future. And that is something that most are very poor at doing.

5

ENABLING VALUE

Introduction

The previous two chapters have explored the core processes by which the Intelligent Organisation generates value for its customers and itself and manages that activity. The next task is to develop the value-enabling processes. These are essential to the control and development of the organisation as a whole; they act to create its future. Like the core processes, they are designed backwards from their customer (the value-generating parts of the organisation), aiming to ensure alignment to a changing environment and improve performance (adherence to goals) with each iterative cycle. They synthesise information about the present with desires and intent for the future *and* reassess the appropriateness of the established goals in the evolving environment.

The management of the value-generating activities is in a position of internal informational omniscience. That is management can see the performance of the whole operational (value-generating) organisation and modify its inputs in order to improve it; that is good. However, its capability for learning and adaptation is constrained to generating an improved version of its present arrangements. It will be effective in delivering marginal performance gains within the existing organisational arrangements and paradigm, but it lacks the structures, processes and autonomy to reinvent itself.

The value-generating part of the organisation is autonomic; it is fit for purpose but in a market which can evolve beyond it. Doing what it has been designed to do, but nothing else, it has no capability to understand the need for change and evolve at the whole organisational level, no mechanism to enable interaction with the problematic future. It can, to misquote Henry Ford, produce a faster horse, but it will never invent a motor car: it is not adequate for a rapidly changing world.

A head office pathology

It is time for a little more organisational philosophy, a little more thinking about organisation. Every organisation, whether a sole trader or a global corporation, needs what are usually thought of as "head office" functions if it is to survive and thrive. These functions are concerned with understanding the possible internal and environmental causes of risk and opportunity to the organisation and enabling it to deal with them.

These functions (and this may come as a bit of a surprise to the actors who populate them) are not purposeful in their own right. Their purposefulness and utility are measured by the extent that they enable value in the rest of the organisation. Unfortunately, it has been a while since anybody told them this and often head offices have become self-serving, that is, many decisions are made which "work" for the folks in the centre but not for some, or all, of the rest of the organisation. Whether it is the imposition of a solution that only works for one part of the organisation, undertaking activity that is only good for the particular head office function while imparting cost to other parts of the organisation or, in effect, penalising the customers by reducing the level of service offered, this whole suite of behaviours meets the definition of "pathological autopoiesis" (Beer, 1985).

While autopoiesis (Maturana & Varela, 1987) is the natural and essential process by which an organism sustains its own existence, pathological autopoiesis as a sickness is recognised when those essential activities become self-serving. They thereby impart damage or harm to the host organisation either by failing to fulfil their own purpose or by consuming resources which should be used elsewhere. When the value-enabling functions are investing in their own preservation to the detriment of the value-generating functions and the customers, they are, in effect, cancerous. These necessary functions need to be focused on enabling the whole organisation to add value to all stakeholders. By understanding how they contribute value to the whole they can avoid imposing non-value-adding, unnecessary or bureaucratic burdens on the organisation and its customers. If the value added by an enabling function is properly understood, then the costs that necessarily go with it can be properly appreciated.

A little more sympathetically, the tasks of the value-enabling processes are valuable, necessary and often not that simple. They must do several things in parallel in order to maintain the organisation in a state of dynamic stability (allostasis) which

- delivers value to current customers in current markets through existing services and products,
- modifies the future market to more closely align it with the current service and product offer,
- develops or enhances services and products to appeal to future customers in future markets and
- modifies the internal arrangements of the organisation to enhance its viability in the changing environment.

It therefore must

- understand the performance, current and relatively short-term needs of the value-generating parts of the organisation in the context of the present market environment;
- understand the opportunities and threats emerging in the problematic future environment;
- reconcile the two;
- develop strategies and plans for simultaneously and synchronously adapting the organisation (internal) and modifying the environment (external) to ensure its future;
- synthesise the changes across multiple value-enabling functions, e.g. HR, finance, IT, property, marketing;
- negotiate with the value-generating parts of the organisation to deliver the necessary changes.

Doing all that successfully is quite a trick.

The first challenge is that the value-generating parts of the organisation, typically, have the biggest share of the resources. They will assert their autonomy, and with their appropriate focus on the here and now, they will not want to "fix today what ain't yet broke". Humankind has a general tendency to respond more willingly to threat than opportunity (Kahnemann, 2011), but the threat in this case is perhaps only visible to the value enablers not the generators. Perhaps part of the task is information sharing. Figure 5.1 shows a set of value-generating processes engaging with their environment. The processes have been picked as representative rather than real.

The second challenge resides in modifying the environment, the activity often called "marketing". Its first pursuit is to influence the market to demand "our" products and services; it seeks to modify the buying behaviour of customers. Its second pursuit is to interrogate buyer behaviour so that we can understand

- what is being demanded now and into the future,
- what environmental conditions are changing and

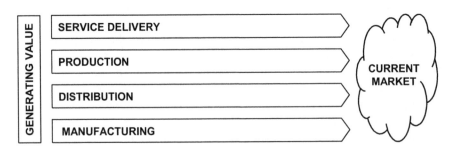

FIGURE 5.1 Value-generating processes

- in what ways the market is seeking to modify the organisation:

  ○ social, demographic, technological, financial, political.

In addition the organisation needs an HR function, to manage its finances both operationally and strategically, to develop future products and services, what in figure 5.2 I have called "engineering". Again, the particular selection is arbitrary, many organisations will have a range of different labels for these essential activities. What can be seen clearly is that the "customer" of these activities is the organisation itself in the form of its core processes. If a "value-enabling" activity is not adding value to core processes, its activity is not legitimate. Value-enabling activities have, or should have, a view of the "future market" to which core processes must be adapting.

The third challenge is the development of new services and products. The value-generating processes of the organisation are adapting and modifying things; they are using information about customers, products, services and performance to "do things right". The value-enabling processes have the responsibility to "do right things". That provides a useful, if rather permeable, delineation between the sets of activities but also provides the basis of potential tension or conflict. Value generation can improve product or service quality, but it cannot define and develop a whole new product or service; it has neither the resources nor the skills to do this and it would not be considered organisationally legitimate. The sustainability of the organisation rests in it enjoying a mutually beneficial relationship with its environment; and that means adaptation for both.

Hence a mechanism is needed, the fourth challenge, through which the internal arrangements of the organisation can be modified to enable its adaptation. Such mechanisms are often cast in change or transformation programmes, managed by

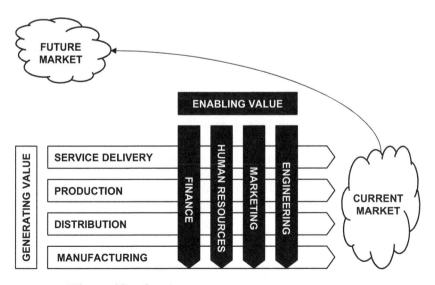

FIGURE 5.2 Value-enabling functions

"change management specialists", consultants and various other hired hands, and are, frequently, enabled or driven by information system changes.

Intelligent organisations are thoughtful about this external expertise. They recognise that, if adaptation is an ongoing requirement (and it is) then they need to develop in their own workforce, their managers and their processes, the capability to deal with it. Goulding and Shaughnessy (2017) provide some good practical insights to how this can be done, particularly in the world of digital transformation. Continuing to hire in short-term expertise to "unfreeze, change, refreeze" (Lewin, 1947) is expensive and doomed to failure. It may be that the temporary engagement of particular technical, managerial, training or consulting skills is a necessary part of accelerating a transformation but ultimately the capability must belong to the host.

Very large organisations may have within their boundaries all of the skills and knowledge that they need. It is certainly the case that they should employ enough people with the right skills and knowledge to address the vast majority of areas. However, unless they wish to close the organisation off to innovative, new or different thinking and ideas or simply to challenge, then there is a legitimate role for external or specialist internal expertise, so long as it is genuinely value adding. Without such expertise, the organisation risks remaining informationally closed, only able to deal with that which already exists within its boundaries. In a rapidly changing environment, that is probably more weakness than strength.

Ultimately it is critical that the processes of change are owned, sponsored and driven by the people inside the organisation, however difficult that may be. Often the help that is most needed is to support them to become intelligent managers, to help them recognise that stability (of the things that are important) arises through change, that permanence is illusory, and, perhaps for the first time, to deal with the new and unknown and all of the risks and challenges that go with it.

Figure 5.3 shows how the organisation uses a dialogue between the management of the value-generating processes with that of the value-enabling processes to formulate a strategy which sustains the organisation, that embeds adaptation.

The role of management in the Intelligent Organisation, regardless of position, seniority or size, is to enable its continuous adaptation to changing circumstances at the same rate as the changes in the external environment. They must keep things the same by making them different, i.e. to maintain dynamic stability through managing change. Each can be thought of, perhaps, as a gyroscope, a device for maintaining orientation. While mechanical gyroscopes generally consist of a spinning wheel or disc (expressing the energy in the system) in which the axle assumes any orientation that achieves dynamic balance, in the organisational gyroscope the axle is the managerial posture (the orientation), the spinning wheel is the flow of information (energy). In both cases the desired outcome is dynamic stability.

Enabling value: dealing with the problematic future

It will, I am sure, come as no great surprise to find that at this point we revert to the homeostat and remind ourselves that the desired output of the value-enabling processes is to create the future of the organisation.

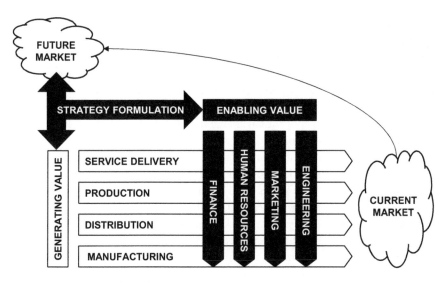

FIGURE 5.3   Strategy formulation

Value-enabling activity needs the creation of a higher order homeostat containing a "model of the model of self" (MoMoS), which consists of more highly aggregated information. The MoMoS reflects the structure and performance of the organisation at the operational level but filters out the operational detail. This aggregation acts to sustain autonomy at lower levels. It avoids being overwhelmed with data and unnecessarily, unintentionally or incompetently constraining freedom to adapt.

A second need is to generate a "model of world" (MoW), a representation of the environment in which the organisation exists. That must contain a requisite abstraction from everything that surrounds the organisation, whether political, social, economic, scientific, environmental or competitive, i.e. all those aspects which impact upon it and those on which it seeks to have impact. This is necessarily an abstraction, "the only perfect model of a cat, *is* a cat" (Weiner, 1948): the only "perfect model" of something is that thing itself. So, we must accept imperfection and the need for judgement. We should be conscientious in our model building while recognising that, to some extent, the model built will reflect the assumptions, preferences, prejudices and biases of the model builders.

These two artefacts, the MoMoS and the MoW, constitute a representation of the organisation in its world and generate the potential to understand possible outcomes from changes in either. The generic question is "what happens if. . .?" The combined models act as the centre point of two processes. The first captures data about the performance of the organisation, compares it with the desired performance and understands the gap. The second captures data about the changing external environment of the organisation and compares it with the current MoMoS and understands that gap. The decisions that emerge from those processes are relatively simple (in principle anyway). They are

- change the organisation in *this* respect,
- change the market in *that* respect and
- a combination of actions that do both.

In figure 5.4, starting at the extreme right, the model of self (MoS) becomes aggregated into the model of the model of self (MoMoS), the informational abstraction of the essentials of structure and performance. At the extreme left the exploration of the environment generates the model of world (MoW), an abstraction of its essential characteristics as they impact on, or are impacted on, by the organisation. The simulation at the centre allows the development and testing of hypotheses about the possible futures of the organisation and the formulation of strategy for realising them. It is a thinking space allowing us to ask "what if?"

For those of a conventional turn of mind these can be recognised as the core activities at the corporate level of formulating and implementing strategy. The environment-facing actions arising from this are often limited to marketing, while the organisation-facing ones can cover a range of things from research and development to product development to structural change (often undertaken in the absence of any more thoughtful approach) and change in skills and/or behaviours.

Figure 5.5 presents the managerial homeostat, an alternative way of considering the argument, and, yes, you have seen it before in chapter 3 – it is after all

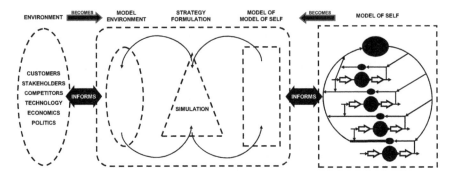

FIGURE 5.4 The value–enabling process

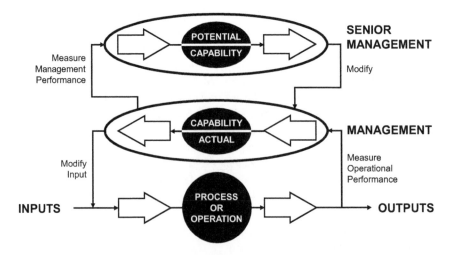

FIGURE 5.5 Enabling value interacting with generating value

a homeostat. The lower loop represents generating value with the management continually striving to improve operational performance. Meanwhile, the value-enabling activity is considering the gap between current capability and potential, the performance that could be achieved if constraints were removed. Their output is fed back to value generation to enable further change, and that stimulates debate about the allocation of resources between current and possible future activities.

For ease of description, this is treated here as a single process. The reality for most organisations is that, as shown at the beginning of the chapter, the value-enabling process happens across multiple functional areas, e.g. finance, property, information services (ICT), research and development, product development, marketing, human resource management and so on.

These parallel processes need to be synthesised, integrated, synchronised and coordinated. All too often an organisational change process, stimulated by one functional team is pulling (or pushing) the organisation in one direction while another is going the opposite way! Figure 3.3 showed how a change reverberates throughout the organisation. Now think about the complexity when multiple processes are stimulating multiple asynchronous changes. Is it any wonder that it feels chaotic at times, that "head office doesn't know what it's doing" and that the value-generating parts of the organisation respond with "keep your heads down" and "ignore the latest fad – there will be another one along next week". The resistance to change in the organisation may simply be a function of too many inconsistent change requirements from too many sources overwhelming the capacity to cope.

In figure 5.6, the information abstraction necessary is segregated into "disciplinary" channels: each discipline is exploring the organisation and environment and drawing data in to a model. In creating a simulation (thinking about alternative futures and actions that happen in the centre of the figure) these discipline-based data sets must be synthesised in a shared model. The data becomes shared information and the implications of possible changes can be explored in a mutual dialogue that focuses on the whole, not the parts. Any one discipline "doing its own thing" and disregarding the implications for the others will engender tension rather than value. It may bring about damage to or the demise of the whole organisation.

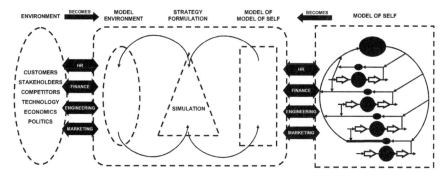

FIGURE 5.6 The multichannel value-enabling process

In a recent experience with a pharmaceuticals organisation, I noticed the commercial function was determined to do things its own way. While there was much merit in the ideas being proposed, they were not tested or agreed with other functions (especially regulatory and finance), and as a result, far from being successful in the long term, they generated an "immune system response" in the regulatory and finance functions which acted to inhibit the commercial strategy.

Corporate strategy

Enabling value in an integrated manner relies upon good process, appropriate information (structure and content) and appropriate skills in data gathering, synthesis, analysis, reflection and debate. It requires willingness to take time to explore, test and reflect. Strategic decision-making should not be measured by short-term responsiveness (how quickly we can make a decision?) but by long-term contribution to "survival worthiness". In biological terms, it is about how well the organisation adapts its environment to itself and how well it adapts itself to its environment, a process of co-evolution.

There are a wide range of tools for strategic thinking which, whilst good in isolation, can have far greater value when used in the context of this argument. Underpinning all is the common language of accountancy, used for the conveying of information about certain aspects of performance. It should be noted, however, that the "financial position" is a product of the activity of the organisation and that financial reports are a proxy for performance, describing only a single, monetary, perspective on performance. Financial reports are a particular representation of the result of the organisations activity, not a driver of it. Not everybody, in some circumstances almost nobody, understands what the accounting numbers mean.

Porter's Five Forces model (Porter, 1980) is powerful in helping to interpret the competitive position of the organisation in its environment relative to existing and potential actors as well as in the value chain of the industry. Ansoff (1987) offers models for considering choices about growth, looking at present and future markets and products, possibilities for further penetration of existing areas and development and diversification into new areas. Adding further to this area is the Boston Consulting Group Matrix (Johnson & Scholes, 2007) and others like it which seek to help understand future possibilities in terms of the market position of existing products and services and how they might be adapted to ensure future success. This includes the action, often regarded as heretical by the value generators, of stopping unprofitable products or services. It seems inherent in many organisations that we continue flogging a horse until well beyond the point where there is any hope of it springing back to life. Adjacent to the strategy literature is that of marketing. Here the work of Kotler and Armstrong (2013) is probably of greatest value and significance. They focus on formulating a marketing strategy by looking at the information required to understand the market and consumer behaviour. Since we have designed our organisation backwards from the customer, the approach has much resonance.

The tools and rules of accounting and financial management are spread across a wide literature and, in some cases, statute law. The most obvious and frequently used tools with which most readers will be familiar are budgeting, forecasting and reporting. There is limited benefit in rehearsing that material here; I could never work out what to include or exclude. Interested readers might look at Bender and Ward (2008) for inspiration.

The people also need to be thought about – how many, what skills and knowledge are required now and tomorrow? How will they be recruited, developed, retained and rewarded? Torrington, Hall and Taylor (2008) offer a range of tools and ideas for developing what is now known as a human resource strategy.

The methods, approaches and ideas for formulating strategy need to be brought together in a supra-disciplinary conversation, one which integrates and synthesises the discussion into coherent and cohesive organisational adaptation. Here the organisation can again draw on the whole body of systems thinking (see Beckford, 2017) and a wide literature from risk analysis (Vose, 1996; Malik, 2008), operational research modelling (Moore, 1986), simulation and modelling (Goodwin & Wright, 2004). These tools allow for the development of decision models and demonstrably valid, integrated and harmonised solutions that use the information in a consistent and coherent way.

Managing tension: leadership and nurturing identity

In the meanwhile we have created a source of tension. While the value-generating homeostat is managing the present, the value-enabling homeostat is creating the future. The first acts to "do things right", it usually has control of the bulk of the organisation's resources. The second acts to "do right things", redefining what "right" means in terms of organisational purpose, opportunities, products, services and all the myriad things that define the organisation. The two processes may be in conflict with each other (figure 5.4), perhaps pulling the organisation in different directions.

In many organisations the value-enabling activity is addressed sporadically; usually after something has gone wrong. Typically falling sales of existing products, an economic downturn, a shift in customer behaviour are unanticipated because the organisation as a whole does not scan its problematic environment effectively. If we think about information systems and managerial activity in the organisations with which we are familiar, we should recognise that much management decision-making about the *next* period is done by considering what happened in the *last* one and assuming a continuation of that into the future. This is, quite a lot, like driving a car down the road whilst only looking in the rear-view mirror – you can see in great detail what has already happened, can align your vehicle with the forecast flow of the road based on what just happened (this right hand bend will go on for ever) and can see all the obstacles you didn't hit. What you can't see is what is happening ahead of you. Organisations which do not have an effective process for creating the future (and there are many of them) necessarily become dominated by short-term,

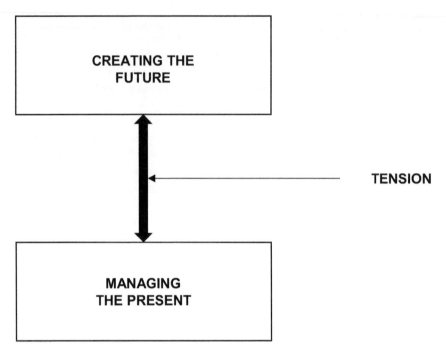

FIGURE 5.7   Managing the present and creating the future

reactive decision-making – and fail. A point worth emphasising here is that resolving the tension between the present and the future is not about administration; it is a question of leadership, the expression and realisation of the values of the organisation and the changes that go with it.

The tension cannot be effectively resolved in the "traditional" manner. That, for many organisations, comes down to an adversarial boardroom battle in which there are winners and losers, with the losers "moving on to explore alternative career opportunities". That approach to resolving the tension is often more about benefit to individuals (promotion and bonuses) than it is the organisation. Decisions arising from it will often contain a "political" element. There must be a better way.

Two things are missing. The first can be solved within the information structure we have already created. In the Intelligent Organisation, information is available to deliver a level of objectivity into the discussion. Stating things objectively distances the discussion from, often irrational or ill-informed, "I think" conversations and allows all parties to view the facts and assumptions rather than attacking individuals and defending personal views. The information, of course, can never be perfect. The future is inherently uncertain, and any discussions or decisions about what to do must acknowledge that uncertainty. The information entering the debate from within the organisation should have a higher degree of precision in reporting what has happened. There will be less certainty about what might happen in the future since there is limited insight to that. The second element that is missing and that will allow resolution of the debate is an understanding of the purpose of the organisation: its mission, the reason it exists and the societal values it brings to bear.

It is easy to say that, for commercial organisations at least, the purpose is to make money. However, as was established earlier, making money is but one part of the value exchange between the organisation and its environment. So, yes, generating a surplus of income over expenditure is important to shareholders but from the perspective of the survival of the organisation itself, making money is a consequence of being efficient at what it does. It is a necessary constraint upon its existence, but what it does is done by the core processes that deliver services and goods to the customers. If we are in doubt about the purpose of the organisation, we can look to the outcomes it generates in its environment and the process outputs that lead to them. Outcomes are, for the observer, the realised purposes of the organisation – whatever the intent.

The third and, somehow, more difficult element of this is to consider the values that underpin decisions. Bear in mind that the overarching objective is organisational survival in a world where both customers and internal actors can exercise choices about what they buy and where they work. It would be reasonable, then, to adopt a set of values that support sustainable coexistence; a set of values shared internally and with our customers that represent our "identity", that tell people who we are, what we stand for. We should perhaps look to the literature on ecology here for inspiration, as words like "collaboration", "co-operation", "co-evolution", "symbiosis", "partnership" might most usefully define the style of behaviour most likely to succeed.

This conversation in three parts inspired by Beer's (1985) "metasystem", was defined by Dudley (2000) as the "trialogue" (figure 5.8). It allows the logical closure of the internal conversation whilst sustaining the dynamic, open relationship with the environment. The purpose of our organisation is ultimately an expression of the beliefs and values of those in leadership – whether they recognise them and espouse them or simply live them. The choices the organisation makes about its present and its future are a product of those beliefs and values.

The whole organisation is brought together in figure 5.9.

Thinking about growth

Economic theory has it that the enabler of economic growth is savings, that is, the excess of income over consumption, reinvested. We are not going to argue with that convention here, but we are going to explore and, perhaps, extend the definition of "growth".

The Intelligent Organisation seeks viability (Beer, 1985). It is designed to act in ways which enable its adaptation and survival in a changing environment. Thinking about that purely in economic terms is inadequate because it fails to consider all of the other dimensions of organisations and their place in complex societies. If our

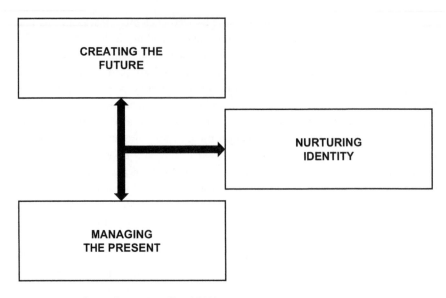

FIGURE 5.8 The trialogue (Dudley, 2000)

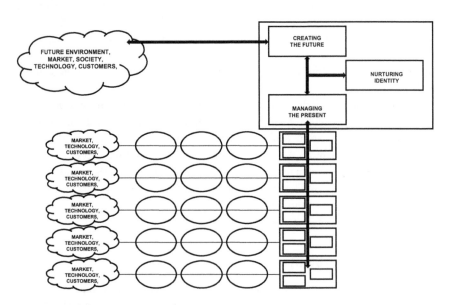

FIGURE 5.9 The Intelligent Organisation

Source: Adapted from Beer (1985) and Dudley (2000)

organisations are going to be survival worthy, then we need to think about growth in at least two dimensions:

- physiological: getting fitter or bigger (or both);
- psychological: getting smarter.

Conventional economic thinking only really addresses the first of these. Physiological growth is the stuff of market penetration, product penetration and product development and of mergers and acquisitions. Market and product penetration means that the organisation sells its products and services to a bigger audience in its existing markets, whilst market development takes those products and services to new audiences. Product development is concerned with the creation and sale of new products and services primarily to existing customers. These can, of course, be combined in a variety of strategies, all of them intended to increase the revenues flowing to the organisation, and they are equally applicable to commercial organisations, charities and not-for-profits. The sources of the revenue may vary, but the intent with all is to increase both market and revenue share. The economic benefits may be several – improved cash flow, improved profit, lowered unit cost through volume increases. The net effect is to increase the surplus of income over consumption. For the avoidance of doubt none of that is necessarily a bad thing. Mergers and acquisitions are, in effect, shortcut attempts to acquire additional surplus through access to larger volumes of sales, a new market for products, complementary products and services, complementary cash flows or, sometimes, to take a competitor out of the market. A business that sells heating products in the winter might well want to sell cooling products in the summer; the customers are the same, while the market needs are different.

A word of caution: there is some evidence that mergers and acquisitions do not "add value" to shareholders because of the difficulties and challenges associated with such transactions. It sometimes appears that they work better for the executives than they do for the companies and their shareholders. We would do well to understand whose interests are truly being served by such activities.

Untrammelled physical growth is not always good. Once the organisation exceeds a particular position in the market or is in a position with few or no apparent predators, then through its sheer size and weight it may become lethargic, slow to recognise and react to threats, perhaps even culturally complacent, convinced of its own "rightness". It will certainly become more self-interested. It may act to preserve the status quo and be less able (and willing) to respond to opportunities ("oooh! too risky") or threats ("oooh! too big to fail" or "hmmm, not big enough to harm us"). Alternatively it may become so convinced of its own greatness that it ends up "taking over the world! Tech giants are blowing billions" (Lynn, *Daily Telegraph*, 20th February 2015). These constraints may apply to organisations whose dominance, in effect, enables them to slow product progress (particularly in applied technologies). This can occur where the cost (capital requirement or customer acquisition) of market entry is very high, e.g. aerospace or motor vehicle design and manufacturing, or where natural predators are inhibited by structural lack of meaningful competition, e.g. rail franchising or regulated utilities. In some cases the only true predator is the regulator, and it is not in their interest to catch the prey. That thought takes us to psychological growth.

Here again we can start with the conventional thinking. If one of the keys to survival is economic fitness, then being smarter is a good start. That might mean pursuing strategies such as "operational excellence", "quality" or "lean thinking" (Beckford, 2017). That has been built into our process and structure. All such strategies are intended to improve the efficiency and productivity of the organisation, doing current things in current markets, increasing output and lowering (relative) costs to increase the surplus of income over cost. That, at the organisational level, can be seen as a good thing.

These conventional thoughts, though, rely on the assumption that "growth" is in itself a universal good; that being bigger will ensure the survival of the organisation. It is interesting to note that the economic growth (accompanied by inflation) that has been seen over the last century is an aberration in the very long term. The norm over many centuries has been much greater stability of value, with increased savings arising from genuine productivity improvement rather than price rises. So a challenge to convention that arises from the lethargy, inertia, bureaucracy, risk aversion and, perhaps, power that results from dominance: the human actors in the organisation may come to believe in their own "rightness", use that power to manage (manipulate) the market, the products and the customers, potentially ending up, in effect, abusing their position. Some banks and bankers may be considered to have achieved such power during the early part of this century as the inquiries into rate-fixing, payment protection insurance and other financial scandals have suggested. The good news is that, however powerful they may be in the short term, these organisations ultimately always seem to fade, to struggle, to collapse. This is brought about by the emergence of new competitors coming to the market with innovations that are disruptive, whether through technology, process, service, product design or some other factor. A concern at the time of writing, emerging first in the USA, is that "tech giants" are becoming too powerful and are, possibly, acting to stifle innovation that may threaten them (Titcomb & Pagnamenta, 2018). The invulnerable, dominant player or players are ultimately unseated, though that may take some time and is delayed, if not stopped, by the barriers to entry, particularly those of capital and regulation (and sometimes by government intervention). So, those organisations are not survival worthy. Large they may be, but they fail to truly build a sustainable position. Why? Because they are often not smart.

We need to think about smart organisations powered by psychological growth; organisations getting smarter, learning, learning about learning, maybe even learning about learning about learning! This also means that we, who give the organisation life, need to be (encouraged to be) smarter. We constitute a "brain", an organisational "collective consciousness" (Wilson, 2002). Instead of "throwing bodies at problems", we should throw intelligence. We are the agents of the organisational memory, its connectivity, knowledge and self-awareness. Brains are neuroplastic: they change and evolve through new data and experience. Perhaps psychological growth can arise by us raising the organisation to consciousness of its actions and impacts, and that will occur through individual psychological changes in affect, behaviour and cognition. We should be smart about being smart.

Psychological growth means that the organisation can apply its collective intelligence to improving itself informationally – perhaps this what is really meant by knowledge management? We have already demanded this in the shape of the MoS, a representation of "how well I am". This must be honest, perhaps brutally so; otherwise it is, at best, unhelpful. The human actors interpreting the MoS must be aware of the risk of "black swans" (Taleb, 2010), "optimism bias" ("that was a one off – it couldn't happen again"), and "availability bias" (Kahnemann, 2011). We typically react to the most recent events as if they are either blips or a long-term shift in things, and there often appears to be little between these reactions other than the interpretation of a rapporteur. We must consider the trends and shifts in the environment to which a response is required and, unlike individuals, information in the organisation can give access to the unconscious organisational self (Wilson, 2002). All this is enabled by the constructive use of information, data filtered through tools, techniques and models that aid understanding. They should have their biases exposed by the honest challenging of their underlying assumptions and assertions about the organisation and its world which, inevitably, influence them.

I accept the argument of one discussion about this: that "any CEO explicitly not aiming for physiological growth is likely to be sacked". However, psychological growth may mean recognising that the organisation has reached an optimum physical size relative to its competitors and its environment. It may be that it has reached a size which actually suits the human actors, its philosophy or the opportunities available to it. It may mean accepting that a technology, product or service is reaching the end of its life and understanding how the pattern of changes around it will demand a new approach. This contrasts sharply with the apparent application of market power to hold back innovation, delay technology or inhibit competition through lobbying and the application of perverse standards which preserve the status quo. The reality is that the innovation, the disruptive technology, will, ultimately, find a way through, and in the medium term that leaves the organisation exposed.

The Intelligent Organisation recognises that, with the aid of contemporary technology, it is in a position, through its people, to use data to develop a robust, honest, model of itself and its environment and can use the resulting information to support decisions about the future which are able to maximise opportunity whilst minimising risk. That requires that the autonomy of individuals within the organisation is maintained.

Practically, how does psychological growth get expressed? It will mean maintaining (or creating) the time and opportunity for people throughout the organisation to find better (faster, cleaner, more efficient, different) ways of both delivering the present products and services and tomorrows. We must build into the way the organisation functions specific freedom to challenge the status quo, to think and explore. This needs to be expressed in job design, in meeting structures and agendas and, most of all, in the behaviour of managers, supervisors and leaders who must learn to welcome being challenged rather than taking it as an affront to their position or supposed superiority.

Summary

Some readers will no doubt object that I have reified the organisation, that is, I have apparently given it a life independent of its human actors. The story has been represented that way consciously and deliberately. People give life to organisations. Within the limits of current technologies and for most purposes, it is largely people that make decisions. Nonetheless, it is a useful artifice, just for the time being, to suggest that we can both observe the process and be part of it. The complexity entailed in observing a process in which we are ourselves actors will be pursued later. It is also sad but true that in the absence of any particular individual most organisations and processes will continue to function regardless. The established organisation, particularly a bureaucratic one, will have a momentum, an operating rhythm that will suborn the efforts of the individual. Large organisations do seem to develop a "life" which is beyond the capabilities of individuals to influence (Robb, 1989).

That has been quite a walk through the essential principles and logic of the value-enabling activities. In the next chapter we shall bring it to life by looking at some case studies.

6

ENABLING VALUE

Cases

Introduction

Maintaining the rhythm of the book, we can now return to the case studies already considered in chapter 4 and add some new ones to demonstrate how they enable value. The cases are:

- Fusion21
- Canal and River Trust
- Southern Mill
- The Sisters of Nazareth
- UKCRIC: A multi-university research organisation

Fusion21: creating the future

Two corporate objectives were left unfulfilled in our first look at Fusion21:

- to undertake research and development in improving products and services;
- to maintain "fitness for purpose".

The fulfilment of these objectives is led across the business by the Heads of Corporate Services and Business Improvement. They work together to constitute a nexus for the interaction of the present with the future. Corporate services leads the challenge of maintaining fitness for purpose and deals with a range of matters:

- operational and strategic finance,
- operational and strategic HR management and
- applied information systems.

Business improvement, meanwhile, leads the research and development agenda, including

- marketing,
- product and service development and
- information strategy.

The whole enabling activity relies on the aggregation of information from value generation and its integration with that discerned by value-enabling activity. This whole is represented in figure 6.1.

We needed to develop an understanding of the current operating status of the company, its MoS, and interpret that not just through the operating activity but also by understanding how well corporate services were enabling that through the provision of

- skilled and knowledgeable people,
- budgets and operating finance and
- information systems.

The directors of the three business units – procurement, TES and consultancy – were in parallel able to provide performance information about each of the units. Taken together these information flows enabled the creation of the MoMoS, a rich understanding of the current situation from all perspectives.

The Heads of Corporate Services and Business Improvement developed, through processes of research and enquiry, information about the problematic future. To enable Fusion21 to expand the fulfilment of its mission, they looked outside the company to explore

- the opportunities in the markets served by the company (by segment and geography);
- information about competitors and customers (in particular their apparent strategies);
- sources of government and other funding opportunities.

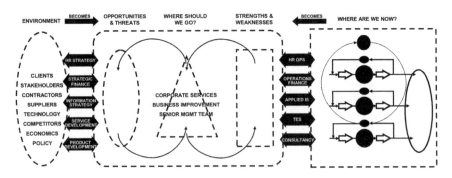

FIGURE 6.1 Enabling value for Fusion21

In parallel they looked inside the company to find opportunities

- for different approaches to strategic finance (especially in the light of the business ambition);
- for extending the use of information throughout the business (with associated technologies);
- to enable improvements in operating performance (especially through reduced transaction costs);
- for delivery of strategic growth.

All that information was brought together in a rich, complex and, very importantly, continuing conversation. Since Fusion21 is an intelligent organisation, their strategy formulation is not a "once every five years and put it on the shelf" report but the basis of an ongoing dialogue between all of the relevant people in the business. This allows learning, adaptation and, through the information systems, management of knowledge about the organisation, its staff, suppliers, contractors, clients and beneficiaries. This process selects from all of the tools available in the strategy and management literature those which, at any given time, cast the most useful light on the debate. This is illustrated in figure 6.2.

The behaviour and approach of the senior management team (the operating business Directors plus the Heads of Corporate Services and Business Improvement) were critical to this process. As I engaged with them, it was important to develop their understanding of the 'Intelligent Organisation' model so that they recognised the need to develop a strategy for Fusion21 as a whole and not prefer or defend any particular part of the business, position or individual. They needed

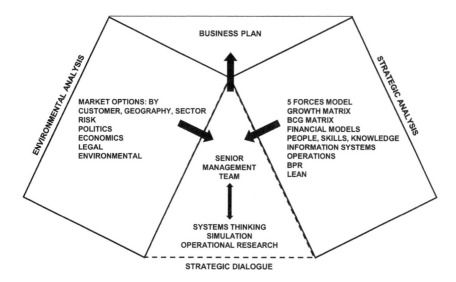

FIGURE 6.2 The strategic dialogue

to trust the process and set aside personal feelings, issues of power, control and all of the other personal preferences that can get in the way of relatively objective decision-making.

I say relatively objective because, for all the tools, analysis, rational debate and quantification, we are all humans with preferences, prejudices, hobby horses and bees in our bonnets. We all make decisions which are emotionally informed regardless of the apparent facts. On good days we call this exercising professional judgement. The tools and approaches used to support and enable the debate were drawn from the literature on systems thinking and, in particular, Checkland's Soft Systems Methodology (1981). The outcome of the initial running of the process was to inform and modify the business plan, which expressed greater ambition for the business than had previously been articulated. The Chief Executive took on the task of engaging Board support for the strategy.

Implementation of the plan had its challenges, not least because the continuing process maintains openness to debate. This has been accompanied, as it always will be for every organisation, by changes in personnel and skills, by competition in the marketplace(s) in which Fusion21 does business and in changes in the overall economic position of the country. The process persists, as does Fusion21.

Fusion21: five years on

The organisation continues to be successful by developing its market position, improving the products/services and attracting (and retaining!) more and more customers each year; arguably the most significant update to the case study can be seen in how the organisation responded to these challenges from a leadership perspective. The original case study describes an organisation that is rooted in the value-based thinking (enabling, delivering and creating value) but was organised in a more traditional functional pattern with "Operating Business" Directors and Corporate Services and Business Improvement Heads.

Today the leadership structure more closely resembles the philosophical stance, with each value element having a single senior lead. This has enabled a sharper focus to materialise within each value element and also improve the synergy and interaction with others. Each has a clearly defined remit and can demonstrate how it takes lead (and also supporting) roles to achieve corporate objectives. The successful integration is managed using the trialogue with an acknowledgement that the leadership team share a joint responsibility for all value elements (which is a conscious decision to avoid empire building and the associated silo mentality!).

Benefits include the improved engagement with customers and the link between customers and the research and development process. Customer engagement information is used to drive the research and development process and in doing so increase the speed to market of new products. This is also supported by effective information flows that enable timely information sharing and an increased ability to rely on information-led decision-making (see other chapter updates).

Canal and River Trust: enabling change

In chapter 4 we considered the overall structure of the Canal and River Trust and how that needed to change and focus the organisation on first engaging its (wide variety of) customers and then its two underpinning value-generating activities of asset maintenance (engineering) and investment and income (revenue). It was apparent that more detailed change at the operating level needed to be consistent with the emerging strategic shift from the traditional focus on asset maintenance to an external focus on the user experience and benefit.

Historically experiencing a siloed, bureaucratic, and, more recently perhaps, over-centralised decision and power structure, the executive understood the need for an inclusive, integrated approach to delivering the desired transformation. Recognising that such integration would be achieved through a synthesis of behaviour, process and information enabled by a shared conversation, the CEO brought together an "Information Strategy Group" (ISG) as the forum in which the necessary dialogue could be held. Taking collective responsibility for the transformation process, this group included senior representatives from throughout the organisation who became the principal agents of change.

The group was led by the CEO, informed by its own membership and challenged by this author. The most crucial issue was that the transformation itself needed to be owned by those internal to the organisation and that the management team should become the managers of the change. The role of the external advisor became threefold: to illuminate the dialogue with insights rooted in the ideas of Intelligent Organisation, to challenge the status quo where appropriate and to bring to bear insights and knowledge drawn from other organisations and experiences – to act as Beer's "guide, philosopher and friend".

Alert readers will recognise that effect of the ISG is to constitute the simulation at the heart of the value-enabling process (see figure 5.4 for a reminder). The representation of people from across the organisation ensures that data, information and knowledge about the whole of the situation can be shared, discussed, considered and challenged. The modelling emerges in the discussion and debate about how best to deliver the purpose espoused by evaluating proposals and suggestions for change against the extent to which they deliver the desired change. Thus, because of the way the conversation is constructed, what in some instances could be thought of as "just a meeting" becomes a device for sharing and learning. The meeting is purposeful, the ISG becomes the management element of the change process homeostat, the process for delivering the desired change.

At its first event the ISG confirmed the adoption of the principles of Intelligent Organisation to underpin the process, agreed the needs, recognised the demand for early action and an initial plan to go with that. Issues of particular concern, and the first value-enabling activity arising, at that time were to determine what established reporting activities were no longer required, which needed revision and what new ones were needed. In parallel the provisions of the General Data Protection

Regulations were coming in to force in relation to data about individuals. The Trust needed to establish how it was going to reconcile the legal requirement to be parsimonious in the capture and retention of data with the commercial imperative to know and understand its customer, user and volunteer base. This tension, always in existence, was brought in to stark relief with the realisation that the information systems were not fully aligned to supporting the business needs. Three further value-enabling workstreams emerged from that meeting to determine how best to comply with GDPR, to develop options and choices about future information systems design and to develop a fuller transformation plan dealing with issues of performance, processes, decision schemes and so on.

The Canal and River Trust is a large and highly distributed organisation with many offices, around 1600 employees (and more than double the number of regular volunteers) and, of course, substantial daily operations which must continue while the change processes are in course. Nonetheless, only about six weeks after the first ISG a second meeting saw individuals reporting substantial progress in identifying how key individuals were losing time in supporting reporting activity and a series of proposals were brought to the table, addressing

- systems improvements,
- automation of some reporting,
- investment in skills and
- decision-focused reporting.

These proposals included short-term deliverables enabling the organisation to function more effectively under the structure recently implemented, a restructure which had seen a substantial reduction in the number of senior management positions, thus demanding the decentralisation of some decisions.

A second workstream had considered the requirements for executive information and developed a set of principles to guide how they should be addressed. These included the following.

- Information should enable decisions and actions;
- Decisions should drive demonstrable improvement versus targets and objectives with each cycle;
- Information availability should be through "dashboards" enabling simple comparison of actual performance with standards and norms;
- Information should be simple, transparent and available and should support control and accountability.

Overall the executive demand was for "information that will enable us to deliver sustainably higher performance on agreed outcomes at sustainably lower cost" (Canal and River Trust, Internal Report). Figure 6.3 highlights principal areas of interest and concern at the time, highlighting the need for change.

CHIEF OPERATING OFFICER	CHIEF INVESTMENT OFFICER	STRATEGY & ENGAGEMENT DIRECTOR	ASSET IMPROVEMENT DIRECTOR	FINANCE DIRECTOR	HR DIRECTOR
PROGRESS V OBJECTIVES	ASSET PRODUCTIVITY	OUTCOMES V OBJECTIVES	DIRECT SERVICES PRODUCTIVITY & UTILISATION	FINANCIAL CONTROL	HEADCOUNT & SKILLS/TRAINING PERFORMANCE
PRODUCTIVITY	LONG TERM ROI	DONOR & SUBSCRIBER INFORMATION	COMPLIANCE TO STANDARDS	STATUTORY OBLIGATIONS	ABSENCE, SICKNESS, GRIEVANCES
ATTRACTIONS PERFORMANCE	IN-YEAR PERFORMANCE	COMMUNITY ENGAGEMENT	PERFORMANCE VERSUS PLAN	MANAGEMENT REPORTING	SAFEGUARDING
CUSTOMER CONCERNS	CAPITAL ACCUMULATION	COMPLIANCE WITH STATUTORY OBJECTIVES	PROJECT PERFORMANCE – TIME, COST, QUALITY	INFORMATION SYSTEMS PERFORMANCE	EMPLOYEE PERFORMANCE
ASSET PERFORMANCE	LETTABLE ASSETS PERFORMANCE	INFORMATION FOR THE TRUSTEE DAHSBOARD	ASSET CONDITIONS & PERFORMANCE	RISK & CONTINUITY	TRAINING & DEVELOPMENT
VOLUNTEERING	MUSEUMS	VOLUNTEERS	VOLUNTEERS	AUDIT	GRIEVANCE AND COMPLAINTS

FIGURE 6.3   Initial executive information requirements

It was a clear outcome of the second ISG meeting that the pace of change in some areas needed to be increased while, in contrast, there was a need for further investigation of how the needs being expressed could best be met – and how quickly!

Committing to realising an overall change in spend profile of about 25% over five years through a combination of increasing income and reducing costs, the ISG proposed identifying systems upgrades and replacements as a matter of urgency with rolling implementation of revised reporting in the proposed dashboard format to enable early gains to be realised. We shall return to this case to consider more of the "how" later.

Southern Mill

We left Southern Mill in a state of recovery; vital performance characteristics were improving but the whole business remained under risk of sale or closure.

Considering this organisation, we have to realise that whilst effective enabling activity is critical to its performance and survival, it did not enjoy the strategic freedom seen in the Fusion21 case study. Southern Mill was constrained in a number of ways:

- A single (and old) paper machine had a limited capacity and product range;
- A "speciality" market required high frequency, small batch deliveries;
- Capital investment was controlled by the owning group;
- The group controlled raw materials supply and cost;
- Southern Mill was in a rural location (with limited workforce options).

Within those constraints, the strategic choices were effectively limited to market growth and market penetration: either selling more product to existing customers or finding new markets to which the existing products can be sold. Physiological growth would, ultimately, be limited by the capacity of the paper machine, but might the existential threat be overcome through psychological growth? Could a "smarter" Southern Mill achieve sales volumes that would utilise all the capacity? Could it use information to manage itself better, to make better use of skilled and knowledgeable staff? Could it improve processes and systems and increase overall revenue, reduce unit costs and increase margin.

Frankly, being smarter looked like the only way forward.

The costing and pricing model in conjunction with the daily dashboard and the operations meeting were taken as the key starting point for the smarter strategy. The first provided actionable, unarguable information which informed decisions about

- what products should be made;
- what products could be eliminated from the range (very small demand, difficult to make, unprofitable);
- what priorities should be set for customers, products, conversion, delivery;
- production order (the sequence of colours and weights).

With a range of around 3000 shippable products, two sites and the knowledge that the Finance Director had been unable to produce an accurate costing model in two years, this might sound like the wrong place to start. However, in the absence of accurate costing and pricing Southern Mill was doing business blind to the implications of each purchase or sale decision. It was unable to respond to increases in supply costs (energy, materials) and incapable of a meaningful pricing conversation with its clients.

Building on the process understanding, the first step was to review the costing work already undertaken to see if it could be made useable. A number of significant flaws were discovered in the structure, organisation and utilisation of data which inhibited the accuracy and speed of the established costing model. It was jointly agreed to start again. A new approach was developed that replicated the process structure but was expressed in the languages of both finance and production. The two functions have a direct informational equivalence but use different languages. The approach was developed and tested tracking a single product through from despatch backwards to inbound materials. All functional and enabling areas were included in the development, each making a contribution and pushing the limits of the model. The initial manual costing approach produced what looked like reasonable answers but took 30 minutes per product at the first attempt. Several days were subsequently invested manually costing each product. The validity of the model was established by applying production volumes to the total production costs for the year to date generating a difference of under 1%. The model as constructed very faithfully reflected the actual situation. Once that test was completed and signed off by the relevant directors, the costing process was automated so that it was possible to reanalyse *all* 3000 products in under five minutes given any change in input costs or conditions.

The pricing model was built using the manufacturing cost results with the addition of despatch costs, exchange risk and flexibility on pricing (enabling management of margins). This meant that the sales team were able not only to understand product costs but also to negotiate from a position of knowledge with customers, understanding for the first time the implications of discounts and the sensitivity of the business to price. All of that work was designed to enable the senior managers of Southern Mill to be more effective in decision-making. All of it drew on existing information sources and the final version was deployed across the corporate network.

It may sound a little complicated, and there were numerous challenges in bringing the whole model together. What you may find more remarkable is that the costing and pricing model were not built by a qualified accountant (who had failed miserably) but by a 19-year-old engineering undergraduate (with a little guidance), who understood process and information. It took only a few weeks from problem definition to implemented solution. Thanks, Allen!

The second focus was to look at how the skills of the "enabling" individuals in the organisation might be enhanced. Drawing on the generation of more useful information on a more regular basis, the daily operations meeting became a learning, knowledge-sharing event. Using the information presented each day, the attendees were able to objectively explore what was working well or less well, what perhaps had gone wrong and, crucially, the cross-company effect of errors or failures in one area. Initial interventions were facilitative but moved rapidly to a coaching approach as the participants began to learn from each other, to develop and test ideas, to behave differently together (for example being collaborative rather than competitive) and, for the sales team, to take different ideas and propositions to customers.

Great progress was being made, the work together was bearing fruit and the results were showing through on the bottom line. Production, sales volumes and revenue were increasing, stocks were falling (in particular eradication of old stock and previously uncalled orders), low-volume and/or high-cost products were being eliminated through substitution reducing product and production complexity and increasing throughput. All was going in the right direction.

Unfortunately, at this point Southern Mill was sold to a new owning group, and the intervention ceased; but we know the mill is still there and has received some of the strategic investment it so sorely needed.

Creating the future with the Sisters of Nazareth

The Sisters of Nazareth are a Roman Catholic Religious Order founded in 1851. Their ministry today is primarily fulfilled through the residential care of the elderly and takes place in five regions: the UK, Ireland, Southern Africa, Australasia and the United States. In 2006 there were around 300 sisters.

When I met the Superior General, the elected leader of the Congregation, in 2007, it was apparent there were several significant challenges. At the height of the sisters' fortunes there had been 66 houses. In 2007 there were 37. Most of the closures had taken place in the previous 20 years. Sisters were aging and increasingly unable to take direct operational responsibility for the care operation; there were few new vocations, especially in the UK and Ireland; the care work was operating at a loss; the lack of modern processes and business systems made it hard to measure the extent of losses never mind manage them; regulatory standards and public expectations were rising and the fabric of many of the care homes was outdated or in poor condition; increasingly residents were highly dependent and arriving near end of life. The sisters were in a business in which other, arguably more well-equipped operators were struggling with the basic economics of residential care. The quality of care remained high, but the operation was not sustainable, and both the religious order and the ministry faced a challenging future. House closure had become the default strategy.

We worked with the sisters on what became a global turnaround, a project that lasted for ten years. Throughout, our approach was informed by "the trialogue", and the associated concept of the Intelligent Organisation.

Some of what needed to be done was obvious – e.g. the establishment of professional business management standards and new businesses processes and systems – but it was also clear that other things had to happen to make that possible. The "hard" features of the system could not be addressed without first addressing the "soft" features: the people, their behaviours and their sense of identity. This was not just a matter of principle: it was a practical necessity. The sisters had to be reassured that the changes that would be required would not violate the Congregation's charism and vocation and that change would not be possible or sustainable without the sisters' support. Secondly, the sisters had to renew their sense of common cause. For historical and geographical reasons, regions and houses operated virtually autonomously. Now the sisters would need to work together. The process of change and what followed from it would need enough central control to ensure that congregational objectives could be met while preserving sufficient local autonomy to ensure fitness of organisation and mission in the highly diverse circumstances in which the sisters' work takes place.

We started by reviewing the Congregation's purpose and values with the Superior General and the General Council (an elected body of five sisters, charged with overseeing the total life of the Congregation for a period of six years). We went back to the governing constitutions and explored the history of the Congregation. We noted that the apostolate was to the "poor and needy". Although the decision was made quickly to retain the focus on the elderly, this distinction between core purpose and historical role created a new and liberating sense of choice and possibility. The Council then developed a hypothesis about the future. Key features included the creation of a new partnership with non-religious staff, a new governance and management structure, new roles for sisters as trustees rather than managers and the commitment to achieving an operational surplus.

This was followed by two rounds of engagements which included all the sisters in all five regions in which the hypothesis was shared and developed. There was then a round of planning engagements (with non-religious managers and staff now involved) which led to the creation of plans at congregational, regional and house levels. This all involved well over 100 meetings over a two-year period.

The next stage was a management development programme for sisters and managers which was held in each region. In the UK, this was complemented by a course leading to a post-graduate diploma at Loughborough University for a group of sisters and managers.

The implementation of plans led to significant changes: new business processes supported by new IT systems; the appointment of new managers and regional support teams (often where none had previously existed) and the establishment of new regional governance structures.

Of course, nothing happened as neatly as this suggests, but by the 2012 General Chapter (the principal representative and decision-making body of the Congregation, meeting every six years), considerable progress had been made and the new way of thinking and working established. The Chapter charged the Superior General and General Council with continuing the work but shifting the focus to the renewal of the Congregation itself. The period after 2012 to 2018 (the most recent General Chapter) saw continuing implementation of the original plans, but also a programme held in all the regions (tailored and designed in detail within the region to meet local needs) aimed at helping sisters to renew their personal and community lives.

A great deal of discussion and concern centred on the concept of "business", and this was linked to a suspicion of the "men in suits" who had become part of the sisters' lives, as staff or trustees or advisers. "Business" tended to be thought of as implying a commercial, instrumental mindset. The Superior General constantly emphasised that business served mission and that managing their affairs properly was essential to maintain the mission, and this became accepted over time.

The process of change brought sisters together in ways they rarely experienced before. The sense of renewed bonds, discovery and spiritual renewal was striking. For all the hard work, it was also a lot of fun. Staff too (many unaware that there were other Nazareth Houses) found the process involved becoming part of a larger world. This links to another key feature of the project – the need for the sisters to make staff partners in the mission rather than merely helpers or employees. The sisters had to develop ways of educating staff about the mission to ensure that the vocation behind the mission did not entirely depend on a shrinking group of religious. Staff had to come to terms with the fallibility and humanity of the sisters; sisters were surprised by the readiness of staff to become their mission partners.

There are regional and local variations in performance, but the new structures and business models are established in all the regions. In 2016–2017 there was a surplus worldwide on a substantially increased turnover. One house has closed, but another one has opened. Houses have been refurbished or rebuilt, or there are plans to do so. Most (but not all) the sisters are embracing the new world, and many are finding it liberating. The ministry is sustainable. The number of sisters continues to fall, but there have been several new vocations (chiefly in Southern Africa) which give encouragement for the future (though, with it, a cultural challenge!).

The efforts made to engage and co-create with sisters and staff were undoubtedly unusually thorough and open and were critical to the project's achievements. But, at a time when there may be a fashion for underplaying the role of leadership, it must be noted that the drive, determination and complete commitment of the Superior General and the General Council were the precondition for success. This was not because they had the answers but because they were determined to find the answers and see the process through. It was also crucial that they were both able and willing to give their time to the process and allow the process to take the time it needed. They created the necessary confidence and the environment for change and encouraged the sisters to "trust the process" through times when it became easy to lose heart, become confused or forget why so much change was necessary.

The transformation required a great deal of the sisters at a stage in their lives when most might have been supposed to have preferred a quiet retirement. They had become used to expressing their identity through doing the practical work of care. The turnaround required them to develop new ministries of pastoral care (for example) and/or operate as trustees or proprietors – to oversee the work of others. It was only possible because of the power generated by the basic sense of religious purpose in their lives – for most this trumped the power of custom and habit.

The sisters' achievement is remarkable. It required strong moral and practical leadership, both a respect *for* and a renewed sense *of* identity which in turn allowed new ways of behaving, all allied to a rigorous process of consultation and planning which engaged everyone. This took time, but the time taken has meant that change is solid and sustainable, making it possible for the sisters to make and maintain all the necessary practical and business changes.

UKCRIC: all about the future

Increasingly, organisations do not respond to the traditional and formal structures of ownership but, unincorporated, emerge as more or less formal collaborations between legally bounded entities. When that happens the bureaucracy of conventional organisation needs to become subordinate to the fluidity of the Intelligent Organisation. In the case of UKCRIC (The UK Collaboratorium for Research on Infrastructure and Cities), that need is further amplified by the recognition of it as an organisation whose present is only about creating the future.

UKCRIC is an unincorporated organisation that brings together academia, industry, government and end users to improve the nation's infrastructure. It was founded by 14 universities, which represent the UK's academic experts in infrastructure, civil and construction engineering. These included the University of Birmingham, University of Bristol, University of Cambridge, University College London, Cranfield University, Imperial College London, University of Leeds, Loughborough University, University of Manchester, Newcastle University,

University of Oxford, University of Sheffield and University of Southampton). The vision is to create, operate and coordinate a national and international multidisciplinary research programme that addresses strategic infrastructure needs and the societal benefit arising from research informed innovation.

UKCRIC offers

- leadership and support for the development and growth of a coordinated and coherent, world-class, UK-based national infrastructure research community;
- collaboration and engagement with government, local authority and commercial policy makers, investors, citizens and academia – a joint venture that drives innovation and value creation in the exploitation of services provided by national infrastructure;
- central coordination to drive knowledge transfer, UKCRIC supports a step change in the nation's approach to infrastructure investment.

The first step has been enhanced capital investment of £276 million in a portfolio of state-of-the-art research and innovation facilities which include

- a set of interlinked national facilities,
- a network of "urban laboratories",
- a modelling and simulation environment (figure 6.4) and
- a Coordination Node (CN).

In the 2015 autumn budget, HM Treasury announced public funding of £138m to support this investment. This funding was allocated to UKCRIC facilities on a matched funding basis through a suite of research grants awarded by UKRI and EPSRC. Research work commenced through two initial collaborative research grants.

UKCRIC is developing a wide range of multidisciplinary research and teaching programmes alongside the convening function hosted by the Coordination Node to help create, build and strengthen new and existing collaborative partnerships.

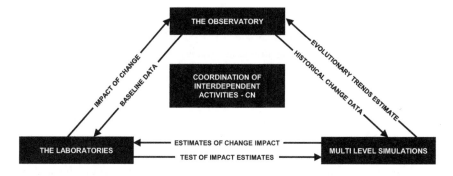

FIGURE 6.4 Overview of UKCRIC facilities and founding partners

Strategic need

All societies and economies are enabled by economic infrastructure systems. *The purpose of that economic infrastructure* is to enable the production of the goods and services needed to underpin the normal operations of society and to act as a catalyst for growth by enabling wider economic and social activity. Effective economic infrastructure investment supports a "multiplier effect" in enabling societally beneficial outcomes that simply would not occur in its absence. Given this purpose, economic infrastructure systems are essential to delivering social outcomes such as the quality of life, social cohesion, economic prosperity and productivity, sustainability, resilience and inclusiveness of our societies.

A number of factors combined to make a compelling case for the creation of UKCRIC. These include the following.

- The Council for Science and Technology (CST) warned that current approaches to infrastructure are allowing systemic resilience to decline: *"we do not believe national infrastructure can continue on its current trajectory. . . . Delivery and governance are highly fragmented and resilience against systemic failure is significantly weakening"* (CST, 2009; author's emphasis).
- The cost of ownership of the infrastructure in developed countries is unaffordable;
- It is expected that the UK will invest at least £400bn in economic infrastructure over the next 20 years;
- The value extracted by services using national infrastructure is insufficient and unsustainable.

HM Treasury have acknowledged the importance of infrastructure systems to the UK economy and now advocate a systemic approach to infrastructure, stating:

> Ultimately, it is infrastructure networks and systems as a whole that underpin the effective operation of our modern economy, and infrastructure spend should be valued and considered within this system-wide context
>
> *(HM Treasury, 2015).*

Alongside this, the UK Industrial Strategy (BEIS), acknowledges the role of infrastructure systems in supporting industrial strategy priorities. It has outlined four industrial strategy grand challenges and four societal missions, and it committed to funding investment in research priorities through the Industrial Strategy Challenge Fund (ISCF).

Nations, including the UK, need infrastructure systems that are resilient to the disruptive impacts of future systemic challenges such as climate change, natural hazards, malicious manmade hazards, digital transformation (or system transformation of any form), demographic transitions, aging infrastructure, greater demand on existing capacity, changing patterns of regional population growth, global demand for scarce resources and urbanisation. These are a prerequisite for wider societal or economic resilience.

Organisation

UKCRIC's purpose, expressed through its missions, is to align infrastructure research with societal needs, where a step change in the nation's approach to infrastructure thinking is required as a central component of a wider portfolio of actions to support an overarching societal change.

UKCRIC has no legal existence, it is a distributed virtual organisation, an emergent product of the interactions of the representatives of its founding partners and their funding bodies. All physical research facilities belong to the institutions from which it emerges. Taking the idea of UKCRIC to incorporate all of the relevant research activity of the partner institutions then all of the activity that constitutes "value generation", that is research activity leading to new discoveries, new science and the evidential output in the form of papers, products and other publications are undertaken by those partner institutions and their resident researchers, either alone or in other collaborative arrangements. The tasks of UKCRIC itself are to

- comprehend societal needs and expectations,
- develop a research agenda to address those needs,
- act as a linking device to create the systemic mindset and
- synthesise the outputs of discipline-based research activity to deliver societal outcomes.

UKCRIC must respond to the principles of Intelligent Organisation or else it will cease to exist. In the absence of intelligent behaviour and processes and the use of shared information, it will simply collapse back into the partner institutions. UKCRIC is an enabling device which recognises that the systemic benefits of interdisciplinary infrastructure research, ultimately embracing both engineering and social sciences, also require sustained disciplinary expertise at the level of individual researchers. It requires institutions with a common understanding of and commitment to a shared mission. The interaction of the partners is facilitated by a "coordination node" physically present (for convenience and low cost) at one of the partner institutions. It is not purposeful in itself but is a pure enabling function supporting two sets of interactions – those of the research leaders and those of the researchers undertaking synthesising activity on behalf of the partners. UKCRIC uses the Coordination Node to creating the tight-loose control of a "virtual" intelligent organisation. This work of coordinating the research and arranging for the synthesis of outputs is of a logically higher order than the individual research projects; it is of no greater or lesser importance but provides the research architecture from which UKCRIC outcomes can emerge.

UKCRIC has not started from scratch. All founding partners were already active in the field of infrastructure research prior to its emergence, and many of the collaborative relationships on which it builds emerged through earlier grants. The research grants to support the investment are individually granted to partner institutions. Therefore, it neither owns nor operates the research facilities. Rather it is constituted through a suite of research grants supported by matched funding from UKCRIC founding partner universities. The initial Grants awarded to partner universities were capital grants to create the facilities rather than fund research itself. UKCRIC aims to create open access to all its research facilities for all founding partners and collaborating communities of interest.

Value enabling

The UKCRIC value-generating system requires support from a value-enabling system if it is to generate value as effectively as possible. Therefore, it needs a value-enabling system that is fit for purpose for a virtual organisation comprised of a portfolio of research facilities distributed across the UK, and it needs a convening function which brings together the partners to discuss and develop the research agenda, engage with advisory boards and disseminate findings.

Developing a dynamic value-enabling system capable of this has been a strategic priority. It recognizes that it needs a value-enabling system that is inclusive and in the first instance draw on the skills, knowledge, experience, relationships, strengths and goodwill of all participants at the founding partners.

Additionally, the organisation recognizes the need to continually adapt and update this value-enabling system if it is to successfully draw on and be shaped by the skills, knowledge, experience, relationships, strengths and goodwill of all future participants and collaborating communities of interest.

The value-enabling system for UKCRIC is largely based on the work of the Coordination Node (CN) (figure 6.4). The CN is working to ensure delivery of emergent synergies between research facilities and outputs and ensure that they are appropriately exploited. Through integration of resources and robust mechanisms for cooperation and collaboration UKCRIC will enable all relevant academic and user communities to work together on the challenges of current and future generation infrastructure in complex urban and non-urban environments. The CN is also driving and supporting the overall direction of the co-developed UKCRIC strategy, governed and steered by national and international public and private sector experts and "future leaders".

However, the purpose of the CN is to coordinate not direct. Therefore, it is recognised that the value-enabling system will be insufficient if solely comprised of the CN and that complementary elements of the valuing-enabling system are provided by each UKCRIC facility and research grant as well as a number of advisory bodies which have taken the form of an International Advisory Board (IAB) and a Management Board (MB).

Value generating

Value generation is primarily undertaken by the various partner institutions. Value generation at the level of UKCRIC as a whole consists in individual researchers and research groups collaborating to synthesise research outputs into societal outcomes.

This means that individuals and research groups at partner universities undertake much of their research in the traditional manner, but they come together to derive additional value from that research by synthesising and integrating research outputs to provide higher-order outcomes to society. Such work is undertaken on behalf of UKCRIC as a whole even though the individuals contributing will continue to be employed at their individual institutions. In this instance they are generating value at a meta-level to their own institution, working on behalf of the whole and giving "ownership" of the outcome to UKCRIC as opposed to that individual partner.

Information

An information system is needed to facilitate the flow of information between the value-enabling and value-generating systems and to support UKCRIC engagement and collaborations. The information system is supported by a number of formal structures such as the Coordination Node, the IAB, the Management Board, as well as a number of electronic tools for communicating information internally and externally and, very significantly, by all individuals involved.

The element of the information system supported by UKCRIC individuals is to a large extent organic, spontaneous and informal. It is based internally on relationships between individuals and externally on the established networks of UKCRIC individuals. Informal does not, however, imply insignificant or unsupported. Because of the scale and distributed structure of UKCRIC as well as its multidisciplinary, multi-institution focus and the large range of potential partners, the informal information system is an essential complement to the information system as a whole.

Furthermore, the creation of regular opportunities to enable the interactions required by the informal elements of the information system is a key component of the value-enabling system. Opportunities for information flow are enabled through regular meetings of the formal devices and through the convening function which collaboratively hosts workshops, events, and conferences and seeks to have UKCRIC represented on external groups, at external meetings, workshops and conferences.

Additional elements designed to maximize opportunities for flow through the informal information system include

- the Coordination Node being populated by individuals involved with one or more of the research and innovation facilities (figure 6.4);
- a number of research grants held in collaboration between multiple founding partners;
- the creation of two pump-priming grants to promote collaboration between different labs (PLEXUS) and urban observatories (CORONA);
- an intentional overlap between the individuals named on the suite of UKCRIC grants to ensure it has multiple people engaged simultaneously with either
  - one or more activity at a single tip of the triangle (figure 6.4)
  - or multiple tips of the triangle (figure 6.4);

- UKCRIC CDT (Centre for Doctoral Training) grant applications developed involving multiple founding partners;
- plans for an additional collaborative grant to extend the number of urban observatories.

Moreover, the efficacy of this informal element of the information system must be underpinned by a shared sense of identity amongst the UKCRIC community that is nurtured through UKCRIC's identity system.

Nurturing identity

For UKCRIC, long-term and short-term success are different concepts. It will have succeeded in the short-term once the initial facilities are constructed. However, for UKCRIC to be a successful organisation in the long term it must consistently enable value generation over and above that which could otherwise be enabled if the research facilities were to operate on an independent basis. To do this it must nurture its identity, a critical component for ensuring its long-term success.

This has two significant components: internal identity and the ability to meaningfully use that identity to engage with its environment. UKCRIC as an unincorporated, intelligent, virtual and distributed organisation must develop identity through a shared sense of purpose and a collaborative culture. Pragmatically, this must be supported by an evidence base to demonstrate to all involved the benefits to their research, their research facility and their host institution of being an active member.

Engaging with the environment depends on the ability of UKCRIC to project its internal generated identity, purpose and potential value to those outside in order to raise awareness of the advantages of collaboration. Demonstrating the actual benefits of engaging with UKCRIC will help to establish a reputation as an invaluable collaborative partner for all communities of interest involved with infrastructure.

Two complementary tasks have recently been undertaken to stimulate development of a sense of shared identity amongst those already involved with it and how it should project itself.

The first task was to work with independent branding experts to develop a value proposition. The exercise produced a set of succinct statements to describe UKCRIC, its purpose, its proposition, its values and how it would like to be perceived by those not already involved with UKCRIC. The task served a number of purposes in nurturing shared identity between members. Moreover, the statements themselves serve a number of purposes:

- to succinctly communicate UKCRICs purpose and priorities,
- to communicate the values driving UKCRIC and
- to frame the value proposition for collaborating with UKCRIC.

The second task, led by an external convener, drew on the mission-oriented approach advocated by Mazzucato (2018). The objective was to develop a set of succinct, clearly stated missions. The process again nurtured shared identity while the missions themselves serve a number of purposes:

- to succinctly communicate UKCRICs purpose and priorities;
- to emphasise that infrastructure systems have a pivotal role to play in addressing grand societal challenges;
- to explicitly link UKCRICs purpose and priorities to the grand societal challenges, Missions and objectives stated by other influential communities of interest;
- to create a basis for future collaborations.

The two exercises were conducted independently. Both sought input from as many UKCRIC-connected individuals as possible and followed a clear process prompting discussions that might not have otherwise taken place.

The value-enabling success of these activities to create the internal shared identity and purpose will directly shape the success with which UKCRIC projects its identity to all communities of interest (the environment of UKCRIC). It is these communities of interest that will shape UKCRIC's value-generating activities to the achievement of the intended outcomes.

Summary

We have shown in practice many of the ideas about the value-enabling parts of the organisation and how they can be applied to full strategy formulation, to using information as the key to value. They have developed understanding of how we can use information about the present to understand potential value in the future and, most critically, how that can help us to appreciate the sort of virtual organisations which are possible in a digital world. In the next chapter we shall look at the autonomy of the individual in the organisation and how to exercise tight-loose control.

7

MANAGING AUTONOMY

People are at the heart of the enterprise.

Stafford Beer, The Heart of Enterprise (1979)

Introduction

Having established the value-generating and value-enabling structures of the Intelligent Organisation, we see it will be evident that within those structures we run the risk of either over-constraining the organisation or having it run riot. We can have insufficient autonomy or too much. The dilemma of the Intelligent Organisation, as Weiner (1948) expressed it, is that, rooted in changing technologies, it "embraces technical developments with great possibilities for good and for evil". The information-processing capability of contemporary technology has the potential to massively centralise potential control, or it can guarantee our freedom. For now we have a choice; just because we can do something doesn't mean we should! The appropriate point of balance will be, to draw on Henri Fayol (1916) in Beckford (2017), "a question of continuously varying proportion".

For me, we must ensure that everyone is free to exercise their skills, knowledge and judgement. Doing this effectively will allow those people to be "all that one can be" (Maslow, 1970). It will also enable us to reduce costs, flatten structures and devolve decision-making. In our Intelligent Organisation we need to manage what people do, not where they are, and as far as is possible we need to equip them with the skills and knowledge to manage themselves. Our Intelligent Organisation needs intelligent managers, as the cases in the first chapter showed us.

Power, communication and organisation

Power and control have a tendency to centralise in organisations of all types (Beer, 1993), and ultimately that will have a deleterious effect on performance as it imposes delay in responsiveness and increases costs. Quite apart from anything else, if the small group of people at the centre of the organisation are going to make all the decisions then:

- Why do we need all the other people?
- Who wants to work where they are not trusted or valued?
- How big will managerial heads need to be to contain all the information needed to competently make all decisions?

Woodward (1965) suggests that organisational form (the structure and hierarchy) is determined by the technology employed by the organisation. It is true that technology constrains some aspects of organisational form; however, that research was undertaken before the revolution in technology of the last 50 years. Perhaps it is time to reconsider?

Contemporary technology enables the radically different form of the Intelligent Organisation, which, if it is to be truly sustainable, must

- distribute decisions widely;
- have a shallow, logical hierarchy;
- have wide spans of control;
- constrain autonomy no more than is necessary to sustain cohesion of the whole.

Enabled by the effective use of information, organisations with distributed control are leaner, faster, and more responsive to both customers' desires and their own needs. Distributed information enables local empowerment and effective self-regulation. So, what gets in the way? We do – in particular, the habit of imposing our will on others.

The Industrial Revolution, from about 1760 in the UK, saw the formation for the first time of "manufactories", large-scale organisations bringing together significant numbers of often unskilled or semi-skilled people to carry out a range of tasks. These were dark, dank and dangerous places (no labour laws in those days), and the owners understandably drew on the only organisational models available to run them. These models were essentially either religious or military. Both drew on strict hierarchy, centralised command and control, adherence to orders and severe (but different) disciplinary controls.

This approach may have been appropriate, even necessary, at the time. Only a few lucky people were educated or skilled, and communication was primarily oral, not written. Communicating with large numbers of people simultaneously meant giving a speech or, in a noisy environment, shouting. The limited new skills of the majority of the workforce together with unsophisticated, dangerous, unfamiliar, unguarded machinery made close supervision essential. Of course, there will always be some people (at every level of organisation) who would rather talk about work than do any.

Historically, then, large organisations relied upon a command and control hierarchy simply to continue existing. Knowledge and power were held by a very small, educated and often business-owning elite at the peak of the hierarchy. Orders were expressed orally and in writing through intermediaries (middle management). It was perhaps, given the limits of communication and the skills and knowledge of the workforce, the only way to run things successfully. Compare and contrast, as they say in the exams!

What is different about our circumstances? Globally, and of course to different levels in different countries, many individuals are much more highly educated and skilled than was the case in the 1700s. Organisations are often several orders of magnitude larger than they were. Walmart [webref 9] employs around 2.2 million people globally (more employees than the population of some countries), operates around 11200 retail units under 55 banners in 27 countries. Microsoft [webref 10] has "only" 135,000 employees and operates in about 123 countries. The number of individuals and PCs using its products changes so rapidly it is probably subject to Heisenbergian uncertainty. Even Jaguar-Land Rover, [webref 11] one of the world's smaller motor manufacturers (and owned by Tata in India), has 10 sites in the UK, has more than 43000 employees and distributes its products to 170 countries.

Nobody can shout loud enough to be heard across such vast distances; no centralised process can manage such numbers. It is essential to distribute control. Contemporary information technologies enable that distribution but also enable the opposite. Whether through smartphones, tablets, laptops and personal computers, corporate applications, intranet, Internet or rapidly multiplying social media platforms, transmitting a message from the centre of the organisation (and verifying that it has been received) has never been easier. Verifying that it has been understood and acted on as hoped is a different problem. Where is the equivalent mechanism for upward transmission?

Absolute centralisation of control will calcify the organisation. Absolute control by each individual militates against the idea of the organisation as a purposeful, unified entity in which is implied a number of people working in concert to achieve a shared end. To have complete freedom within the organisation would, in contradiction, be anarchic. However, once individuals become spatially or temporally distributed, even for relatively small organisations, control necessarily distributes itself (e.g. a policeman on the beat, a delivery driver, a surgeon in an operating theatre, a worker on a production line – all activate their understanding of the work requirements; they do what they comprehend is required of them). Individuals with different levels of skill, knowledge and experience will, simply because they are operating at a distance from the command centre, interpret things in different ways and need to exercise discretion and judgement. If we want to both achieve coherence *and* accept that individuals will necessarily exercise some level of discretion, then we must reflect on freedom and belongingness and build those characteristics into the logic of the organisation. We cannot regulate, legislate or manage them out and survive.

Much has been written over many years about freedom and belongingness in organisations of all types. This ranges from the aristocracy of the philosopher-kings in Plato's *Republic* (Plato 390 BC in Lindsay, 1906) to Mill's (1974) discussion of liberty, Sampson's (1993) concern with Britain's "democracy in crisis" and Beer's (1974, 1981, 1993) insights into "designing freedom". There are explorations of this in the "human relations" school of thought in the management literature, e.g. Mayo (1949); Maslow (1970); Herzberg (1959), the soft systems work of Checkland (1981) and others and the critical systems work of Ulrich (1983).

The individual, in many situations and in circumstances where the choice truly exists, expresses their ultimate freedom by choosing whether or not to work with (or for) a particular organisation. Making the choice to join a particular organisation means we relinquish some portion of our freedom. When we choose to belong, we commit, at some level, to follow organisational norms. Those norms include values (beliefs about how to operate in the world) and certainly include rules. This will extend to using the technologies provided for us and, for some organisations, clothing. It used to be said of individuals joining the armed forces in the UK that "if you take the Queen's shilling, you agree to wear the Queen's uniform, you follow the Queen's orders". Whilst being able to recognise a member of the military forces by way of his or her uniform seems reasonable, the widely reported requirement by Disneyland Paris in the 1990s that attempted to specify the employees' underwear seems somewhat less so!

The challenge for contemporary leaders is to create the behavioural and cultural conditions under which individuals within the organisation are able to empower themselves. The legalistic meaning of "empower" is to "invest with authority, to authorise". Might we consider that as of the basis for developing appropriate autonomy throughout the organisation? What is the scope of empowerment? What are the conditions and opportunities that need to be created? What skills and knowledge do individuals need in order to empower themselves?

We cannot empower people; that is a nonsense. We can, however, create the cultural and behavioural conditions under which people can choose to empower themselves *and* act upon that choice. That is, we cannot simply state that "you are hereby empowered" (although I have witnessed the attempts) but must create the whole situation under which that "authorisation" can be exercised. What might that mean for leaders?

In the Intelligent Organisation the logical hierarchy is based on the flow of information. It follows that the individual best placed to make any particular decision is the person who can resolve three dimensions of any decision simultaneously:

- What is the optimum solution for this specific instance?
- What are the implications of and on that decision for the wider organisation?
- What is the impact of the outcome of that decision upon the environment of the organisation, and what is the impact of that environment upon the decision?

That of course is a very bald and simplified list. There will be simple decisions, ones with obvious, simple or transparent information and implications; they need not detain us here. However, many decisions will be complex, rooted in uncertainty, perhaps fraught with risk. In these cases being the boss doesn't make you right, it just makes you the boss. It seems that in order to make effective, risk- and judgement-based decisions and to engage the support of others, it will be helpful to the decision maker to amplify his or her own capability by leveraging the knowledge and capability of others. This will also reduce the need for a manager to have a brain the size of a planet and either or both an eidetic or photographic memory.

That means it is OK, in fact it is essential, to acknowledge that other people may know far more about something than you do. It means it is essential to recognise the talents and capabilities of all the people in the organisation. Perhaps it requires a certain Socratic humility on the part of leaders and managers to accept that a hierarchically "superior" position does not demand of them that, sophist-like, they have all the good ideas, solutions and answers. What it demands of them is that, using the best information available, they make the best decision to steer the organisation towards its desired outcome. That requires human judgement. If it didn't require judgement we would certainly buy a machine to do it, as is increasingly the case (Kaplan, 2015).

That judgement means that we, as managers, have to allow ourselves to be wrong. We have to allow ourselves to simply not know an answer. We must support, educate, encourage, teach, coach and rectify in such a manner that we continually develop the capabilities of others and invest in their freedom to apply them. Whilst management is also work, creating the conditions under which each individual will empower themselves will mean, over time, that the "work of management" is much more interesting, productive and fruitful.

If our intelligent organisation is going to survive and thrive, then populating it with people blindly following orders will not suffice. Those so able will exercise their choice and leave; those in charge will not have requisite capacity to control everything. Equally, an organisation populated by anarchists, or perhaps prima donnas, each doing their own thing will not suffice either.

How much autonomy is enough?

Some? That is probably not an adequate answer. At this point it would be great to say "here is a simple rule" – I wish it was so. In the absence of such a thing, I shall have to try and explain how I see it! Stafford Beer (1985), not terribly helpfully, states the rule that each individual part of the organisation should have "as much autonomy as is consistent with cohesion of the whole". We can take that to mean that constraints upon any individual within the organisation should be minimal. They should be free to fulfil their tasks so long as they act in a manner consistent with its espoused purpose, its values and the legal, regulatory and performance requirements which constrain it. An intelligent organisation develops autonomy based on sound, repeatable, reliable, sustainable principles. We must create conditions under which people can "know" the right thing to do in any particular circumstance without having to be told on each occasion. Those principles, developed and jointly owned with each individual, will themselves increase the perceived level of autonomy.

The organisation and the individual can, in effect, jointly determine the degree of autonomy, and both can actively seek through dialogue to modify it. That is a good starting point for the discussion: enough freedom to do the right things, not so much that it damages the cohesion of the organisation. When we work within agreed constraints because we recognise and accept them, because we see them as self-evidently appropriate, we will be low cost to manage. We will most likely manage ourselves within the boundaries and will be able to develop authentic, consistent relationships with customers and colleagues. Very importantly, having chosen to accept the constraints, we will be likely to wish to remain with the organisation in the long term. Contented people appear to have higher levels of satisfaction with lower staff turnover, reduced absenteeism and sickness. These things are good for the financial health of the organisation.

One of the very interesting aspects of military management (and similar "disciplined" organisations) is the extent to which it is outcome focused and operationally decentralised. Such organisations seek to recruit people whose values are aligned with those of the service (or to develop that alignment in early stages); they set out to find "people like us". All recruits, whether commissioned or not, go through basic training, which is designed to both turn them into soldiers, sailors, airmen or marines *and* to help them identify for themselves whether or not they fit (sometimes, I am sure, with a little guidance). Only once the civilian has been turned into a serviceman does the focus shift to training in the technical content of the particular service, whatever aspect that might be. Once the individual both "belongs" and is fully technically trained to a very high level, then he or she is deployed into active duty. Such active duty will be specified in the form of an outcome, "achieve this". It matters not what the particular activity is. The officers, with inevitably the occasional exception, know that the servicemen, with inevitably the occasional exception, are willing and able to achieve the outcome (the "what") and of developing the means for themselves (the "how"). The "why" is a given, it is ingrained in their belongingness to the organisation. In simple terms, because they are trained and tested thoroughly in advance, great autonomy can be allowed in the delivery of the outcome. An interesting paradox: the more tightly certain aspects are controlled in the early stage (selection, alignment, behaviours, skills), the more freedom the individual can have later.

Figure 7.1 shows how in the logical hierarchy of the Intelligent Organisation each level is constrained by belonging to the level above and in turn constrains the level below. Autonomy, in terms of the purpose for which the particular level exists, is constrained by belonging to the next higher level and constrains the one below it:

- Procedures are constrained by the required outputs of tasks;
- Tasks constrain procedures and are constrained by the outputs and outcomes of processes;
- Processes constrain tasks and are constrained by the required outputs of management;
- Management constrains processes and is constrained by its required contribution to senior management.

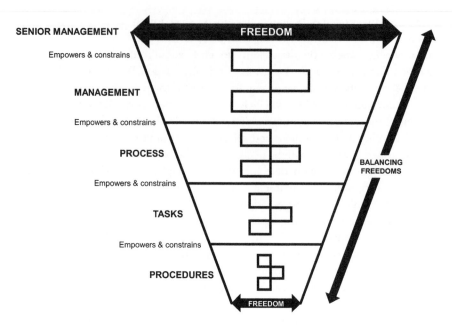

FIGURE 7.1 Managing autonomy

Recall the homeostat: the information about outputs and outcomes flows from each level to the next higher level as the enabler of management activity. The regulatory activity of the homeostat works to maintain it within the defined limits. Any tendency to move outside given parameters is rectified by control action already embedded in the system and keeps the system under control – all of which sounds potentially terribly oppressive. However, having already embraced Beer's principle, an oppressive regime cannot be the answer.

The answer is that the Intelligent Organisation embraces the principle of subsidiarity which, in context, means that "functions which subordinate or local organizations perform effectively belong more properly to them than to a dominant central organization". (WebRef 12)

Embracing this principle and maximising autonomy acts to

- decentralise the organisation,
- enable local responsive to local customers,
- minimise the cost of supervision and
- maximise the sense of control for the individual.

Efficient manufacturing is very reliant on a high level of automation. This creates conditions in which, in general, people are employed only to carry out those tasks that cannot be completed by automatons or, it has been determined for reasons of cost or complexity, will not be automated. In such circumstances the work of the individual is controlled by the work rate of the production process to which they contribute. Autonomy in relation to the task or procedure is low; it is governed by the machine. Individuals may be making some specific, limited choices and should have the power to stop the process if they observe it to be failing (Shingo, 1987). Here the technology (automation of the process) largely governs autonomy although even the most automated process relies on the skills of individuals, for example, those required to set up the technology and keep it operating within its constraints.

Fast-food outlets rely on production technology, repeatability and process optimisation. Reliable low-cost, high-volume output is the basis of the business model. However, while there may be only one machine process to cook a burger, staff members must apply their skills to assemble it according to the instructions and the required presentation. That is something only a human can currently do; it requires judgement. Equally, while the counter clerk is constrained in their process by the operating method of the cash register, they must also deal with the customers who will vary widely.

The blend of skills required by the burger assembler and the counter clerks are different. The autonomy required by the counter clerk is greater. They are not simply dealing with the need to follow the process in a consistent manner but also with the vagaries of the requirements and behaviours of individual customers (largely but not completely constrained by a menu). Given that customers will not arrive at regular intervals, the employees must deal with varying arrival rates and the variances in behaviour of those customers, who will, inevitably, range from delightful to downright rude. One junior banker I met very early in my first career had all these skills back to front. He was a delight with the customers, could always handle any mood or situation however strange, but he couldn't cope with process; his till never balanced. More often than not he did the wrong thing for the customer, but they loved him anyway!

The less the organisation relies on process technology, the more it relies on individual skills and behaviours, and the greater the autonomy or discretion required by the individual in order to fulfil the task. Even in a notionally "pure" service environment, such as banking, there is still a significant and increasing constraint imposed on the individual through process technology, the banking system. Customer service cannot be built in to the process, it has to be part of the authentic skill set of the staff member. Stupidities arise in any human system, even with the best of intent.

Technology versus autonomy

It is fascinating to consider what happens when we are late, for whatever reason, to pay a bill. The processes of the people and the technology are not synchronised!

The standard process can cope with an unpaid bill. A gas bill was paid on time, and the full value deducted from the payer's bank account when the cheque was presented. However, the value recorded was transposed in the records, which resulted in a demand for the balance from the utility. The utility's help line was helpful, understood that the customer was trying to get the error corrected with an intermediary (where the transposition had happened). A week later another letter arrived. Another phone call. Another helpful conversation, but those letters are automatic. There is no intervention. The issue was resolved, the bill showing as cleared, just in time for another letter. Apart from the obvious concern about damage to the customer's credit rating, the main irritation was with getting repeated automatic standard reminder letters, which did not reflect the conversations with the supplier. The supplier had set the standard process, with a letters protocol that addressed the majority of standard issues. On this occasion, there appeared to be no intervention that an intelligent manager (in role as customer) could make, without the (large) organisation itself being willing to add more flexibility into their procedures. Technology drives efficiency (we hope). Autonomy may require inefficiency, but without it we will always be ineffective.

Binding employees in to process compliance through overbearing scrutiny has, ultimately, the same effect as bottling gas under pressure. It is very expensive to achieve and will inevitably find the weakest point and leak or be triggered by a spark into an explosion. Sustainability for any organisation demands that it build harmonious relationships with the people that make it real. The Intelligent Organisation rests on an underlying assumption that most individuals, most of the time, want to do a good job, reflecting Theory Y (McGregor, 1960). They want to help the organisation succeed; that is good for both parties.

Greater reliance on skills implies greater autonomy. That, in turn, drives an opportunity for further skills. These skills are not technical, requiring the ability to carry out the task, but self-managerial, requiring judgement and discretion, the ability to decide which task should be carried out, when and to what standard with what level of risk.

A decision model for autonomy

We, in our organisations, desire that people do at least four things with their autonomy.

- Deliver: apply requisite skills to the process and deliver the required output and outcome.
- Learn: reflect on how well they applied the skills and ran the process and teach themselves how to do it better next time.
- Communicate: provide relevant information to prior, subsequent, contained and containing activities about performance.
- Alert: highlight to management those constraints on the whole system (skills, process, information) which limit performance and where they do not have the power (the limits to autonomy) to change the system.

How much autonomy is enough is perhaps largely determinable by certain characteristics of the whole organisation, such as the

- business model;
- processes and their degree of automation;

- competences and skills of the individual;
- probability and consequences of error or failure;
- alignment of individual, organisational and professional interests.

We shall consider each in turn. The business model is probably best represented in the form of a grid (figure 7.2).

In this grid different business types are categorised according to two dimensions: volume and value. Essentially, production of a low-value, high-volume product or service will probably rely on a low autonomy process with a low to moderate level of skill, production of a high-value, low-volume product or service will probably rely on a high autonomy process with a moderate to high level of skill.

Figure 7.2 contains four possible examples. Our fast food franchise is considered as making money from high-volume, low-value transactions. It needs a process which is repeatable and reliable, likely to drive down unit costs and enable survival on a low price and margin. This suggests low cost per transaction, which typically implies a low level of skill or a very high volume relative to cost. Sales of power stations are considered high value and, at least relative to fast food, low volume. The high value of each power station suggests that whilst it is important to have a process for design and construction, the unique circumstances of each one will demand a more customised approach. This implies a significantly higher level of skill. Information technology products are seen as lower volume than fast food (most people buy more burgers than they do laptops or tablets). As relative commodities, value is higher, but reliability must also be high. Technology products are either right or wrong, they either work or don't. This suggests sound technical design and, again, a repeatable and reliable production process with a medium level of skill. Car manufacture is considered high on both dimensions. A car, in the hands of the purchaser is a high-value item (the second most significant purchase for most consumers after

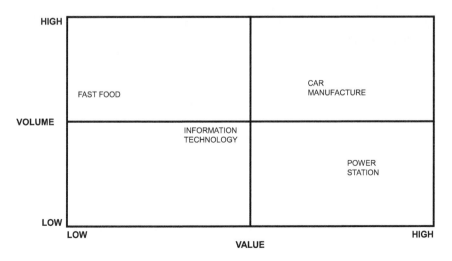

FIGURE 7.2 The business model

their home). Whilst individual cars are low in value to the manufacturer, their total volumes are high (around 10m cars per annum for the largest manufacturers). The technical complexity of the individual product needs to be matched by the technical skills of those assembling the product.

Taking this into consideration, we can now look at the processes and their degree of automation (figure 7.3).

At the left-hand end of this continuum are processes in which the level of automation suggests that a low level of individual autonomy will be appropriate. Those towards the right-hand end (requiring higher levels of skill or judgement) will enable a higher level of autonomy. We can apply this to the skills of the individual as shown in figure 7.4, in which we represent a progression from unskilled worker to seasoned professional.

It is important to note that these continua will never reach 0% or 100% on a scale. However customised a process may be, there will always need to be some level of process consistency, otherwise there will be no effective output. Equally, when considering skills, it is unreasonable to suppose that even a fully automated process requires no skill whatsoever. In some cases the level of skill may be very small; in others (and automated ticket machines are a good example of this) the skill requirement is outsourced to the operator (the customer). Think about this next time you are queuing to use an automated checkout in a supermarket or DIY store. It is not the case that no labour is required for the process. The store has simply outsourced the skill, and the cost, to its customers. Stores do not always think this through fully. I was recently in a store queueing to pay the member of staff because there were "not enough staff to open the self-service tills".

The fourth element in the decision model is to consider the probability and consequences of process error or failure by individuals, i.e. risk. Represented in figure 7.5, this works best as a grid. I suggest that fast food production is a low-probability but high-consequence activity (food poisoning). Demonstrable adherence to an approved process will mitigate (comprehended) risk, reducing scope for autonomy. Information technology, on the other hand, is low probability, low consequence. While the risk to life from information technology has historically been low, the risk to reputation will be higher. However, the latter is likely to have less immediate consequences and the manufacturer will have the opportunity

TICKET MACHINES	FAST FOOD	VEHICLE ASSEMBLY	POLICING	CONSULTANCY	RESEARCH
HIGHLY AUTOMATED	SEMI AUTOMATED	BALANCED		GENERIC	CUSTOMISED

FIGURE 7.3 Process progression

TICKET MACHINES	FAST FOOD	VEHICLE ASSEMBLY	POLICING	CONSULTANCY	RESEARCH
UNSKILLED	SEMI SKILLED	TECHNICALLY SKILLED		PROFESSIONAL	SEASONED PROFESSIONAL

FIGURE 7.4 Skills progression

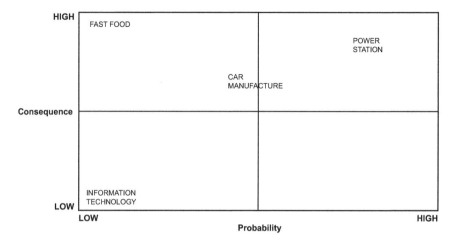

FIGURE 7.5   Risk, probability and consequence

to rectify matters. As the "Internet of Things" and 5G grow to reality (especially around connected and autonomous vehicles) and as we increasingly rely on them, the risk profile – especially that of potential threats to life will change dramatically.

A power station carries a much higher probability of incident in all its phases. The consequences of unmitigated risks are significantly higher, not least the potential for loss of life. These present a particular problem, needing reliable, repeatable processes in all of the design, build, operate, maintain and decommission cycles over 50 years or more. At the same time they need technically skilled and professional people to operate them. The power generation technology of the station will delimit the extent to which autonomy can be possible.

Finally, we can consider alignment of individual, organisational and professional interests. Represented in figure 7.6, this gets a little tricky; I have identified three sets of interests that somehow must be reconciled.

First is personal interest. An individual for whatever reason may be disengaged from the organisation's values. Those not so aligned are likely to act primarily in their own interest. Autonomy is likely to be minimal, but such a situation imparts a duty to those managing the organisation to consider how to rectify it.

Second is organisational interest. Individuals in this position are wholly aligned with the values of the organisation and likely to act primarily in its interests but may neglect their own interests in so doing. Here we may wish to constrain autonomy to mitigate the risk of damage to the "self" through overcommitment to the organisation. Members of religious orders and Type A personalities tend to be here!

The third set of interests is technical or professional. Here our interests are in a state of tension. The primary interest alignment is professional, second and third are personal and organisational. Doctors are a good example of individuals whose primary loyalty is often to their profession. The hospital or medical centre in which they work is a convenience rather than one to which they necessarily feel they owe allegiance.

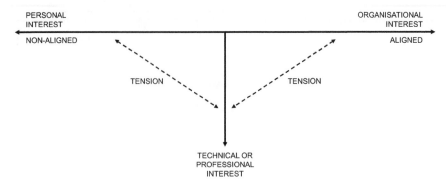

FIGURE 7.6 Aligning values

And yes, I have made all those choices a little stark, exaggerated for effect. For most of us, in most situations, we are trying to manage the tension between our self, organisational and professional interests. We must appreciate the existence of that tension and then design in the "right" amount of autonomy to dissolve it for all parties. In particular we must test the principle of subordination, that the "interest of the organisation is more important than that of the individual" (Fayol, 1916). More than 100 years on that principle may not hold in a wide variety of circumstances and for a wide variety of reasons.

Pulling all of that together, what do we need to do? And no, I am not going to make this easy; there is no arithmetic solution or silver bullet. We are going to have to think and then exercise our judgement:

- Locate your organisation in the business model.

  - Low Volume: Low Value
  - Low Volume: High Value
  - High Volume: Low Value
  - High Volume: High Value

- What does that suggest to you would be a good way to use process?
- Locate the process(es) on the process progression continuum:

  - Where do you think it fits?
  - Is that consistent with the business model?

- What does that suggest to you would be a useful level or autonomy for individuals?
- Locate the skill levels on the skills progression continuum:

  - Where do the skills fit?
  - Is that consistent with the business model?
  - Is it consistent with the process progression?

- How does that modify your perception of the level of autonomy?

- Locate the organisation on the probability and consequence grid.

  - Low Probability: Low Consequence
  - Low Probability: High Consequence
  - High Probability: Low Consequence
  - High Probability: High Consequence

- How does that modify your perception of the level of autonomy?
- Locate the people on the interests alignment chart.

  - Where do you believe they fit?
  - What evidence do you have to support that belief?
  - What, if anything, is being done to manage the alignment?

It would be surprising if in many organisations there were not favourable overlaps, that is overlaps where the skill level of individuals is higher than is required to safely operate the process. In these circumstances it may be appropriate to increase levels of autonomy, to allow for further delegation of decisions, to increase the sense of freedom within the organisation.

It may also, of course, be that there is unfavourable lack of overlap. That the extent to which the process is automated is insufficient to compensate for the lack of skills being applied to it. Usually there will be evidence of this in poor product, failing customer service, complaints and so on. The interesting thing is what you do to fix it. Do you reduce autonomy (quick fix, looks cheap and feels powerful), or do you invest in resolving the skills deficiency and preserve the autonomy in the system?

It is usually the case that once autonomy has been removed (usually on cost or risk grounds) it becomes impossible to restore to its previous level.

Summary

What this decision model alerts us to is the need to link back to the value-enabling activities of the organisation. Where we have discovered a bias towards automation and process, then value-enabling activity needs to focus on ensuring that these aspects are appropriate, robust and that the people have the appropriate skills to deliver the required outcomes. Conversely, where the organisation has low reliance on process and high reliance on skills, the value enablers need to ensure that they are investing appropriately in employing the right people with the right skills and that both the organisation and the individual are investing in them suitably.

Both of these actions can be conceived as addressing the matter of "risk". Appropriate investment in processes and skills will be one of the tools for mitigation. One measure of success in this regard might be *not* that individuals have been trained or processes enhanced, but that the perceived level of risk exposure has declined as a result.

Alignment of individual and organisational values will also require investment. This might be achieved through evaluations in recruitment processes for new employees but will also need to be tackled for individuals already in post. Quantitative indicators of alignment can be found in such things as staff turnover, sickness and retention rates. Qualitative indicators will be discerned in the myths and stories that pervade the organisation, the sense of coherence and collegiality that is sensed rather than directly measurable. Investment does not mean that "beatings will continue until morale improves". Value-enabling actors need to understand the organisational benefit of aligning interests and ensure that mechanisms are in place through which lack of alignment can be recognised and addressed, particularly by encouraging and enabling managers to "model the way".

That was all a bit thoughtful and thought provoking. In the next chapter I shall try to put it into practice.

8

MANAGING AUTONOMY

Cases

Introduction

We did lots of thinking about autonomy in the previous chapter, explored the decision model for autonomy and considered the implications for enabling value. We shall now return to the ongoing case studies, apply the model and see what the implications are for each one. I have (figure 8.1) consolidated the five diagrammatic elements of the model into a single diagram. This is informationally equivalent to the individual elements and allows us to see, holistically, each element in the context of the others.

We return to the continuing case studies of Fusion21, Southern Mill, the Canal and River Trust and UKCRIC.

Fusion21

You will recall that Fusion21 has three value-generating elements – procurement, training and employment services (TES) and consultancy. Each has a slightly different business model, and while the guidance for determining appropriate autonomy in each are the same, there are differences in the outcomes. The rules have been applied and are shown in figure 8.2. Different symbols are used for each of the elements in order to ease comprehension: the star is procurement, the heart is TES, and the cloud is consultancy.

For Fusion21 as a whole, the procurement business model is relatively high value (it generates the greater part of the income) and high volume. It undertakes the majority of the work with in excess of 300 projects per annum. The process was developed in partnership with those who deliver it and, as far as practical, was codified into information systems. One element deals with the procurement of materials and labour for projects, while the other deals with the project process

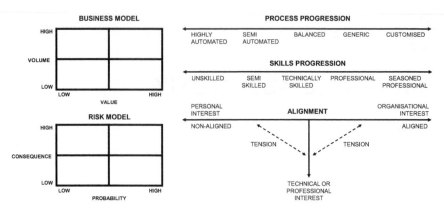

FIGURE 8.1 Integrated decision model for autonomy

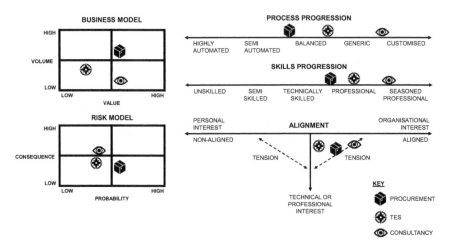

FIGURE 8.2 Autonomy in Fusion21

itself from inception to completion. The whole is more than semi-automated, giving it high-reliability and repeatability, but it also relies heavily on the professional skills and knowledge of the procurement team. They are specialists, mainly quantity surveyors and project managers. On balance, procurement relies slightly more on skills than it does on process. There is a lot of judgement involved.

From a risk perspective procurement can be thought of as higher probability but with relatively low consequences. The probability arises in the volume of the projects, while the consequences of failure are important but unlikely to be life threatening. The consequence of process or skill failure is likely to manifest itself in rectification work or loss of future opportunities. When we consider alignment and look across the team as a whole, they are most likely to be aligned to technical/

professional interests first and organisational interests second. As professionals they have a duty to act in a manner consistent with professional standards first and organisational standards second.

The procurement team have no autonomy to change the business model; they are constrained to operate within it. They do need sufficient autonomy, within the constraints of the process that they designed (a higher level of autonomy), to exercise professional skills and judgement about how they do what they do. From the value-enabling perspective we must ensure that they have sufficient process to deliver against the business model whilst maintaining and investing in the skills and knowledge necessary for the professional standards to be maintained. It would be appropriate to reflect on the degree of alignment between the technical/professional interest and the organisational interest as a means of recognising and, if appropriate, reducing tension.

Turning our attention to the TES team, we find a slightly different situation. The business model is very different; it has relatively low volume and relatively low value. The first of these is because it is "batch based", a small number of intakes each year, each of which has multiple participants. The second is because TES, to some extent, fulfils the purpose of Fusion21 (remember: profits into people not into pockets). The desired outcome of the TES activity is employed people, not profit. The process is clear but more balanced. It is reliant on manual rather than automated processing, placing a higher emphasis on skill. It is therefore no surprise to find that the skills progression position is more professional than technical. Quality delivery of the process, one which involves education, training, personal development, is highly reliant on the judgement and applied expertise of the staff. Considering the risk position, it is low and low. The probability of failure is mitigated (through, for example, good classroom and workshop practice) and the consequences of process failure for Fusion21 are also likely to be low. There is a need to draw on the process, but it is not dominant. Alignment is more balanced, though leaning towards the technical and organisational interests. What draws it back towards personal is that there is a perception that people working in that area do so because of the intrinsic reward of the work itself rather than the extrinsic reward of salary, professional recognition or standards. They do the work because they care.

Again, the TES team cannot change the business model, and they were involved in defining their own process. Discretion is important here: the TES team are not dealing with physical artefacts but often with vulnerable people. It is easy in these circumstances for the process to get in the way of a good outcome. They need to have discretion, up to a point, to minimise the amount of process and emphasise the application of skills, knowledge and judgement. The limit is reached when there is insufficient process to make the whole thing viable. This is easily attained if there is failure to keep essential records about trainees, their skills and qualifications or to sustain safe working practices in the workshops.

The value enablers need to be considering and investing in the skills and knowledge of this team and, in particular, developing mechanisms for capturing and retaining it in the business – something often called "knowledge management".

Consultancy is a small part of Fusion21. It is low volume but relatively high value business (the margins are very good). From a process perspective it sits at the generic/customised end of the progression. Consultancy projects are characterised in this context as unique and complex, requiring a method to be developed for structuring a problem and then solving it. There must be a level of process, but that is at a level of principle. The real emphasis is on the skills where the focus is on seasoned professionals. The nature of the industry and the actors within it are such that the routine challenges can largely be solved by the clients within their own businesses. Where a consultancy project arises it is because the problem or challenge is not tractable to the normal tools employed. Risk probability here is relatively low (assuming the people are competent), but consequences potentially high. These consequences are primarily reputational. If Fusion21 does a good job, the clients will probably take the credit. If they do a bad job (or the client doesn't like the outcome), they will blame Fusion21. This is not uncommon.

From an alignment perspective, consultancy staff will largely align themselves to the organisational interest whilst leaning on professional/technical interest as the base of their capability. As employees they have chosen to exercise their skills within an organisational context rather than a self-employed one.

In terms of the value enablers, the critical issue will be in maintaining and developing problem-solving and consultancy skills and ensuring that the context continues to be conducive to maintaining the values alignment. Consultants can often "model the way" for other, less seasoned professionals. They should be encouraged to act as mentors in developing capability and need to be granted the autonomy that lets them do so.

Fusion21: five years on

The original case study outlined how Fusion21 had chosen to address its commercial and social purpose primarily from a functional perspective (i.e. having three distinct functional propositions to its customers). Since then, the internal conversation has progressed to discuss how the organisation most effectively delivers its commercial and social purpose, which led to the creation of a charitable arm of the business.

Within the new "group"-based organisation, there is now provision for commercial activity (both procurement and social value) that is expected to deliver a commercial return, and there is provision for purely social activity that is expected to deliver social benefit. What remains largely the same is the approach to autonomy outlined in figure 8.2. This change has given the organisation the ability to maintain the model but change the organisational structure that supports it.

The change to the respective business models has created a structure to maintain the appropriate/desired level of autonomy for each area. However, these business models are now more closely aligned to one or both of the dual purpose.

Canal and River Trust: necessary and constrained autonomy

The Canal and River Trust needs to consider autonomy in two dimensions. Not only are the three core processes constrained vertically (they "belong" to the

organisation), but also both investment and income, and asset management/mainte-
nance are constrained horizontally (i.e. internally to the organisation), because their
"customer" is customer engagement. Fulfilling the needs of customer engagement
is the purpose of the other two and meeting that purpose defines the legitimacy
of their actions. It can be argued that if an activity of investment and income, or
asset management/maintenance does not contribute to the outputs required by
customer engagement, it does not contribute to the whole and cannot be sustained.
It ought to be possible to define a "golden thread" that runs backwards from the
desired customer engagement outputs to the inputs to each of the prior processes.
Of course it is not that simple. The "vertical" belongingness, the logical hierarchy
of the whole organisation, also places demands on the core processes. These may
range from the regulatory (operate in accordance with the law) to investment criteria (generate sufficient income to sustain the organisation and set aside a certain
percent for future years). This double constraint generates an interesting tension
and challenge – the individual working in this setting may be capable of responsi-
bly deploying greater autonomy than the constraining circumstances allow or can
allow. They may have capability, or ambition, that the "system" cannot benefit from.

Turning to the model as applied to the Canal and River Trust, we can see a
number of differences and similarities. Note that all numbers have been drawn
from the Canal and River Trust, Annual Report and Accounts 2017/18. In the
business model section, the value of the investment process is ranked most highly
with a portfolio value of over £850m and revenue of around £150m. In addition
there is a fixed grant, of around £50m from DeFRA until 2027. This portfolio and
the associated earnings are crucial to the financial sustainability of the Trust. The
volume of transactions is medium. Customer engagement is high volume: there
are over 4m visitors to the canal network's towpaths each fortnight in addition,
particularly, to the 35,000 boaters using (and in some cases living on) the network
and the many other community, day-trip and holiday-hire boats as well. While the

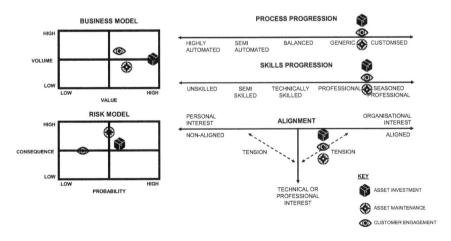

FIGURE 8.3   Necessary and constrained autonomy

earnings and cost associated with each individual may be low, the aggregate is high. For asset management/maintenance, this has been interpreted as medium/low in volume when considered relative to the other two; however, its value is considered to be higher than customer engagement, with a direct spend of around £100m and, critically, the greater part of the task of maintaining the waterways – the activity that underpins attracting customers.

Each of the core processes has a different risk profile and different risk factors. Lowest risk in terms of both probability and consequence is customer engagement. This reflects the individual nature of customer engagements (so that a failure or problem typically affects a small number of people), and both the risk to life and risk to money may be considered moderate. With investment and income, especially in a volatile investment market, the probability of an adverse event must be considered as higher (though a well-diversified portfolio mitigates risk), with the consequential "risk to money" being higher because that risk applies not only to revenue but also to the value of the underlying investment. Asset management/ maintenance, on the other hand, may be considered as medium risk but with high consequence. Risk in this area is heavily mitigated by adoption of appropriate engineering and operational standards and through regulated and inspected activity. Risk is further mitigated in some activities by outsourcing both design and delivery to other organisations. A significant element of the risk is associated with the nature of the assets themselves. Designed and built over 200 years ago in many cases, their original design and current condition can be to some extent unknowable until either they are stripped for working (with water removed!) or some adverse event occurs. The consequence of failure is potentially significant in relation to injury, life and finance.

It is important in managing both the business model and the risk elements, particularly given the diversity of the activities, that the leadership of each process is granted significant technical autonomy in the delivery of the outcomes. It is unlikely that any one individual at a higher level in the logical hierarchy would be sufficiently expert in all areas to competently intervene. That leads us to consider the nature of the processes themselves. Here, all three have been considered as being between generic and customised. There are, for all three processes, but particularly for both investment and income and asset management/maintenance, well established and highly regulated norms, standards and processes to be followed which are designed to ensure the safety of works undertaken, of the employees (or contractors/volunteers) doing that work and, in the investment arena, to ensure compliance. However, in each case these are complex, dynamic activities which require those responsible to exercise professional judgement drawing on significant practise and expertise. The positioning on the continuum recognises the underlying regulatory processes and the professional discretion needed. It is almost redundant to say then that the individuals must be, or be near to being, seasoned professionals on the skills progression continuum.

Turning finally to alignment, again, we see the positioning is common to all three processes. Here the positioning shows the alignment as towards the organisational interest combined with technical/professional interest. The thinking here is first that the reward system of the Canal and River Trust reflects its status as a charity; the people who work with it are typically aligned with its values and active supporters of its purpose. They will therefore be inclined towards doing what is both right for the Trust and technically and professionally defensible rather than pursuing self-interest.

All of these factors taken together support a proposition which seeks to maximise autonomy and to distribute control albeit within a system of very clear accountability and transparent performance management.

Southern Mill

You will remember we left Southern Mill as it was sold to its new owners. Nonetheless, we can apply the decision model to the organisation as we left it.

When we consider the model here, we shall apply it primarily to the core process of paper making. The business model is based on high volume and moderate value but operates in a high input cost environment where the key to profitability is reliability and throughput. That it is not in our gift to change; it is a property of the global market itself, not Southern Mill or its owning parent.

When we consider process progression in Southern Mill, we find that it is both highly automated (paper making) and manual (paper conversion). The paper machine only works one way; productivity is primarily a function of the capability of the machine itself and its inherent technology. There is an undoubted level of technical skill required to make good paper, but that is constrained by the limits of the machine. The operator can adjust speed, weight, volume and colour and, by setting the machine well, can ensure that good paper comes out, but that is it. They cannot change the process. On skills progression, therefore, the evaluation rests on

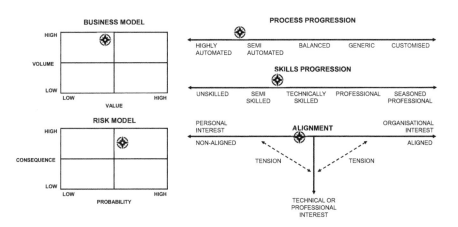

FIGURE 8.4 Autonomy in southern mill

a combination of semi-skilled and technically skilled people, applying those skills in machine set up and minding. Paper machines are big, fast, loud and have lots of dangerous, rotating, heavy parts. They process prodigious quantities of water (the "soup" going in to the front of the machine is around 97% water) and energy (energy is around 25% of the base cost of making the paper in this instance). They are easily capable of maiming or killing their operators.

Although the machines are well guarded and protected, paper making is a high-risk process. The consequences of failure to follow safe practices are high, even fatal. Alignment with organisational interests in this particular case were low, tending towards the personal end. This was a function of a number of circumstances. The mill had been in its location for several generations and employed more than one generation of several families as well as several members of the same generation. It was seen as "our mill", physically distant from its parent and the single largest employer in its community. Decisions were seen to be made by managers within the mill that were clearly in the interests of individuals rather more than they were the organisation.

In this case, autonomy was primarily constrained by the process technology employed. Skills development needed to focus on two things. First was working within the safe processes defined, i.e. individuals could not simply modify the core process for reasons of technology and safety. The second matter was to emphasise the development of semi-skilled and technically skilled people so that they would be able to reflect on their own performance and deliver improvement in those elements which were under their control.

Whilst the conversion process is less technologically constrained, it still had high risk. Handling large reels of paper (say five tonnes each) and using powered guillotines whilst manually inserting and extracting blocks of paper carried with it risk of injury. Conversion required greater autonomy in relation to process, and a number of innovations were conceived and implemented during our time there. The emphasis in skill development for the value enablers in this area was much more on process improvement than was possible on the paper machine itself.

UKCRIC: inverted autonomy

In the studies considered so far, autonomy is achieved through schemes of delegation to the individual actors which they exercise through positional power. The position in the organisation, in effect, legitimises the exercise of authority. In UKCRIC this does not apply: autonomy is relinquished by the individual in order to belong. In UKCRIC,

- The individual participants are employees of academic institutions. They do not have to participate in UKCRIC. They choose to do so and, in doing so, necessarily relinquish some of their residual autonomy (remember they have given up some to their host institution) to the service of UKCRIC.
- The participants embedded in the Coordination Node recognise that their task is to enable and facilitate the collaborations, not to direct or control them.

- The International Advisory Board influences but does not direct the research agenda.
- The Management Board can only exercise "control" of that limited range of activities undertaken directly by UKCRIC itself, not of the activities undertaken at the individual partner institutions *nor* of the individual participants.

There is therefore a need for a robust value proposition. There must be a greater "value" to the individual in belonging to UKCRIC than the "cost" of the marginal loss of autonomy experienced through that belonging, taking account of the opportunity cost of not belonging. Let us start by considering the individual, as we have done for the other studies.

In figure 8.5 we can see the suggestion that the individual academic in UKCRIC is undertaking high-value work but typically at low volume. This is consistent with a research agenda that is focused on long-term change to infrastructure design, implementation and maintenance. As an indicator of potential value, the National Infrastructure Plan for the UK contains in excess of 700 projects with their cost estimated at £400bn plus at the time of writing. Research grants to pay for the work undertaken are themselves measured in millions. Whether you consider only the cost of the research or include the value of the outcome, you end up recognising that this is high-value research. While the processes of research are well understood in this community, research by its very nature demands innovation, new forms and means of inquiry, and with changes in technology and our understanding of information, it is to be expected that a customised, individual process will be adopted in most circumstances. Academics engaged in UKCRIC activity are necessarily highly qualified, highly experienced and are closely engaged both in developing the research agenda and in the design and delivery of the research programmes themselves. They are seasoned professionals and, notably, draw a lot

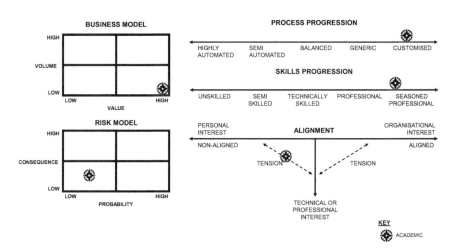

FIGURE 8.5 Autonomy in UKCRIC

on the notion of academic freedom to defend their autonomy. Academic freedom is the right to pursue their research without unreasonable or undue censorship or interference from their paymasters or the state. The extent of academic freedom remains an open and continuing debate. Turning to risk, we have cast that as low in both probability and consequence. The research work undertaken by UKCRIC itself does not involve dangerous materials or significant threat to life. The immediate consequences of research failure are largely confined to the involved individuals.

An alternative view of this can be argued here. The very existence of UKCRIC is predicated on a comprehension, set out in the case study in chapter 6, that the infrastructure of the UK, in common with many mature economies, is failing, is beyond its design life, is insupportably expensive to maintain, at risk of failure. This suggests that building further infrastructure on the historic basis is contributing to the incipient failure and to risks associated with global climate change. Hence, it could be argued that the consequence of research failure (for UKCRIC in the aggregate) is very high, possibly contributing to a failure to support the population of the UK and other countries, failure to secure infrastructural conditions for economic growth, failure to enable the society that the population as a whole desires. It can also be suggested that the perceived risk associated with failure is contingent on the inclusion of the opportunity cost of doing nothing. This allows consideration of the counterfactual alternatives:

> Counterfactual 1: In the absence of any change to current practise, business-as-usual (BAU) performance levels can be projected as a stable baseline to predict future infrastructure system performance.
> Counterfactual 2: In the absence of any change to current practise, BAU performance levels must be projected as a declining level of performance because current practise is not fit for purpose against future needs.

The constraint to this is one of "contribution". UKCRIC can contribute to and enable change, but it is not and cannot be solely responsible for all of the potential consequences.

Finally, we can turn to the issue of alignment. This is challenging. As already mentioned, the individual researcher will rightly defend their academic freedom and, in doing so, be loyal to the science (whatever the discipline) and the scientific findings. That loyalty is, in effect, to their integrity as a scientist (a follower of the scientific method in their research) and to their sense of self, and hence we have positioned them on the diagonal between personal and professional interest. If we choose that position, it can be argued that alignment to the organisational interest has been, at best, underestimated, at worst simply ignored. For this author, while recognising that loyalty to the organisation is perhaps the key to some aspects of career success, promotion and additional income, loyalty to the truths revealed by the science accompanied by publication and dissemination of findings will, ultimately, be more sustainable.

Summary

It was stated at the outset that there is no arithmetic solution or silver bullet to solve the problem of how much autonomy is enough. It is, re-citing Fayol, a continuously shifting balance, a negotiation perhaps, always a matter of judgement.

Of course it would be possible to develop a complete prescription for (nearly) everything, to state in unequivocal terms the absolute boundaries to everybody's freedom. But every day something changes; every day each individual is different; every day somebody leaves and somebody joins, an old machine is removed, a new machine is installed. Do you *really* want to spend all your time modifying what one organisation called "The Empowerment Manual" – and no, I am not joking – a manual which prescribed everybody's freedoms!

Think about starting with the core processes of the organisation (those processes which generate value) and assume at the outset full autonomy (with the potential for anarchy).

Then proscribe only that minimal set of freedoms which would breach the values of the organisation or are inconsistent with the business model. Prescribe only those matters which are required by the technology employed. Define those skills and behaviours which are required to do the rest. Then actively manage and develop those skills and encourage the behaviours and create a culture where individuals are able to empower themselves to do the right things right.

Under the right conditions, enabled the right way, autonomy will manage itself.

9
THE INFORMATION FACTORY

Introduction

In designing the Intelligent Organisation, we have established the need for change in the way we use information and realise its value. The processes and structures for generating and enabling value have been explored, and the need to sustain appropriate autonomy articulated. Making all of this work relies on changing the way we structure and use information. If we want our people, processes and systems to act intelligently, then we need to provide the necessary information in a timely manner and in a suitable format to achieve it. Then perhaps some of the intelligence needs to be built in to the systems. We need to educate and enable people and create our organisation and its systems to use information in ways which activate decisions, without human intervention where that is appropriate, to close the gap between where we are and where we want to be, between actual and desired states. In a world of work in which "humans need not apply" (Kaplan, 2015), the strategies currently employed by many organisations can only have one outcome, failure.

We need a strategy for information itself, not an information technology strategy, not an information systems strategy: an information strategy – the difference is huge.

Information strategy

An information system is not purposeful in its own right. It is an enabler of the purposefulness of the rest of the organisation, i.e. it must meet customer expectations, and the organisation is the customer. Its performance and its value, in a broad sense, is measured by the extent to which it fulfils that obligation. Unfortunately, many of the technical community do not recognise or respond to this obligation.

The data genie

A small manufacturer has a highly complex product portfolio, several thousand possible combinations, in a low-volume, small-batch-size factory. Their information systems consist of non-networked, non-integrated SCADA systems, a stand-alone (and largely manual) manufacturing planning system and a stand-alone accounting system.

The business is out of control. Through the separate systems, the data genie has escaped from the lamp and is wreaking havoc. Data lacks integrity and is duplicated and triplicated – there are multiple possible "right" answers to every question, all depending which system is looked at and, importantly, who is answering the questions.

There is no effective information function within the business. Systems are, by and large, provided by a remote head office department, and nobody thinks about the value lost or what could be gained through more appropriate information and systems.

Held back by thinking which is rooted in delivering a slightly better version of now, justifying investment in information systems, gets progressively more difficult with each new generation. Gains through conventional thinking become more marginal, payback becomes harder to achieve; the dead weight of established practices, applications and data clog the organisational arteries. I once thought it would be mischievous to suggest that organisations with established information systems should abandon them on a wholesale basis and start again; I am now thinking that may be the most effective (or indeed only) way forward. It is my experience that some organisations are in such an informational mess that it might be the best thing to do.

Working backwards from the savings

A brief project with a public sector organisation highlighted the challenge (and no, I can't name them; it would be unfair on the individuals). Working on a broader challenge exploring the potential for merging with others, we came to consider the implications for the back-office systems (HR, payroll, finance, property) of the three organisations. All had, to some extent, been outsourced to third party providers. One was in a state of flux; a business case had been prepared for its replacement but not yet approved.

The business case as presented showed a need for significant investment in upgraded or replacement systems including further outsourcing to a speciality service provider of some aspects ensuring compliance with "sector best practice". The payback period was under three years, an investment of less than £5m (over two years) generating a saving of £2m per annum after the first year.

So far, so good, so conventional, perhaps even worth pursuing.

Discussions and interviews revealed that the whole business case had been driven by a desire to operate within the sector norms and a requirement to generate a particular (and organisationally headline-grabbing) level of saving rather than to explore what might be possible. When we were comparing what was proposed (sector best practice) with benchmarks of other sector equivalents, it was obvious that a larger saving could

be obtained against a smaller investment. Implementation of the proposed plan would have generated a sub-optimal outcome both informationally and financially.
Good enough is not good enough!

The unconventional thinking of an information strategy needs to be rooted (figure 9.1) in

- understanding the information needed for decisions – throughout the organisation;
- understanding the value of that information;
- determining what, if any, applications and hardware are needed to provide the information;
- commissioning information projects – the success of which are measured in the provision of information required.

The information strategy can be prioritised against appropriate criteria – for example, urgency, importance, economic value. The whole can then be measured in terms of information value and impact on business effectiveness and financial performance. If an investment cannot be expressed in terms of its multi-criteria benefit to the organisation, then, perhaps, it is not an investment!

The information needed, together with an assessment of existing applications, systems and technologies, will determine what, if any, further application(s) and hardware are needed, and they can be chosen accordingly. Completion of an information project is measured jointly by the delivery of the anticipated information and by the value added to the business.

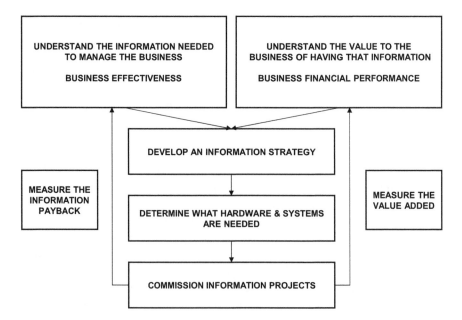

FIGURE 9.1 Information strategy

It is critical to note that "new-tech" tools are not necessarily the best answer. Technology can only solve a technology problem – *not* an information problem! The best answer to an information problem is "right-tech". In one recent instance the information was provided via a simple "counter" display answering the key question: "how many have we produced?" In another, where the size and complexity of the site meant that simple counting was not quite so straightforward, whiteboards were used adjacent to each workstation and updated half-hourly with rolling results. It may have looked a little Stone Age, but the operators could see for themselves what was going on across the whole process and the supervisors' role became primarily the provision of information.

The silent information system

A habitual observer of organisations, I was sitting in the café lobby of a hotel in Kuala Lumpur between meetings, something I did several times over a few days.

The staff glided around the floor, never speaking to each other but seemingly always doing the right thing for each customer, always asking the right question. Intrigued, I became determined to work out how they were doing this. They never spoke but were clearly communicating with each other. What was the information system that enabled this?

As I paid careful attention, the solution quickly became apparent. Upon a new customer arriving in the café, the staff would approach the customer and ask for their order, and upon taking the order they would take the menu card and lay it down, signalling that the order had been taken.

Serving the drinks, they would pour roughly half the contents of a bottle of beer or a pot of tea, then place the bottle or pot beside the cup – a signal to the next member of staff to complete the pour when the glass was half empty.

Upon the second pour, the empty bottle or pot would be placed in the centre of the table, a signal to the next member of staff to offer another drink. If the offer was declined, the member of staff would remove the empty bottles or pots whilst the customer finished their drink, which was a signal to the next member of staff to present the bill which would be placed beside the evident host. The next member of staff would then accept the payment, by whatever means, and leave the paid bill in the centre of the table: a signal that this customer was leaving and had settled their account.

All of that occurred without a word being spoken, with no bureaucracy, no centrally managed process (although one was clearly being followed), no orders or instructions being given. Simply thoroughly trained, hard-working staff were doing the right thing because the process contained its own instructions. The information is in the actions. Genius!

Solving the information challenge: the lean information system

If we want to be effective, then we need to minimise data proliferation whilst maximising availability of information. That should make us think in terms of a "lean information system" (LIS), one in which the decisions that need to be made at each point are understood and generate, by themselves, demand for contextualised information.

That determines what data needs to be captured, by which actors and processes within the system and for what purpose. This "information-demand" approach to information is consistent with lean production (Dennis, 2007). It can be expected to have a similar impact for organisational information as it has for manufacturers and service providers who have adopted it: reduced waste, greater operational efficiency, lower storage requirements, increased productivity. This thinking applies just as much to the data for value-enabling decisions as it does for value-generating decisions, and the two orthogonal views of the organisation will be sharing "common" data, i.e. data which can be held once but used many times by different processes.

We can begin developing the lean information system by recognising that the information architecture must map isomorphically (Beer, 1966) to the organisation (figure 9.2). The information architecture must be a direct function of the organisational architecture. Change in one demands equivalent change in the other, with all the implications for the technology and system layers (presentation, integration, applications, devices and network) and for the behaviours and skills of the users. This mapping must extend beyond the boundary of the organisation into the channels through which customers and the organisation communicate. Unless the mapping between the organisation and the information is maintained then one or the other, or quite probably both, will not work effectively. While I was in a recent consultancy assignment, it became apparent that the structure of the information system and the cost of changing it (effectively a reimplementation of all systems would have been required) were inhibiting the ability of the rest of the organisation to change. The information system had become "pathologically autopoietic", in effect serving its own ends and inhibiting the achievement of organisational purpose.

When we map the information architecture to the organisational architecture, we both simplify things and reveal embedded complexity. Simplicity arises from consistent application of the notion of the homeostat to the process, task and procedure levels which become very specific in the actual application. Complexity is exposed in the decisions that we are now asking people to make, wherever they are in the organisation. This is unlike conventional, functional decision-making because we

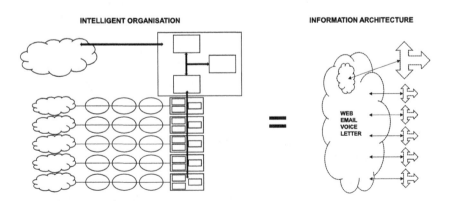

FIGURE 9.2   Mapping organisation and information architecture

make explicit the complexity of such multiple criteria decisions and the need to meet multiple outcomes and constraints. Decision makers are asked to decide which input (or inputs) to modify to generate outputs closer to the desired goal. They do this in the context of all the other decisions being made in the organisation and its environment. Looking at figure 9.3 we can see how decisions (the diamonds) are distributed throughout the organisation. Information is "demanded" by the customer, and that stimulates a chain of decisions horizontally and vertically through the organisation.

It is evident from this wide distribution that there will be a range of different information requirements and implications. Consistent with earlier discussion, we need to generate and distribute information both horizontally and vertically through the business.

Unless (or until) we can rely upon the information provided, the appropriate reporting mechanism is most probably some form of dashboard showing both the capability (what should have been achieved) and the actual (what was achieved); the difference should be highlighted (using colour indicators to draw attention to the points where action is required).

The information heartbeat

Information provision enables self-regulation, and that works when the information in the system acts to damp error so that in "going out of control" the system uses information about its own performance to bring itself back under control. Self-regulating systems act to reduce error, which saves the manager a job. Given the ability of technology to deliver fresh data, there is a need to moderate the rate of its arrival and to synchronise it with the cycle time (the "heartbeat") of the processes and decisions which it both informs and is informed by. Reporting and

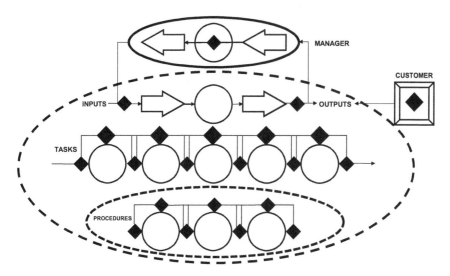

FIGURE 9.3   Distributed decisions

PROCESS PERFORMANCE

	INPUT	39656		TARGET	40000		OUTPUT	36664.22				

	POTENTIAL	UNIT CAPABILITY	PROCESS CAPABILITY	MOST LIKELY	UNIT LATENCY	PROCESS LATENCY	UNIT PRODUCTIVITY	PROCESS PRODUCTIVITY	UNIT PERFORMANCE	PROCESS PERFORMANCE	BACK	POSSIBLE	TRANSLATION
RCF	53100.00	39656.00	39656.00	36028.85	0.75	0.75	1.00	0.91	0.75	0.68	40000.00	39656.00	1
PPP	50978.00	49080.00	39656.00	34803.59	0.96	0.96	0.81	0.87	0.78	0.84	40000.00	39656.00	1
PM	41043.76	36664.22	36664.22	35242.67	0.89	0.89	1.00	0.96	0.89	0.86	42920.00	49080.00	1.073
WINDER	60743.38	55852.16	36664.22	39166.08	0.92	0.92	0.86	0.99	0.60	0.91	40000.00	36664.22	1

RCF	SETTINGS	FPP	SETTINGS	PM1	SETTINGS	PM2	SETTINGS	WINDER 1	SETTINGS	WINDER 2	SETTINGS	REWIND	SETTINGS
LIMIT	37.50	LIMIT	36.00	LIMIT	910.00	LIMIT	1700.00	LIMIT	1000.00	LIMIT	1200.00	LIMIT	1000.00
RATE	32.00	RATE	33.00	RATE	905.00	RATE	1850.00	WEIGHT	48.50	WEIGHT	44.60	WEIGHT	44.60
LINES	2.00	LINES	2.00	WIDTH	5.40	WIDTH	9.40	WIDTH	5.40	WIDTH	9.40	WIDTH	9.40
HOURS	20.00	HOURS	24.00	WEIGHT	48.50	WEIGHT	44.80	HOURS	20.00	HOURS	20.00	HOURS	20.00
DAYS	31.00	DAYS	31.00	LINES	1.00	LINES	1.00	TLOSS	3.50%	TLOSS	2.48%	TLOSS	0.00%
PSHUT	12.00	PSHUT	12.00	HOURS	24.00	HOURS	24.00	JR LOSS	0.90%	JR LOSS	0.90%	JR LOSS	0.00%
UPSHUT	12.00	UPSHUT	12.00	DAYS	31.00	DAYS	31.00	BEATER	3.00%	BEATER	0.52%	BEATER	0.00%
TARGET	39656.00	TARGET	49080.00	PSHUTS	2.80%	PSHUTS	2.90%	CULL	1.00%	CULL	1.00%	CULL	0.00%
				UPSHUTS	5.80%	UPSHUTS	2.90%	PSHUTS	2.80%	PSHUTS	2.90%	PSHUTS	0.00%
				BREAKS	3.00%	BREAKS	3.00%	UPSHUTS	5.80%	UPSHUTS	2.90%	UPSHUTS	0.00%
				JR LOSS	0.90%	JR LOSS	0.90%	BREAKS	3.00%	BREAKS	3.00%	BREAKS	0.00%
				BEATER	3.00%	BEATER	0.52%	LINES	1.00%	LINES	2.00	LINES	1.00
				GROSS	10680.55	GROSS	30879.54	NO. OF DAYS	31.00	NO. OF DAYS	31.00	NO. OF DAYS	31.00
				NET	8840.57	NET	27723.85	GROSS	9401.89	GROSS	36501.49	GROSS	15695.73
				UNIT MAX	10275.85	NET	30788.11	NET	7850.41	NET	32406.02	NET	15695.73
				COMBINED TARGET	13 & 14	UNIT MAX	30788.11	UNIT MAX	9428.40	UNIT MAX	38222.34	UNIT MAX	15092.64
						COMBINED TARGET	36664.22			COMBINED TARGET	13 & 14		55652.16

FIGURE 9.4 A performance dashboard for a paper maker

response then become consistent with each other and conform to the notion of using the process homeostat as both the organisational and regulatory device.

Failure to achieve this synchronisation increases the risk that what we respond to is "noise" rather than "signal" (Silver, 2012). Responding to noise leads to inappropriate actions which amplify rather than attenuate error and can risk "catastrophic collapse" (Beer, 1974). Our mental "hot" systems (Mischel, 2014), our emotional selves, receive information first and respond intuitively to perceived opportunities and threats. We need to use process design and the synchronicity of arriving information with process outcomes to ensure that our "cool" system, the rational self, is able to intervene and modify our responses.

Fast data delivery appeals to our inner "chimp" (Peters, 2012) but drives us towards correcting for every small variation. Sometimes it is better to wait. Good examples of this can be found in a sport where the novice responds to every minor event; watch six-year-olds playing soccer. Experts demonstrate much greater economy of effort by observing the pattern, reacting only to significant events (with significance being a matter of judgement, so sometimes they get it wrong) and positioning themselves in anticipation of the next event rather than in reaction to the last one. Snooker players take the current shot not just for the "pot" but also to position the cue ball where it will be most useful next; drivers of rally cars (whilst appearing insanely busy from outside the car) demonstrate amazing economy of effort within it, relative to the movement of the car – notably they are driving the car; it is not driving them. We must use information to ensure that we are driving the organisation, and it is not driving us.

To do this we must design our decision models to get the right information in the right format and language at the right time. Then we can reflect it in our behaviours so that our human response can be dominant, not our inner chimp.

Damping "hot" response

A healthcare organisation had an established unit whose task was to clean and sterilise surgical instruments ready for reuse. They handled about 1m packs a week, with each pack containing between one and one hundred instruments and a contracted maximum eight-hour turnaround time for every pack. The essentially manual process was simple:

Collect, Unpack, Check, Rinse, Wash, Check, Pack, Sterilise, Despatch

Packs were received at irregular delivery intervals and batch sizes, a function of activity volume and availability of delivery staff. The staffing pattern had evolved over many years to accommodate the needs and preferences of individuals. This generated a typical queuing problem; both the flow of dirty packs and the staffing capacity had irregular asynchronous heartbeats leading to pulses in the workload.

Unable to see the whole process because of the physical size of the facility and the incomplete information, supervisors undertook what Peters and Waterman (1982) called "management by walking around". Whilst this can have merit, in this instance they would observe a backlog occurring in one area and, in hot response, call for staff from other areas to "come NOW" and address it. Meanwhile, of course, the processing in the other areas would slow due to the lack of staff and a backlog would start to arise there. The backlog in the first area would become under control, and the staff, respecting the command and control ethos arising from the "come-NOW" style of management, would wait to be given fresh instructions to be sent to the next identified backlog.

The natural ebbs and flows were thereby amplified rather than damped. This caused frequent breaches of contracted turnaround times and, of course, a need to insert "urgent" packs and fast track them, drawing at least one, and often more, members of staff out of the standard workflow, increasing the workload on others, further increasing delays.

The challenge was addressed in five ways. First we developed a process and data model of the whole system allowing its status to be seen at any time, creating a context in which cool decisions about staff allocation could be made. Second by establishing priorities for different pack types, giving priority to bigger and rarer packs for neuro and cardiac surgery over the thousands of single instrument packs containing only one scalpel or pair of scissors. Third by regularising the flow, initially establishing a heartbeat for introducing packs into the flow, which meant accepting that it was OK for the stock of dirty packs to ebb and flow. Fourth, a collection and delivery schedule, based on the planned hospital activity, was introduced to induce a regular heartbeat in the supply chain so that the frequency of deliveries became stable.

Fifth, over time and in consultation with the staff, shift patterns and staffing levels were adapted to balance against the anticipated flow of work. The outcome was that the contracted turnaround times were always met, and overtime costs were reduced by £330k per annum (all but eliminated).

Design for decision: exploiting the model of self

If the information architecture is mapped to the organisation, we know what decisions need to be made where. Managerial action can then be focused on deciding what to do to close the gap between the actual and desired performance rather than collecting and collating data. Doing that requires us to have a robust, rigorous understanding of our intentions, and that is the MoS embedded in the homeostats.

For many managers and in many situations, decisions can almost be regarded as programmatic and, given properly designed, constructed, authentic and useful informational models of self, they can indeed be so. Given a desired output, the manager should be able, with the right information, to determine which input(s) to change in order to close the gap. The algorithms of computer programmes are ideal where a good level of relative certainty exists. In those cases we can design the application and reporting programmes to do what they are good at and free up the people to deal with relative uncertainty and do what they are good at, and that is making judgements.

With the organisational and informational architecture aligned, the key to reducing uncertainty (where possible) in decision-making is to attenuate variety where practical and appropriate. Such attenuation can be applied to many business decisions by generating rules for reporting and decision models which rely on known and agreed assumptions and definitions of the meaning of "data". Where these do not exist, then the models themselves are inadequate.

Obtaining value from information relies on competent users, but now anybody with a PC and a spreadsheet can be a data analyst! But can they? What if they are using the "wrong" data? What if they are using a wrong tool, one not designed for the particular job, or a problem-solving model developed for a different purpose or are making different underpinning assumptions (or even simply putting the decimal point in the wrong place)? What they will get is a perfectly correct, often beautifully presented and utterly wrong, right answer.

Beware of geeks bearing GIFs

At one time, when I was working with a major logistics organisation, we were developing a performance reporting and modelling tool. This tool took a data feed at the close of business each day (the network for their system could not deliver a live data feed) and through a series of algorithms produced reports by shift, sector, line, infeed, outfeed, process and team covering work done, rework, failures and stoppages. It enabled the active balancing of workload with staffing level and was saving the client around £15k per 24-hour period, delivering real value to the business.

We decided to look at the pattern of activity over the course of a week to identify regularities (or irregularities) to enable further performance gains. The in-house data analyst was asked to take the raw data set (about 1GB of data per day in 43 columns and about 500,000 lines) and represent the activity through the week as a time-series graph.

Very pleased with himself, the analyst arrived to present the results, complete with a first interpretation of what they told him. They contained some surprising results; in particular the workload peaked much earlier in each time series than we expected, with a dramatic mid period slump followed by a second peak and a further slump. This needed further investigation and validation, but where to start? The results did not match our combined experience and expectations.

A difficult choice was made – perhaps if we reordered the data so that the days of the week were in order of occurrence, rather than sorted alphabetically. . .

Nearly all established organisations use decision models, though often they will not be recognised as such. In functional structures they may well be inadequate or dysfunctional. Nonetheless they provide "rules" for decisions. Such models might embrace issues of performance (of individuals, teams, business units and divisions), investment payback, return on capital, presence (or absence) of staff, numbers on payroll, asset performance, reliability, quality, yield, revenue and a whole host of others considered important to any particular organisation. However, they are most frequently only brought together in a single place as a debate or discussion in the boardroom, rather than integrated with the workflow at the operational level. Similarly, because each of these elements is managed and measured separately, it is difficult to bring them all together in one coherent story.

There are a wide variety of sources from which decision models can be identified, all of which rely for full effectiveness on the operational definitions, i.e. structure and meaning (Oakland, 2003, 2019), of the underpinning data (values) being properly defined and the data itself being timely and accurate. While Mark Twain suggested that there are "lies, damned lies and statistics", if you want to be effective in your lies, then refer to the work of Darrell Huff (1991) or read the work of Goldacre (2013) on the pharmaceutical industry. If on the other hand you would like your decision models to be rigorous, transparent, verifiable and useful, I suggest you draw inspiration from a more broadly based literature. Harper and Lim (1982) provide a sound insight to mathematical analysis of business problems through operational research while Knott (1991) gives a sound grounding in models for financial management (though the relevant professional bodies in this field provide the contemporary standard and statutory models to which the finance director will refer). Tennent and Friend (2005) provide a useful and well-worked-out set of tools for business modelling and demonstrate good use of computers for this purpose. Goodwin and Wright (2004) offer a range of methods for modelling decisions under conditions of uncertainty. Between these four sources the greater part of the business decision world can be addressed, although many others are available. All of these models should also be used to enable organisational learning (Senge, 1993) and knowledge management (Hislop, 2013). We need to ensure that the models we use enable us to solve the problems we already have, not to generate new ones. We need to learn from our past errors and to carry new knowledge into a future that we have learned to anticipate – to provide feedforward information that allows us to dissolve error as well as feedback that allows us to self-regulate.

When we understand what decisions need to be made, the information needed for them and the data that underpins them, we can determine how to capture and store it – once.

We started to address the lean information system (LIS) by identifying the decisions we need to make, developing the information needed to make them, establishing the decision models that we need and the data that is required to populate them. In this demand-led world it is reasonable to question what other internal data needs to be held and what mechanisms we should use to archive (forget?) material that no longer has relevance to our decisions. One of the tasks of the managers throughout the organisation is to understand how the information architecture needs to evolve – that is *not* just a job for the IT crowd. This is necessary to ensure that the relevance of "new" data is recognised, that the relevance (or not) of "old" data is understood and that the information architecture and its supporting systems are enabled to ensure adaptation of the whole.

The information (systems) hierarchy

Most, if not all, established organisations, even those that are very small, have an information technology system comprised of five essential layers:

- Presentation: programmes used to display outputs;
- Integration: programmes which allow programmes to "talk to each other" and share data;
- Applications: the programmes through which we work and in which data is structured and organised;
- Devices: mainframes, servers, PCs, tablets, smartphones, peripherals that physically store the data;
- Network: the telecommunications infrastructure that carries the data.

The top three layers are what we have been concerned with so far. Presentation and integration deal with the decisions we need to take, the process models we adopt and the data requirements that go with them. They constitute much of the executive, management or business information system and deal with the business process (or processes). Applications cover value generation (customer relationship management, sales management, enterprise resource planning) and value enabling (asset management, human resource management, procurement and finance). These should be thought of as IS and require data sharing between applications. Applications are typically functionally oriented and hold a set of data, data which may be required in other parts of the business. Unfortunately, this requirement is often met by developing and storing multiple similar data sets – back to the idea of the Borgesian library, a database of all possible versions of the truth? In the Intelligent Organisation we recognise that data can be used for multiple purposes and that there must be only one source of the truth within the organisation. That requires the development of master data sets (and their custodianship) which hold only one version of the present truth (and its history) and makes it available to all the applications that need it.

Organisations typically have one set of customers, one set of staff, one set of assets, one set of suppliers. Is it not better, then, to hold one set of data about each of these and make it available to all who need it within the organisation? A decision model for asset maintenance needs to draw on the shared data set (what assets have we got?) but addresses questions specific to the maintenance processes. The core data (what assets have we got?) is *also* relevant to the production system, but the decisions they are concerned with are about utilisation. So asset data must be stored once (to avoid duplication, error and decay) and contain everything necessary to allow it to be used for all legitimate purposes. This compares with the common practice of holding the base data in two separate systems – one for asset management, the other for production. Immediately after this latter situation occurs, there is either unnecessary work to maintain synchronisation or else the data sets diverge, leading very rapidly to a situation where there are two versions of the truth and neither is authoritative.

The bottom two layers, devices and network, constitute the "T" in IT. They are the technologies which carry, store and distribute data, and their job is just that: to carry the data around the network and deliver or store it as instructed.

Contemporary technology offers a plethora of devices which individuals might use to carry out their work. The LIS considers these devices from the viewpoint of the work the user needs to do with them, i.e. the decisions they will make, the processes they will operate or control, the data they will transmit and receive and the locations in which they are expected to work. These then drive the type of devices that are necessary, their size and data processing capability. There is little more entertaining when commuting, at least for the observer, than to see the frustration on the face of a fellow commuter trying to work on an unsuitable device. This embeds a further hidden inefficiency in the business, in addition to causing unnecessary frustration. It is unfair to blame that only on the provider; often the user should recognise the stupidity of the way they are trying to work – and where.

The information "feedback" loop between the device and the organisation's network needs to be taken into account in application choice, device choice and network design. The network is the data conveying capability of the organisation (its wiring diagram) and, to be effective, must have

- sufficient access points (network nodes) that every user who has a need can gain access to, including customers and those working remotely through virtual private networks or mobile telephony;
- sufficient capacity (bandwidth and speed) at each node and through the cables or wireless network to carry the volume and frequency of data;
- sufficient capacity to store and process the required data;
- sufficient resilience both in its internal and external connectivity to cope with service failures.

The LIS must accommodate all of this and, to be resilient, should have more capacity and connectivity than is likely to be needed for even peak demand. Given that networks, network switches and machines are low cost relative to the value of the work that is done on them, this is one area where redundant capacity adds more value than it does cost. Network failure because of poor connectivity or inadequate capacity simply slows the work of the organisation down and generates a flood of unnecessary activity which adds no value.

Long-distance printing

One small organisation I worked with had outsourced technology provision with its servers for data and printing located at the outsourcer's data centre some 200 miles from the office itself.

With data travelling at the speed of light, 200 miles is not a significant distance, but there were substantial delays in transmission and receipt of data, frequent service failures, failed print instructions and much retransmission of failed jobs.

A brief analysis of the situation revealed that the available capacity of the telecommunications lines and associated switchgear was inadequate for the volume of data being handled which was far greater than had been comprehended. For example, for data and documents held remotely, any individual wishing to print a document would first open it on their desktop (involving the transmission of the document from the data server to their PC); they would then send the print instruction to the print server (which involved sending the document again), and the print server would then send the document to the designated printer.

For the document to be printed it had to be transmitted three times across the network, and, with around 30 staff all engaged in this activity, it was no great surprise that the network was struggling and that performance was poor.

The audible signs of this were the gripes and complaints of the staff affected. The invisible cost was all the time that was wasted either waiting for documents to load, waiting for print jobs to complete or retransmitting instructions that had, for one reason or another, failed.

Aspirations to mediocrity

The primary focus of the lean information system is enabling the business processes, end to end, and the end is the outcome for the customer. The process represents the workflow of the organisation, which we need to understand and manage because it is that which delivers value to the customer. It is only when we have grasped the whole that we can make sense of, and meaningful assertions about, the parts. This approach also enables us to capture data as a by-product of the work itself rather than as a series of partial, functional or siloed activities that we try to interrogate after the event through "data mining". Data mining is the attempt, after the fact, to reconstruct what happened; it is inevitably difficult, expensive and, more often than not, wrong. Its necessity means we have not built *in* to the system those elements of data that we subsequently want to take *out*. Capturing data as a part of the workflow is precise, effective and free.

When undertaking this work in practice, it is important that, where appropriate, we design and build the information systems around the process for the particular organisation, its customers, its people (especially their skills and behaviour), its culture and its needs. It is increasingly common to adopt "best practice" from another organisation. This is fine where the process is not core to the existence of the organisation (the processes for procurement, for capturing financial data and so on can very often conform to a generic standard). However, often the practice isn't actually the very "best", does not suit the particular circumstances and needs of *this* organisation and, a little like benchmarking in the quality arena, is often an aspiration to mediocrity. Being "as good as" or "good enough" is not good enough.

Nobody knows the process better than the people who do it, so they must be fully engaged in documenting, reviewing and improving its design. Nobody is in a better position to improve work than the people who spend their days variously baffled, frustrated and enraged by the "stupid way we do things around here". Appropriately engaged people in well-designed consultations will reveal not just the obvious but the hidden, subtle and nuanced ways of working that can really enhance the process. In the Intelligent Organisation, the people who do the work are largely self-regulating; they must then be engaged in specifying the necessary inputs, outputs and outcomes and in developing the tools that will help them to be more effective.

Summary

We have explored the notion of a lean information system (LIS), a radical departure from the organisational norm. The Intelligent Organisation pulls through the LIS that data which it needs to enable its decisions makers, to support process control and improvement and, most critically, to meet its customer outcomes. It eliminates waste and duplication through its architecture.

In the next chapter we shall consider how this can work in practice.

10

THE INFORMATION FACTORY

Cases

Introduction

In the last chapter a lean information system (LIS) was proposed to support the Intelligent Organisation. In this chapter the challenges, benefits and pitfalls are considered, and the focus is on the provision of information for decisions. We are revisiting Fusion21 and considering the Canal and River Trust in this chapter. The first case, updated, continues to give a sound introduction to applying the idea of a lean information system. The second is to consider how a much larger organisation with a longer history and more deeply ingrained systems can address the challenge.

Fusion21 – deal with things as they are!

We revisit Fusion21 to look at the development of the lean information system (LIS) that supports it. The organisational representations remind us that the information architecture must reflect the organisational architecture (figures 10.1 and 10.2): they are alternative views of the same thing.

It would, of course, be wonderful to tell the story of the development of this LIS in the delightfully linear fashion proposed in the previous chapter, starting with a strategy and working from that. Life, however, is not like that.

The initial invitation to work with Fusion21 arose when its growth exceeded the capacity of the supporting technology infrastructure. Presenting symptoms were low quality and availability of data, technology underperformance and excessive costs. The IT (the network and devices) could no longer handle the volume of data traffic generated by the growing business going through the IS (applications, data integration, presentation). The consequence was frequent service failures, delays and disruptions. The "outsourced" provision of the whole system appeared expensive relative to open market costs, and supplier service was slow, causing further disruption.

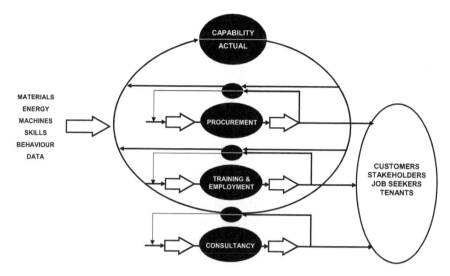

FIGURE 10.1   Fusion21: value-generating activities

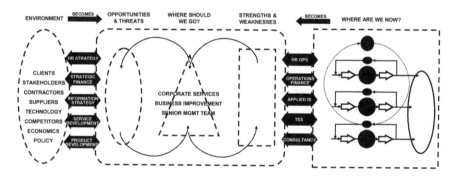

FIGURE 10.2   Fusion21: value-enabling activities

As I was working with the Head of Business Improvement (an enabling role), the performance of the whole system was reviewed. While the organisation had grown, from three people at the outset to around 25 at that point, the overall information system had not grown with it. Costs had grown disproportionately to both volume and performance; information value at Fusion21 was deteriorating.

Exploration continued, as the organisation was seeking to understand how data was being captured, held and used for decisions.

After establishing its initial procurement activity, Fusion 21 through organic growth, both generating and reacting to opportunities, had developed additional lines of business (training and employment services, consultancy). Data storage reflected this; data was held in and drawn from small functional "pots" throughout the organisation. These represented the narrow interest of particular individuals or tasks. They could not be interrogated in a business-wide or systemic manner. Much data was held in spreadsheets which were not systematically maintained, partly because of culture, partly because of underdeveloped processes. The consequence was periodically made evident when the need to report completed projects, invoice clients and settle suppliers accounts caused major difficulties. Each time there was a mass of work to be done to update records and generate the required information spreadsheets. Errors and omissions were frequent.

It was recommended that Fusion21 should do the following.

- Recognise that effective use of information was essential if it was to sustain its value proposition in "intelligent procurement".
- Develop an information strategy which would allow it to sustain its leading position and improve its competitive position by working smarter, not harder.
- Develop an information architecture suitable for the emerging shape of the organisation, consolidate disparate data records.
- Develop information systems to support process delivery, control and reporting across the business.
- Address the information technology challenges through a hybrid strategy:

  - insource those activities that Fusion21 could do better itself (information management, device procurement);
  - outsource those activities which required specialist expertise or were required infrequently (broadband and network provision, server and PC maintenance).

A value-based business plan was presented and approved for implementation. Reflecting continued aspirations for growth, the business payback was addressed through "reducing cost per transaction over time", following Coase's Law (Lorenzo et al, 2011) that companies expand to the point where

> "the costs of organising an extra transaction within the firm becomes equal to the costs of carrying out the same transaction by means of an exchange in the open market".

It would have been foolhardy to seek an absolute reduction in costs, but a relative reduction means that the cost of operation grew at a slower rate than the increase in revenue generating a greater margin. Such is the value of information.

With a new understanding of the information requirements of the business, we addressed the prevailing technological constraints. The following plan was designed and implemented.

- Enhance the wired and wireless networks to provide sufficient capacity to cope with more than the anticipated growth of the business and the frequent visitor and client events. The value of redundant capacity in such a network far outweighs its cost. The benefit showed through in reduced system-imposed delays and downtime, increasing productivity.

- Provide a new high bandwidth Internet connection for performance with a second, lower bandwidth line sourced entirely separately, giving resilience in the event of primary connection failure.
- Establish a small in-house "server farm" (mail, data and print servers) to bring all data within the walls of the organisation supported by procurement of an "online" data backup service. This ensures both local control and business continuity.
- Procure user-specific replacement devices against a rolling replacement plan.

Investment in training and education of staff in the use of the new network and systems soon saw initial challenges and difficulties overcome, and the previous complaints about connectivity and delay fell silent.

A lean information system for generating value

The starting point for the information strategy was to determine what decisions needed to be made throughout the business and what information was required to enable them. These decisions ranged from Board-level decisions about strategy, business performance, investment and reporting social return on investment (non-financial contributions consistent with the social objectives of the organisation) to operational decisions about delivery of outcomes through processes, task and procedures.

The company had already made a substantial long-term investment in a "supplier and contractor" costing system to support its intelligent procurement activity. This system was embedded and working well but only supported the procurement process and only dealt with one critical stage in it. It matched client requirements through house archetypes to produce indicative project specifications and costings prior to on-site survey. This system made excellent use of the notion of a MoS, the various housing archetypes being such models. The IS development needed to capitalise on the established investment, not replace it. This placed a small, appropriate but significant constraint on the project.

In addition to the intelligent procurement system, a number of other areas were identified for which data was being stored in multiple databases and spreadsheets. Inevitably these were different in structure and content (even when being used for similar purposes) and were under the stewardship of individuals. This generated significant risk when individuals changed roles or moved on from the organisation.

Fusion21 now understood that knowing "what", knowing "how" and knowing "why" made information its most valuable resource. Knowledge management was impossible unless information was embedded in the system itself. It could not be left solely at individual discretion. The company needed to use intelligently designed models to ensure sustainability. "Brute force" reporting or throwing resources at a data problem would continue to risk loss of knowledge.

The next step was to map the data flow across the organisation. This outcome-focused flow was developed through "brown paper" process-mapping workshops.

They involved staff from each team for all core processes from beginning to end. We established that any one individual might engage with Fusion21 many times. Someone working in the social housing sector might be a customer of all three of the core business processes at different times. They might encounter Fusion21 as a housing officer with one registered social landlord and reappear in a new role with another. Trainees participating in one training course with TES were likely to appear on others funded by different agencies. Consultancy clients were already likely to be clients for TES or procurement. On the procurement side there were clients, contractors (labour), suppliers (parts) engaged on each project, all employing trainees. The relationship of any one individual with Fusion21 was likely to be complex. The company needed to be able to track those relationships, not only to ensure continuity but also to be able to understand how the relationship was evolving and adding value.

The output of this activity was a data flow diagram (DFD) (figure 10.3) which shows how the data is pulled across the organisation from contact to business process to output (reporting).

In the top left corner ("sales administration process") contact data is captured. This contact data supports activities such as prospecting, networking, key account management, framework management and relationship building.

Data is drawn from that source to inform the sales process ("VS prospects"). This presents the data as a sales pipeline with opportunities contextualised to the requirements of the individuals concerned. The sales staff are thereby provided with information that lets them decide which product or service to target at each individual and the system tracks progress towards a sale.

When the sale process has moved to "pre-contract" (a task within the process) the data is available to the relevant delivery process, whether that be TES,

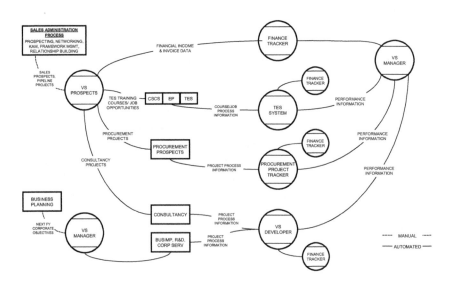

FIGURE 10.3 Fusion21: data flow diagram

procurement or consultancy. Each of these processes has a "tracker" built in, allowing the staff to both draw on and add to current data about individuals, companies, projects, products and services. Simply by doing their job, the staff are capturing the data to inform later decisions.

It is often difficult to judge in professional organisations how much process is enough. In this case we had confidence in the answer because

- the people actually doing the work thought there was too much process or
- the people managing them thought there was not enough.

The process flows represent only a part of the work. For all three core processes, the work draws on the professional knowledge, skill, relationship capability and judgement of the quantity surveyors, project managers, trainers, educators and consultants employed to do it. These capabilities needed to be identified, codified and managed somewhere outside the core workflow. At present this is handled manually to match and develop the skills and competencies required for any process role to the skills and competencies claimed by staff members, verified through evidence of qualification and demonstrated capability. It is reviewed through 1-2-1 discussions and development-focused appraisals. In a larger organisation, or should it become necessary in Fusion21, the information element of this could be integrated to the overall data structure.

Queries built in to the core processes provide information to the "finance tracker" informing the finance team about what projects, products and services are at each stage of the pipeline, what revenue and costs can be expected and when. Importantly, the core process generates the triggers for the despatch of invoices to clients. This integration eliminates a number of reporting activities that would otherwise be necessary and provides an audit loop connecting process activity to its financial consequence. The "on-cost" of reporting is zero.

As each core process is updated, the data is immediately available to the reporting tool ("VS manager") in which the models of self required to manage the business are embedded. These require no interrogation, no data mining no arbitrary connecting or simulation of results; the data is simply available to individuals, to teams, to processes, to finance and to the whole business. The results also inform value-enabling activity such as resource planning, business planning and so on.

The development of the DFD provided the information necessary to develop an information architecture (figure 10.4). Understanding how and where data is captured and used by the organisation enables understanding of how it should be stored and made available. This is "one view of the truth", all data being captured and stored once but available for use many times for different requirements. This reflects the notion of Master Data Management, a powerful and important idea which is sadly not adhered to by many organisations.

At the root of this diagram are two elements. The first are the "core data" tables. These contain the data which, for Fusion21, is universal. This includes clients, contractors, suppliers, funders, trainees, staff and addresses. Complementing those tables

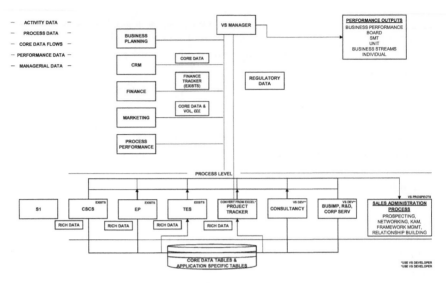

FIGURE 10.4   Fusion21: information architecture

are those which are process specific. These include products and services, and each element is unique to a particular process, so its data does not need to be available to others.

The next level represents the operating (value-generating and value-enabling) processes of the business from sales administration through procurement projects, TES, consultancy to business improvement, research and development. Each embedded MoS is a specific instance, drawing on the underlying data and presenting it in the form of an end-to-end workflow. These provide the staff with a complete record of each project, guidance towards the next steps and, with time cycles built in, alerts to any delays or overdue activities. It enables them to self-regulate, to manage their own work.

The final level of the information architecture is that of reporting. This is both straightforward and extensive. Reports are available for individuals to regulate their own work, for team-level management and for the business as a whole at two levels of granularity (executive team and board). Other reports extend to, though not exhaustively, customer outcome, quality, efficiency, cost, customer relationship management, key account management, marketing, business performance and social value.

All the data required to generate the reports is captured in the system just by doing the work. The biggest challenge was to design and build the data queries that construct the different models of self. It is not good enough to say, "We did *this*"; what is required is to be able to say, "We *did* this, you wanted *that*, *here* is the difference", and to follow that up by explaining what has, is or will be done to improve performance through change in process, skills or standards. This approach is fast and effective in operation because it relies not on fast processing speeds and document retrieval but on rich interconnectivity between the various data.

The staff, having been involved in the design of the workflow processes, were also involved in the design of the numerous reports required from the system. Members of each team were trained in report design, enhancing and embedding capability in the organisation. They determined what they wanted to know, when they wanted to know it and in what format of presentation, and everyone had the opportunity to be involved in the design from the newest and least experienced staff member to the Chief Executive.

As each element of the system was developed, from the workflow to the reporting, all those affected by the particular element were engaged in testing and evaluating it against their evolving requirements, and the system was modified, updated and edited to meet their needs. The lean information system was developed through the integration of people with their process and the information they needed.

This makes it a "lean information system" for the users as well. They are only presented with information which is relevant and useful to their needs, only able to address those parts of the system appropriate to the conduct of their duties.

A lean information system for enabling value

So much for the value-generating IS, but what about value enabling? Here the challenge changes. The value-generating process relies heavily on the professional skills, knowledge and judgement provided by individuals, but those are applied to processes which have to be repeatable, reliable and responsive to the demands of the customers. It is in this standardisation that consistency and coherence emerge in the system – which reduces variability and, in doing so, provides the process and cost efficiency that is valuable to the end customer. However, the value-enabling activities, whilst they must have good process and consistency (particularly around the appointment and treatment of people) are much softer in this respect; that is to say, they do not have the heartbeat-driven regularity of the operational processes. Instead they address three needs:

- support of the operational processes;
- response to emerging requirements of the organisational environment;
- sustainment of the identity of the organisation for it to remain true to its purpose and values.

This is difficult, complex, evolving, shifting over time. We did not, therefore, even attempt to build the complete information system that might be required (though that could be fun). It is of course human activity, wisdom, experience and judgement that are applied, and the challenge for Fusion21 was to determine what information those involved in the value-enabling activities needed in order to be effective.

The first part of this was already embedded in the reporting structure of the operational LIS. Their production was automated so that aggregated data about the overall work of each process was available to the appropriate people.

The support firstly ensured that the operational teams have available to them the requisite resources for their tasks, and the most significant of these is people. Fusion21 chose to deal with this through five elements:

- a "model" establishment;
- job descriptions codifying skills, competencies and experience;
- individual reviews;
- appraisals;
- training and development.

While the LIS could tell them how much (the volume or amount) of a particular skill or knowledge set was being used, the HR processes enabled them to understand how well (efficiently, effectively) it was being used with the reviews and appraisals generating as their outcome the future training needs. Internal resources were used to cross-train and share knowledge amongst team staff whilst Managers and Senior Managers meet regularly to bring together knowledge about the whole business, its performance, needs and aspirations. These meetings and discussions provide the basis of the response to the emerging demands of the environment. That is, they bring together the people who best know what the customers want to buy both now and in the future and how to provide it.

There is inevitably a danger in these circumstances: that Senior Managers, Directors and CEOs will get their hobby horses from the cupboard, put on their bee-filled bonnets and whip into submission anyone who has the temerity to challenge them. To avoid this we experimented with the notion of "the future you are currently in" (Ackoff, 1981). This is the approach that uses the information in the LIS to create a LIS-Sim (lean information system: simulator). This simulation replicates the underlying LIS and allows, by the addition of adjustable parameters of volumes process, skill, finance, customers and so on, the impact of changes to be assessed in terms of the impact on the "current capability". This is set out in figure 10.5 and essentially revolves around the repeated asking of one question: "What if?"

- What if the volume increases or decreases?
- What if the value of contracts changes?
- What if we add or remove staff?
- What if we change the skills applied?
- What if we change the process?
- What if we change the products?

Each of these simulations generates a different "future" for the organisation, and those responsible exercise judgement in choosing the future they want. Most importantly, that is done using facts about the current state of the organisation, not guesses about the future. This allows the debate about change to be set in relatively objective terms; it becomes about things and processes, not about people. It creates a context in which, rather than individuals confronting each other across a table,

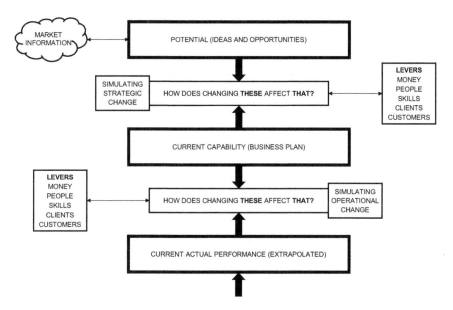

FIGURE 10.5 LIS-simulator: whole organisation adaptation

they can jointly confront the problem and together explore the impact and consequences of any particular proposal (or indeed multiple proposals). The debate is not about winning or losing for the individuals but about the benefit or risk to the business from a particular proposal.

Is this a perfect approach? Probably not. Does it deliver benefits? Yes. In the particular circumstances described, but also with a number of other clients, this thinking has responded to the needs and situation as it is, not as we might like it to be. The sophistication of the simulation is partly about the data and information that is available, partly about the complexity of the debate. It is after all simply a model, and as you will recall "a model is neither true nor false: it is more or less useful" (Beer, 1985). The critical issue is to be stimulating the conversation about alternative possibilities and informing that conversation with data and information about the organisation.

Nurturing identity

Finally there is the requirement to sustain the identity of the organisation, to keep it true to itself. This is very useful because the identity can be expressed as the purpose of the organisation, the reason it exists – and *that* is rooted in answering the question: "What is it we do that is of value to our customers?" We have already established that Fusion21, under the strapline "pounds into people, not into pockets", is an organisation that is built around efficiency in social housing procurement to generate surpluses that regenerate jobs. Resolving any tension between the tendency of those generating value to want to "do things differently" and those enabling value to want to "do different things" is easy. The question and answer become, "Which of these choices best helps us fulfil our purpose now and over time? We will do that one. then". And as for value? The cumulative net gain arising from the application of the LIS in this information-intensive business is around £500,000 against a turnover of around £5m (an increase of about 33%) while staff numbers have increased by only 15%. Proportionately, information is enabling more to be done for less.

Fusion21: five years on

The benefits described in the case study allowed for the business to put information at the centre of its universe. Now that information was more closely aligned to processes, the quality (and reliability) of information increased, and information became more dominant in decision-making processes.

As technology evolves and the demands placed on systems increase, the need to ensure that the technological platform did not become a source of concern was more apparent. As we built on the initial work to develop the LIS, a similar approach was taken to ensure a long-term technological solution was implemented to safeguard the value derived from the LIS.

The period of the original case study was, in effect, a prototyping phase where Fusion21 learned about the information it needed, the format(s) and frequency(ies) it was needed in and, most importantly, the ways in which it would use it. As the business reformed, reshaped and grew, it was clearly necessary to move from prototype to full production systems. A review was undertaken which considered the full range of options from consolidating and making sustainable the systems which had been built internally to replacing them with "off-the-shelf" systems configured to the business need. It was considered that the original systems were too vulnerable in the medium term to redundancy of technology and to availability of programmers. It was considered that the business needed a bought-in system that would emulate the features and capabilities of the prototype systems but with enhanced backup and supportability.

A decision was made to migrate to a cloud-based application and migrate the technology platform to a software as a service (SaaS) model. This ensured that information continued to support process and allowed for improved reporting capabilities to emerge. The business now benefits from increased automation of information processing (saving time and money) and real time information reporting (supporting day to day decision-making).

This has allowed the information strategy to focus on the role of performance information across the business. Driven by the informational capabilities of the LIS, the information strategy identified accessible and interactive performance reporting (which is code for "lots of visual performance information!") as a priority.

The impact of this has been to embed performance information into the consciousness of the organisation and to allow people at all levels of the business to engage with it. The role of information in long-term strategy development has also been a priority. Effective modelling and simulation of the future is now a real capability of Fusion21 and not an aspiration of the information strategy, with the focus now on how to improve the scope and reliability of the long-term business projections using information at its core. The Board draw on both near real-time reporting and increasingly sophisticated performance reporting and predictive analytics to support decisions which balance short-term needs with long-term desires. Fusion21 is using information to create its own future.

Canal and River Trust

In our previous visits to the Canal and River Trust, we have seen how shifting from a functional to a process orientation has enabled a focus on delivering customer outcomes, promoted greater autonomy (increased delegation) and located operational decision-making more appropriately. One consequence of this has been a reduction in the number of senior management posts required. A further consequence is that the established information systems no longer align to the needs of the organisation.

As noted, the Canal and River Trust was previously a company owned and operated by a government department. The formation of the Trust saw this ownership change, and, with the change, the Trust inherited the information systems then in place. Understandably, the first actions of the Trust executive (a number of who transitioned with the change of status) was to ensure the security and safety of the assets, to secure the income and begin the process of developing a new identity. Five years on, with significant progress made on those fronts and the senior management restructuring underway, there is capacity to consider the information systems.

It can be argued that this could have been undertaken sooner, even that it should. While that may have delivered some benefits, it may also have introduced further sources of instability and uncertainty into an already turbulent situation. Maintaining stability, even if inefficiently, during the initial period was a pragmatic, appropriate, rational course. While there was ample opportunity for change in information systems, there was greater need for stability for the benefit of the whole, which a significant systems change could have undermined. The disadvantage of this approach is that the information architecture and systems, albeit operationally modified on an ongoing basis, reflect a lack of substantial strategic investment over a very significant period – including that in the hands of the previous company.

We can use the information systems hierarchy outlined in the previous chapter to interpret the initial situation.

- Presentation: Reports are mainly in the form of Word (and wordy) documents, disconnected from the underlying data, separating financial information from the process data that drives it, requiring expert construction, intervention and interpretation to use. Managers, including very senior ones, complain of lack of transparency and delay in receiving information.
- Integration: Some integration is undertaken, most commonly using bespoke, specially coded, locally owned algorithms, unsupported and unsupportable.

Data is duplicated across systems, the file structures and document sharing systems are overfull, and data is difficult to identify and retrieve.

- Applications: The core finance and HR business application is operated on an outsourced basis and is well beyond its original planned life. Restructured through its long life, it cannot meet the future needs of the organisation. Supplementary applications are diverse, again often outsourced and, in some cases, heavily customised to the historic needs of the organisation. This renders both ongoing support and refreshment difficult, slow and expensive. The underpinning office operations application for email and the like is also ageing and reflects a long-term lack of investment.
- Devices: An early action by the post-transition Head of IT (note the job title: it is significant as a reflection of where the organisation was in its thinking) has seen a significant refresh in this area. This has increased uptime, reliability and availability. There remain challenges with ensuring that all people have appropriate devices for their particular need – but that is being resolved.
- Network: In common with the overall approach historically taken by the organisation, the information systems networks (both wired and wireless) were outsourced to specialist providers. Designed and implemented some years ago, they were no longer suited to the needs of the substantially reconfigured organisation, and, with the emergence of fifth generation networks and the requirement for increased telemetry across the waterways, there was a need for a full refresh of the approach.

In summary, the information management reality was of confused governance, unclear data ownership, poorly defined roles and responsibilities in relation to data and systems design. Much data held, but much of it was poorly structured or unstructured and therefore not searchable or useable. Demonstrating compliance with regulation would have been challenging. Information management was inefficient with a degree of risk and organisation-wide impact.

As you sit back and reflect on your own situation, consider this – your organisation is probably no better! The critique offered above, which might seem harsh, would hold against the great majority of organisations, regardless of size, industry, location or country. Like them, this organisation carries out its functions every day; it realises benefits from its asset investments and keeps the waterways open for its users; it meets the needs of its customers, pays its staff and its suppliers and makes the necessary supporting decisions. The opportunity is to make a step change in the capability, not just to "do things right" but to "do right things", to address the inefficiencies in the way things are done, to reduce or eliminate delays between need and response and to allow all the great capability of the staff to be directed to making and implementing useful decisions, anticipating needs and reducing risks based on information provided, not to have all their talent consumed by the process of reporting. The prognosis for that organisation is that if they do not address the challenges, then they face the risk that some of their systems may fail. All systems will continue to be inefficient and absorb resources that could and should be directed to value-generating activity, and financial performance will suffer. The ultimate impact would be, potentially, an inability to invest appropriately in the assets.

This work reflected in this case study is ongoing at the time I am writing, so what can be shared with you is the information strategy and how that is progressively being realised across the organisation. As mentioned in chapter 4, a cross-organisation delivery group had been established to jointly own and implement the information strategy ensuring that the focus is on the information needs of the various parts of the organisation and that technology design (networks, devices, applications, integration, presentation) was all subordinated to the information need. The information strategy owned by that group is intended to build new capability across the Trust through an organisational development approach which is rooted in synthesising people, process and information. Picking up the five layers it is intended to develop as follows.

- Presentation: The basis of reporting throughout the organisation will be dashboards.

  - These will

    - identify actual performance versus intention/target,
    - identify the cause or location of performance gaps and
    - require and enable improvement action to be taken and recorded.

  - Dashboard "builders" will be located throughout the organisation as "superusers" with expert support and validation of models from the business intelligence team.
  - Dashboards will be "one source of the truth".
  - Business units, *not* finance, will provide commentary and interpretation.
  - Utilise a common "business intelligence" tool with integrated key data.
  - Dashboards will replace existing reporting activity.

- Integration: To provide an appropriately robust platform for the dashboards, it is envisaged that integration will, primarily, be undertaken for data rather than systems, requiring

  - a single reporting tool capable of supporting the dashboard approach to be deployed;
  - data to be drawn from underlying systems into reporting models to enable decision-making;
  - reduction if not eradication of duplication of data;
  - elimination of different performance standards and definitions being adopted across the organisation;
  - insourcing of the capability to handle the integration, increasing staff competence and organisational agility and reducing ongoing support costs.

- Applications: A hybrid approach to applications is proposed.

  - The hybrid will have at its core an enterprise resource planning (ERP) system dealing with, at least, finance, HR and procurement.
  - Customer relationship management and asset management systems may or may not be integral to that ERP depending on a number of

organisation-specific needs in relation to the use and retention of personal and asset data.

- Implementation of any replacement systems will be constrained to "configure, not customise". This reflects the desire for the "intelligent" activities to be embedded in the dashboards rather than the applications themselves. It will increase the speed and reduce the costs of implementation.
- Underlying "office management" systems will require upgrading to remain current and supportable.
- Existing data storage and sharing applications will need to be replaced because

  - benchmarking studies of the approaches taken by other organisations show that no single system can meet all of the organisations' needs;
  - it is supportive of the integration approach;
  - it reflects consideration of the capabilities (present and future) of the Trust.

- Devices: The refresh process is to continue with the caveat that devices offered need to more fully reflect the needs of the users and to be capable of carrying the information outputs necessary to their task.

  - Networks: The Trust had already recognised the need for work in this area and the information strategy outlined highlighted the need for prompt action. A network upgrade process is in course at the time I am writing, which will

    - provide a substantial increase in bandwidth (for increased data volumes);
    - increase security of the networks in all locations;
    - increase resilience to ensure continued capability;
    - reduce costs.

While this last may appear contradictory, the cost of provision is falling, and it is appropriate that the organisation should take advantage of that.

The immediate steps implemented to get the strategy moving were to

- develop a fuller delivery plan;
- evaluate the approaches taken by other organisations to see what could be learned;
- develop initial dashboards on an experimental basis;
- codify the knowledge and skills that will be required to develop and sustain the capabilities;
- understand the staffing implications;
- review support and equipment arrangements to optimise value for money;
- review networks and connectivity for performance, resilience and security.

Summary

This chapter has shown how the idea of the lean information system, developed in the previous chapter, has been applied and worked through in two very different organisations. The scale of the philosophical challenge does not vary greatly between organisations initially, as what is needed is to convince the board and executive management team first of the need for change and second, that this somewhat radical approach, is the most appropriate change. The scale of the practical challenge will vary with the size of the organisation and the extent to which ingrained systems and behaviours combine to cause friction.

It will be essential for the organisation to embrace the essential thinking of aligning the information and organisational architectures. It is critical to then drive this by identifying what decisions need to be made throughout the organisation and to engender the autonomy necessary to make such decision-making legitimate. Finally it will be critical to design the information systems so that the information flows to where it is needed.

11

MANAGING PERFORMANCE

Introduction

We start this chapter by briefly considering the conventional means of managing organisational performance and its limitations. We then explore what performance means for the Intelligent Organisation and the different ways it needs to be considered. The chapter introduces Beer's potentiometer as a framework through which disparate measures can be reconciled and synthesised into a coherent view of the performance of the whole organisation.

> If you always do what you have always done, you will always get what you have always got.
>
> *Mark Twain, Henry Ford, Albert Einstein or, possibly, Anthony Robbins*

Bizarre as it may seem, this is how we typically manage our organisations. The common measures and questions are shown below.

Measure:	**Question:**
• Cost and/or income:	"did we make budget?"
• Output volume:	"did we make target?"
• Conformance to specification:	"were they good enough?"
• Customer satisfaction:	"how many complaints?"
• Employee satisfaction;	"how many complaints?"
• Health and safety:	"any reportable incidents?"
• Environmental impact:	"were we within the legal limits?"

I have perhaps been a little harsh, but not very. Even where these measures and many others are brought together in something like a balanced scorecard (Kaplan &

Norton, 1992), notionally aligned to the corporate vision and strategy and informing the future, they tend to be dealt with

- retrospectively (what happened?),
- functionally (where did it happen?),
- judicially (who is to blame?) or
- independently (the effect of each on the others is not considered).

OK, now I am being harsh; that would be to look backwards to see the future.
Surely nobody would do that, right? Except, in many organisations, performance
reporting is about

- process compliance;
- conformance (budget, volume, safety, quality);
- fault-finding and blame;
- functional, partial, siloed views of actions rather than outputs or outcomes.

Performance management is usually looking inward and backwards, but it also
needs to be looking outward and forwards. Where we are going is, at least, as important as where we have been.

For many organisations there is a whole internal industry concerned with regular reporting. Driven by a periodic management meeting timetable, it is often
dedicated to obfuscation: disguising the errors made in the last period, generating
excuses, displacing blame, making "*my* figures" look as good as they can. The whole
suite of associated activities often adds cost rather than value. This approach directs
effort towards justifying the past and draws it away from modifying the future. It
is designed to "hold people to account" rather than to realise the desired customer
outcome. Targets and objectives are often relatively arbitrary – *last year's budget plus
3% for growth minus 2% for efficiency improvement* – and uninformed by the capability
of the organisation or by the customers' wants. The whole panoply can be a sham.
It demands that often meaningless reports be generated, received and reviewed.
It provides an audit trail for post hoc justification of decisions without actually
improving the outcome. It can be the worst form of managerialism, creating the
illusion of control and accountability whilst adding only waste to the organisation.

Improvement comes not from hiding, disguising, justifying, explaining or rewrit-
ing history but from changing the things that cause the result. That means improving the processes, skills, behaviours and information that generate the outcomes for
customers.

Cheaper not to bother

*The marketing department of an organisation in the travel industry decided to promote
leisure travel between two of its key locations by offering a limited number of low-
priced tickets for journeys during the school holidays. The aim was to temporarily boost*

traveller volume and therefore revenue in a traditionally quiet period. The campaign was duly devised and executed. The promotion was a great success, attracting around 30000 additional travellers at £10 per head and delivering additional revenue of about £300k, an increase of 1% in monthly revenue with a promotional cost of advertising of only £15k – one-twentieth of the revenue.

The Marketing Director exultantly reported this great success to the next executive meeting to great applause until the Finance Director asked how the operational cost of selling the tickets had been factored in. It was rapidly established that it had not been, and it was realised that, at a sales cost of £12.50 per ticket, the successful promotion had cost the company £375k plus the promotional cost of £15k – a total of £390k.

Net, this successful promotion based on an inadequate model, had cost the company £90k. It would have been cheaper not to bother.

Think about your organisation: how is performance managed?

- Lots of people work hard compiling and interpreting reports.
- There are many "business systems", but all your reports in hand-built spread-sheets and carefully written documents.
- Reports are produced by "cut and paste" from last month.
- There are unexplained inconsistencies from period to period.
- Standards and definitions vary across the organisation.
- Activity volumes are apparently erratic and uncontrollable.
- There are inexplicable errors.
- Managing is disconnected from doing.
- The focus is on improving the report rather than improving the process.

You are not alone! Think about organisations in the news in 2018 and 2019, such as Carillion, Interserve, Patisserie Valerie, and consider how their present and their future might have been different if they had adopted different information strategies and ways of managing their performance.

Not solving quality

Arriving one day at the premises of a regular client, I was greeted with some surprise by the receptionist, who was clearly not expecting me:

"They are all very busy today, John."

When I explained that I had a number of meetings organised, she signed me in, and I proceeded to the first appointment. Knocking on the open door I could see the pile of work spread across the desk.

"Hello, Graham. Busy? What are you up to?"

(You have to start the conversation somewhere.)

"Hi, John. Sorry, can't see you today. We will have to reschedule. Should have let you know."

"Big problem?"

Here I was assuming the lid had blown off the chlorination plant or some similar disaster.

"Yes, monthly quality meeting tomorrow, auditor is in, need to make sure I have resolved all the non-conformances for the last month so I keep out of trouble with Gary."

"Oh."

"Yes, will take me all day, need to speak to every customer for every out-of-specification order to get them to sign off the variance to specification as acceptable so that all the "out of specs" become "in specs" for this month."

"Oh."   I was somewhat taken aback. "Why were they out of spec – process problem?"

"They are not really. The sales department has agreed a specification with the customer purchasing department which is far tighter than they need for their process and, frankly, far tighter than our process can reliably produce."

"OK, so the contract is being renegotiated to the specification that can be produced?"

"No, we do this every month. Complete waste of time, but it keeps the quality people off our backs"

"Is there a plan to improve the production process and meet the specification?"

"No, no time for that."

"OK, next time, Graham, bye."

The conversation with the Quality Manager was much more relaxed; he was, after all, confident that at the audit the following day there would be no non-conformances and no follow up actions.

We often manage, and I have tested this in a host of organisations over many years, through a focus on "reducing costs" or "reducing quality issues". That is pointless; the costs or issues just bounce back when we take the pressure off. It is "flavour-of-the-month management": *"Don't worry about this initiative. Keep your head down and ignore it. It will be something else next month".*

There are constraints on performance. Directors, perhaps, have an absolute, legal obligation to maximise the return to shareholders, the surplus in "not for profits", to work within budgets for the public sector. There has to be accountability. Effective control *and* improvement require reporting at a number of levels of organisation. The two objectives of maximum return and minimum cost are not inconsistent. While much depends on how return and cost are defined, performance must be measured by the extent to which the organisation fulfilled its purpose! That purpose is achieved by delivering the outcome valued by the customer and by coexisting with other stakeholders and is likely to have multiple dimensions. Fulfilment of the outcomes required by the customer will enable the survival of the organisation itself.

Organisational adaptedness: the capability for survival

Survival, viability, is a product of the total adaptedness of the organisation to its environment, especially its customers. We must understand and manage the extent to which the organisation is "fit" in the changing environment that is its ecosystem and is able to co-evolve with it. Adaptedness means meeting the needs of all stakeholders including (but not exhaustively), customers, beneficiaries, employees, funders (shareholders, financiers, grant makers, government) as well as meeting regulatory requirements and societal expectations (environment, quality, wider society). Integration and synthesis of performance measures allow the Intelligent Organisation to do that.

Typically, performance measurement is retrospective, asking the question "how did we do?". That is perhaps adequate when environmental change is slow, when we are content that, in the Darwinian sense, only the fittest will survive (those entities most suited to the existing environment are most likely to produce a next generation). However, Darwinian evolution can be considered both socially and economically amoral and not purposeful (beyond reproduction). Dealing with the first of these, both societal and economic productivity and growth depend to some degree on the continued survival of organisations which generate wealth and well-being. Organisational evolution cannot then be socially and economically amoral. The existence of organisations, the services and products they produce and the economic surplus (or not!) that arises from their existence generate a social value and obligation – they may create a dependency. The evolution of human systems, of organisations, is purposeful or intentful. Organisational evolution does not just happen (as reproduction occurs in nature), it happens because somebody, somewhere (or lots of somebodies in lots of somewheres) takes decisions that cause it to happen in order to achieve some output or outcome. If we are going to address the performance issues that arise from this then we must learn not just to rectify the errors of the past but to understand and deal with "the future we are currently in" (Ackoff, 1981). That means we must learn to comprehend performance not against where we are but against where we intended to be and where we are going unless something changes. That gives us two gaps to close, two sets of actions to take:

• to close the gap between where we are and where we intended to be and, simultaneously,
• to close the gap between where we intended to be and where we are capable of being.

This realisation of potential speaks to the work of Maslow (1970) on self-actualisation. "To be all that one can be" does not just apply to individuals.

Performance, that is, effectiveness, is measured by the extent to which an organisation fulfils its purpose. It cannot be meaningfully expressed through a single measure such as profitability but requires a synthesis of metrics suited to the expectations of the organisation's stakeholders.

Sustainable performance is not then one dimensional but multidimensional with dynamic interdependencies between the dimensions. Short-term maximisation of any one dimension may impart harm to another, which, in the longer term, may damage the organisation. For example, profit maximisation through price rises or reduced product quality may both damage reputation and inhibit future demand. Either approach creates an opportunity for competitors. Poor environmental citizenship or poor staff treatment may lead either to loss of revenue or, more immediately, to loss of good staff. Each of these carry existential risk.

Achieving an integrated view of performance in the context of purpose is critical to long-term survival. We must understand, represent and manage organisational performance through a dynamic system with understood limits to each dimension: a performance envelope. Information must be provided at an appropriate rate to allow corrective decisions to be made, and each dimension must be managed simultaneously in the context of the others to ensure adaptedness is achieved at two levels of consideration and with reference to two time frames which are shown below.

- Operational: value generation
- Strategic: value enabling
- Managing the present: "where are we now"
- Creating the future: "where are we going"

Figure 11.1 represents how a number of arbitrarily chosen dimensions interact with each other and synthesise to deliver organisational performance. That performance is measured by the extent to which performance does, or does not, fulfil the espoused purpose of the organisation. We cannot deal with these dimensions individually but must explicitly recognise their interactions and their interdependence. Changing any one will have an impact (positive or negative) on the whole.

That sounds like quite a task, but we have encountered it before in the homeostat. While that dealt with self-regulation (performance management) at the level of process, we are now considering it at the level of the whole organisation. This

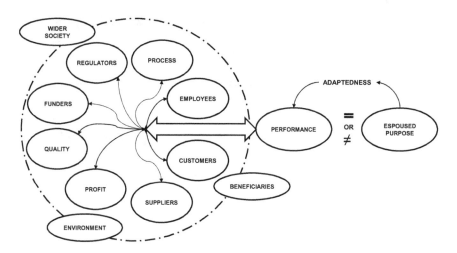

FIGURE 11.1   Dynamic interaction

requires a real comprehension of the total value exchange between the organisation and its environment.

Realising potential

To deal with this rather challenging scenario (synthesis of two levels of organisation and two time frames), we need to embrace its complexity and find a way to handle it rather than, as we have historically done, fragment it into notionally manageable functional elements. The mechanism through which it is proposed that we do this is what I refer to as "Beer's potentiometer" (figure 11.2).

This breaks down as follows.

Potential: a formal statement of what could be done if known constraints were removed or lifted.

Capability: a formal statement of the current capability of a process, i.e. what it is capable of producing.

Actual: a statement of what was done at the last iteration or cycle.

Efficiency: actual performance divided by capability, the gap between output and capability.

Latency: capability divided by potential, the gap between capability and possibility.

Performance: efficiency multiplied by latency (or potential divided by actual); the performance of the whole organisation.

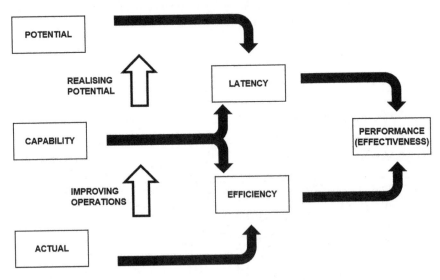

FIGURE 11.2 The potentiometer

Source: Adapted from Beer (1981)

All numbers used in the potentiometer are ratios rather than actual numbers. The use of ratios allows us to make meaningful comparisons of process performance for things which would otherwise look incommensurable. They let us meaningfully compare unlike things such as the productivity of a process plant with that of a quality assurance process or services with manufacturing. This is expressed not in terms of their profitability but by the extent to which they utilise their resources to achieve their objectives. There are, of course, always "real numbers" underlying the ratios, but these can be distorting or misleading when what we are trying to understand is the scope for improvement. Scope for improvement is what the responsible manager can take action upon.

Productivity (or efficiency) measures the extent to which the resources (of all types) applied in any particular process have been used. If the ratio is 1:1, then the resources used in this process were fully utilised with no waste or inefficiency; if the ratio is 0.5:1, then only half the resources have been utilised. The gap between "capability" and "actual" performance is the basis for managerial action; it defines the scope for improvement through process change, application of more appropriate behaviour or utilisation of current skill with current resources against the current standard.

Latency measures the extent to which, by removing limitations or constraints on certain aspects of the process, capability could be increased. Again, a ratio of 1:1 implies that the capability of the process cannot be improved. Any gap between current capability and potential is a measure of what else could be done. Here the change would require some form of investment to overcome whatever constraint is in place. This might mean more, or different, processes, equipment or people. It might mean a change in skill level (demanding investment in training/people development). Reducing latency is about recognising what constrains performance and addressing it.

The productivity gap (the difference between actual performance and capability) is, in general, the responsibility of the managers running value-generating processes. They are charged with "doing things right", and their focus is managing the present, meeting of the needs of current customers and working in the first of the two time frames.

The latency gap (the difference between capability and potential) is, in general, the responsibility of the managers running value-enabling processes. They are charged with "doing right things", and their focus is on strategic change of the organisation to meet anticipated and future needs of customers and other stakeholders.

When there are tensions between these two perspectives, and there will be, reference is made back to the purpose of the organisation, its identity, to resolve it. This you will remember was presented as the trialogue in chapter 5 and the lean information system for enabling value in chapter 10.

We can now think about dynamic interaction as a network of connected potentiometers, each representing a particular dimension of performance (figure 11.3).

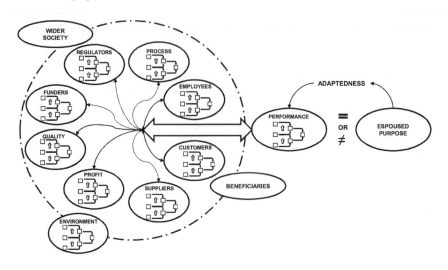

FIGURE 11.3 Synthesising potentiometers

The potentiometer provides the basis for performance management of the whole organisation simultaneously in multiple dimensions. As well as allowing us to manage the present, it allows us to simulate the impact of possible changes and understand the critical issue of interdependence. It allows us to understand the bottle necks and limitations of the whole organisation and direct our improvement efforts to the most beneficial points. This is important: the abstraction of information and structuring of it into a coherent model of the performance of the whole organisation allows us, through a replica of that model, to explore the impact of a range of decisions. We can simulate the future performance of the organisation and understand what actions we may need to take to realise the future we want. Rather than assuming, as so many business plans do, that tomorrow will be the same as today plus or minus financial adjustments, we can explore the likely impact of process, skill or resource change on performance of the whole, we can see how the changes impact on other areas and can then modify our investment plans to take account of all of them.

The potentiometer compiles into aggregate forms. Aggregated vertically, it offers an integrated view of the performance of the organisation from the self-regulating individual through every process level to the boardroom. It offers disaggregated views of individual procedures, tasks and processes and their aggregation through process management. Aggregated horizontally, it addresses interdependent processes – for example, where the sales process and the delivery process for a product or service are dependent upon each other (think about the flow diagram used for Fusion21). Most importantly, it provides the basis of managing over time. It is not simply retrospective but, because of the way the data is compiled, provides the basis for understanding "the future we are currently in" (Ackoff, 1981) and taking pre-emptive action which changes that future.

Within the performance envelope, the organisation can adapt itself over time to further develop in both size (physiological growth) and smartness (psychological growth). What we must do is embed within each homeostat a potentiometer for each critical parameter of its performance. We can then use the information generated to enable managerial decisions about improvement of the parts as well as integrate them to understand the performance of the whole. This sounds more complicated in theory than it is in practice. Simplicity arises from the universal structure that we have already adopted, a process governed by an information loop which enables self-correction called the "homeostat". Because the homeostat structure is adopted for all processes, it is both possible and essential to aggregate the information from each at higher levels of organisation to generate performance information for the organisation as a whole in a consistent, coherent manner. This approach provides information about efficiency, latency and effectiveness to every responsible person and does so in a shared language.

Figure 11.4 shows this structure brought together. Monitoring of output against "standards", "process" and "people" is fed back into the potentiometer enabling

- modification of people (skills and behaviours), process and standards for the next process cycle;
- integration and aggregation of performance of the whole in the context of the customer outcomes;
- reporting to higher order management of the performance of the whole;
- feedback to any predecessor process (or processes) (in effect, *this* process is the customer of its predecessor – so this is the "customer outcome" feedback loop from us to them).

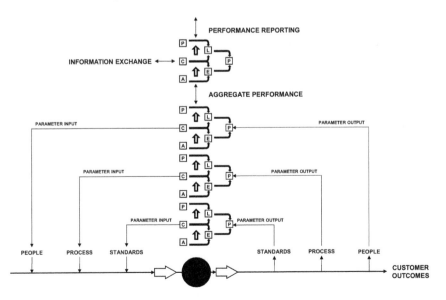

FIGURE 11.4   Aggregating potentiometers

The next chapter will elaborate on this in greater detail for a particular instance. In the meanwhile it is important to recognise that there is an issue of language. I can imagine, as I write this, a number of readers objecting broadly in these terms:

- "but we measure yield";
- "but we measure waste";
- "but we measure profitability";
- "but we measure costs";
- "but we measure quality";
- "but we measure throughput".

Others may object "but we don't measure . . .".

Measuring efficiency or productivity on each parameter is informationally equivalent to these. For example, yield is generally a measure of the output gained from a material input, as such it is a measure of the "efficiency" with which that material input has been used. Similarly, waste is the inverse of yield (and is thus an inverse measure of the same thing) reducing waste or increasing yield amount to the same outcome.

Profitability is more interesting. First, as we have already established "profit" or "loss" are consequences of the operation of the system. Any meaningful action we take to reduce cost or increase profit will be action on the operation of the process itself – that is, on the "causes" of profit or cost, not the things themselves. Second, it is important to recognise that where and how an organisation incurs cost and generates profit are to some degree products of the accounting conventions adopted rather than of the operation of the customer-oriented process. If you doubt this, then I urge you to consider the tales reported over the years of various international companies arranging their affairs to take their costs in one country but their surpluses in another to minimise their tax bills. It would appear at the very least that the notions of profit, loss and cost are matters of choice.

So, I will not be precious about particular words, and nor should you be. The essence of what we need to achieve is to understand, in the broadest sense, those parameters that need to be monitored in order to understand how the organisation can perform within its envelope and take action on them to close the gap between

- what is desired (potential),
- what is currently possible (capability) and
- what is happening (actual).

What is the role of the manager?

In the Intelligent Organisation, management is enabling not controlling because control has been built in to the system itself. The manager is released to add value by acting as a "transducer" (Beer, 1985), bearing information about requirements across the internal boundaries of the organisation, translating the language into that of the receiving party, gaining feedback to ensure the message has been understood, offering insights based on different knowledge, ideating and innovating. The manager provides resources and holds the recipient to account for the use of those resources but measured against the achievement of the intended outcome *not* the input or output variables. This demands that any self-regulating individual asked to generate an outcome *must* be granted the autonomy to do so. One of the resources the manager will be responsible for is people. It is their task to motivate, train, coach and enable those people to perform their tasks, and if the manager is not bogged down in generating fanciful excuses for *their* manager, then they will have time to do this.

One critical aspect to consider is the distinction that must be drawn between the managers' roles of

- looking into the process (resource provision, coach, technical expert) and
- looking out of the process (transducer).

These roles require different behaviours, perhaps different languages, and, of course, require the manager to understand their role in the whole organisation, its expectations, opportunities and constraints. Very often, particularly in operational management roles such as team leader, foreman and chargehand but also quite often in the executive offices, is the tendency of the manager to play technical expert, to demonstrate his or her competence at the job itself, usually by nudging aside the incumbent and saying, *"I'll show you how it should be done!"* Great care needs to be taken here to distinguish roles. It *may* be part of the manager's role to provide some technical expertise to others in the process, perhaps on the difficult or rarer tasks. But when providing that expertise they are doing so as "expert" not as manager; the behaviour and approaches are different.

Similarly, when showing someone what should be done, are they teaching them how it should be done or are they simply doing it for them? Quite often they are doing it for them so that, far from living up to the role of manager as coach, they are simply denying the individual the opportunity to learn. The unintended effect can be to trap people in a state of ignorance.

It is critical to the Intelligent Organisation that the skills, competences, behaviours and values required for its success are understood, codified and captured in such a manner that it is possible to both apply them and manage them. The process-related aspects of this are generally quite straightforward and can be developed in the course of process design and, in particular, the principles for designing in autonomy discussed earlier.

Once we know the constraints that mechanisation or automation of the process may impose on individual autonomy, it is possible to be precise about the technical skills and knowledge that the individual must provide. That is, we can make a formal statement about the technical capabilities required by those carrying out any specific task or tasks, and we can objectively test the skills of any individual and compare them with those required.

Dealing with the behavioural dimension is rather more challenging. Whilst it is possible to make a statement of the values to which those in the organisation should adhere, it is very much harder to generate a fully objective "test" of whether or not they are adhered to on an ongoing basis. There are, of course, a whole battery of psychometric evaluation tools available such as Myers-Briggs Type Indicator, Rorschach Inkblot Method, Strengths Deployment Inventory, Occupational Personality Quotient and Belbin Team Roles. All of these have been developed, polished, redeveloped, tested on large populations and found by many to give reasonably reliable indicators of likely performance. However, Murphy Paul (2005) questions their overall validity. It is certainly the case that individuals familiar with such tests, their underlying logic and assumptions and the behavioural attributes sought by a particular employer are perfectly capable of "beating the test" from time to time.

The role of the manager in managing performance, then, is to gather appropriate, objective information about what is actually happening and to have appropriate and meaningful information about the gap between the knowledge and skills required for a task and those available to any particular individual. He or she can then exercise judgement about the best form of action to close that gap whether that be training, coaching, instructing or, in the limiting case, encouraging the individual to think about their own future.

While that sounds perhaps a little harsh, an individual who is not competent in a particular role, who lacks the skills or training is unlikely to be content in it. That lack of contentment is likely to show through in one or more ways. It may simply show in symptoms such as poor productivity, high sickness or absence rate, poor time-keeping or some other characteristic. The responsibility of the manager is *not* to act on the symptom but to understand and address the underlying cause(s) of that symptom and take action to correct it.

Capturing and presenting the data in the form proposed has generated information for decision-making which locates the challenge not only for the value-generating process but also for the HR value-enabling process on which it relies. With the principles from the examples applied to all processes, meaningful action can be taken by the relevant managers to close the gaps. The whole thing is presented in a form which enables that action rather than seeking to either blame individuals or generate meaningless encouragement, incentives or admonishments. The outcome, rooted in a rigorous understanding of the process and the data that supports it, gives an objective view of both the driver of performance and the adaptive action required to correct it – and the informational logic can be applied to every value-generating and value-enabling process for the whole organisation. It becomes, then, a cybernetic organisation, one in which self-regulation, adaptation and change are built in to the decision-making architecture, where going "out of control" provides its own corrective action to come back "in control".

Summary

This chapter has introduced a very different way of measuring and managing the performance of organisations in a systemic manner. It attempts to embrace all of the dimensions of performance through a unifying framework and will undoubtedly pose challenges to any organisation that attempts to put it into practice.

In the next chapter we shall do just that and see how it all fits together.

12

MANAGING PERFORMANCE

Cases

Introduction

All that has been elaborated so far relies on appreciating the Intelligent Organisation as a dynamic system – that is, as richly interdependent, interrelated and interactive, delivering desired customer outcomes, generating value to sustain itself in the short term while adapting to change in its environment (and changing its environment in favour of itself) through its value-enabling processes. Overall, recognising the Intelligent Organisation in this way, that structure and interdependencies are key indicators of performance, allowing us to understand how, using meaningful information, we can manage its performance. This dynamic, process-oriented approach enables a much richer understanding of the business than is possible from traditional, functionally oriented reporting.

This chapter draws together all those aspects of Intelligent Organisation – structure, information, autonomy – that we have already discussed. It brings the whole to life through consideration of a single organisation, a franchise on the UK railway. This case, developed from a consulting assignment, lets us consider the whole of an organisation from end to end and top to bottom.

Recent history of the UK railway

In the UK the railway was partly denationalised in the 1990s, and what had been a single integrated business was reorganised in a series of separate functional parts.

- Infrastructure: Responsible for the track, control systems, major stations.
- Train Operators: Responsible for passenger and cargo services.
- RoSCOs: Owners of rail vehicles, typically leasing them to the train operators.
- Government: Responsible for overall governance, regulation, system management and performance.

This case study is concerned with a franchised passenger train operator. Franchises based on the "line of route" are open to any organisation to bid for (qualification being a combination of competence and money) and most are run by organisations already established in the transport sector, although, due to a series of failed franchises and continuing challenges, the number of bidders is declining.

While the apparent intent in privatisation was to introduce competition into the railway and improve financial performance, it was and remains the case that the UK rail industry as a whole requires substantial subsidy both for investment in its future and for the provision of low-volume, low-revenue, high-cost services. This is common to mass public transport systems globally which fund their own debt.

Prior to privatisation, whilst safety standards were and, at the time I am writing, remain very high, customer satisfaction was low, passenger numbers were declining and there was a continuing history of poor industrial relations. It is fair to say that since the privatisation process there has been a substantial increase in passenger numbers (although satisfaction shows significant variance), a much more settled industrial relations environment and a massive investment in the network and vehicles, not only to respond to major incidents but also to increase capacity on the railway. The year 2018 was very difficult for the railways with a series of strikes over crew levels, delays in the introduction of new rail vehicles, and in electrification and the already discussed difficulties with introducing a revised timetable. In January 2019 regulated fares rose by an average of 3.1%, which was seen by many passengers as adding insult to the injury experienced in 2018.

A question of purpose

To understand how to manage performance we must first comprehend the purpose of the organisation; without clarity of purpose, performance management is meaningless; to misquote Lewis Carroll, "if you don't know where you are going, every road will take you there". Its purpose is the reason an organisation exists, the customer need it seeks to fulfil, the customer outcome it aims to satisfy and a reflection of the intent of its owners.

For customers profit is not meaningful; profit is rather an internal measure important to the owners of the capital invested in the business. It is fundamental in that, as classical economics tells us, sustainable investment and growth are only possible when there is an excess of income over expenditure; that is inherent in the arithmetic, not a political statement! That is not to say that the income or the profit has necessarily to be derived exclusively from the end user customer. In the case of the UK railway much of the income is provided by the state, and, regardless of the ownership model, that is likely to remain the case. In late 2018 the Principality of Luxembourg abolished fares on its public transport, all of the cost now being funded by government. It will be fascinating to see how the situation evolves when there is an absolute dependence on state funding; the history of state ownership and state funding of utilities (which this has now become) is not encouraging.

The Intelligent Organisation pursues survival, sustainability, in the long term, and that depends on retaining existing and attracting new customers, something with which a focus on short-term profit maximisation may conflict; the fastest way to increase short-term profit is to reduce short-terms costs and, in an industry with high fixed asset, fuel and regulatory costs, the ones most susceptible to short-term reduction are those for customer service!

When we consider a passenger train operator from the customers' perspective, the purpose, the thing we observe the railway to do, is to provide customer journeys, i.e. to move people between locations on the network. The railway also perhaps has a purpose from the perspective of government, a stakeholder in the enterprise. While it necessarily has an interest in the delivery of the journey (the passenger outcome against which the public will hold it to account), it would be reasonable to think that it also has an interest in other outcomes such as financial performance (reducing levels of subsidy or receiving a premium from the franchisee) and that both passengers and government are interested in safety. We can therefore suggest that the desired outcomes, embracing both passengers and government, are

- customer satisfaction,
- employee satisfaction,
- safety and
- financial performance.

The train operator then has four outcomes to meet in fulfilling its purpose. It relies on a set of interacting and interdependent processes to achieve these, as set out in figure 12.1.

Customer satisfaction, employee satisfaction, safety and finance are all dependent upon operations which are managed in real time by control. Control is a regulating

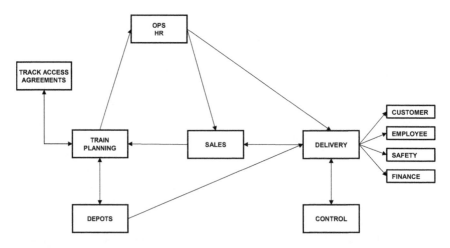

FIGURE 12.1 Train operating company interacting processes

function which manages emerging operational challenges internally and interacts with all the other operators attempting to deliver services on the same line(s) of route. Operations depends on depots to generate serviceable trains and the sales team to sell tickets (generate passengers). All require to be staffed by operational HR activity of recruitment, training, payroll etc. Operations and depots generate demand on train planning (making potential journeys available), which in turn depends on the track access agreement (the license to operate trains). HR operations also depends on Train Planning for the information about the required crew population.

The track access agreement sets out the contract with the infrastructure operator (and franchisor) to run the particular timetable at any given point in time. Successful operation of the business, the achievement of desired outcomes, is dependent upon effective information sharing between these multiple, dynamic processes. Feedback information about how well the business meets its objectives emerges naturally from this.

Track access agreements, which grant permission to run the services, also provide the fundamental, feedforward information needed to plan the business. That information delivers the ability to create the future. From both an organisational and informational perspective, once the track access agreement has been negotiated (an enabling activity), thereby creating the timetable, it is possible to derive a significant number of the volume characteristics (and from them the financial characteristics) of the organisation:

- Value Generating

    - The number, mix and timing of rail vehicles required;
    - The (probable) maintenance schedule for those vehicles;
    - The (probable) need and timing of vehicle parts;
    - The number of engineers required, their skills and their work patterns;
    - The train crew requirements to run the services, their skills and their work patterns;
    - The number of tickets that could be sold (by scheduled service) and the potential revenues of the business, i.e. the potential passenger volume;
    - The staffing requirements for the ticket selling operations, train despatch and so on;
    - The (probable) requirements from the on-board catering service.

- Value Enabling

    - The training and development requirements for all staff;
    - The budgets and working capital requirements;
    - The data to satisfy regulatory expectations in all aspects of the company;
    - The marketing (as opposed to sales) needs.

The company also has to deal with data and information flows to and from external organisations. In the case of the railway that includes regulators, passengers, infrastructure operators, suppliers (e.g. energy, catering and vehicles) and, of course, other train operators and other forms of transport (alternative ways of completing the same journey). Each of the connected elements is constituted as a process homeostat in its own right, self-regulating to meet the needs and expectations of the other system elements dependent upon it, depending itself on those which are its suppliers (of information, materials, people etc.). We cannot improve one part unless we can comprehend the implications of that for the whole. To design an organisation that not only fails to embrace this complexity but also fails to deal with the data generated by it is to design for failure.

Pause for a moment to reflect on the past few paragraphs: what we have is remarkable. Where the relationships between the elements of the organisation have been properly comprehended, the creation of the timetable or schedule (e.g. the product, sales, delivery, production plan in other businesses, the lecture schedule in a university, the operating schedule in a hospital) generates the "information equivalents" for nearly everything else.

The argument for a process view is almost irrefutable when we realise the number of other decisions that are, in effect, made redundant by it. The trick is to understand that the outcome requirements disaggregate to tell us the input requirements. The resulting economy of effort is the key to a step change in performance for the administrative elements of many organisations and shows that there is a level of structural integrity and integration of which we should seek to take advantage. When we comprehend the process, its parameters and characteristics, and accept that it is "information powered", we generate massive economy in what else we need to know.

As we build on the process view, it is reasonable to look at the overall structure of the organisation. Of importance to this was that the company was attempting to achieve two things in parallel. Apart from managing the business to fulfil the existing franchise performance criteria, they were also considering what form the organisation should take in order for them to also be successful in acquiring one or more other franchises.

The established organisation chart, in use at the time and approved by the regulator for safety purposes, is shown as figure 12.2. The headline functional split was between the following processes.

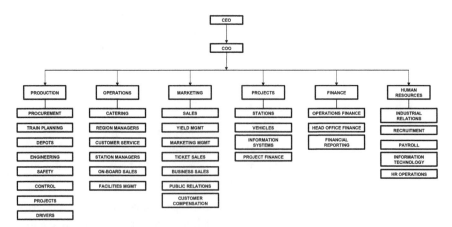

FIGURE 12.2 The hierarchical organisation chart

- Value Generating

  - Production: maintaining, preparing, driving and controlling trains
  - Operations: on-board ticket sales, catering, stations, facilities management.

- Value Enabling

  - Marketing: brand management, yield management, online ticket sales, public relations, customer compensation
  - Projects: projects concerned with vehicles, information systems, station developments and project finance
  - Financial management: corporate bookkeeping and accounting
  - Human resource management: recruitment, payroll, industrial relations, operational information systems and operational HR management

The organisation chart tells us whom to reward for success (the people at the top) and whom to blame for failure (the people at the bottom, obviously) but little or nothing of how the organisation actually worked or of how its performance might be improved. It is particularly difficult to imagine how adding a further franchise could be accommodated without the sort of substantial disruption and change programme so endemic in modern organisations.

Adopting the principles of design of the Intelligent Organisation, we considered it best to redesign the organisation backwards from the customer. We could create a fresh organisation that would be more effectively run with a single franchise (effectiveness being expressed through the measures already established) whilst also able to accommodate one or more additional franchises within the same overall structure.

Reflecting the process relationships outlined in figure 12.1, figure 12.3 identifies the starting point for this redesign. Because there were multiple stakeholders

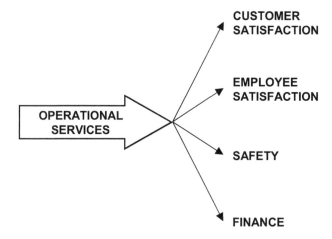

FIGURE 12.3 The delivery process

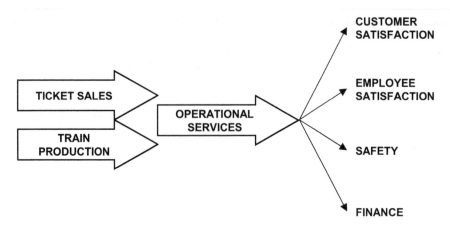

FIGURE 12.4 Operational processes

(passengers, government, safety regulators, shareholders), it was not possible to hold a single outcome as more important than the others; the organisation had to meet all four expectations. The delivery process that ultimately did this was identified as "operations", the operation of the rail services themselves via the timetable, vehicles and crews. It was in the day-to-day activity of the organisation that the company could meet performance expectations.

Operations depended upon the effectiveness of two other processes: ticket sales and train production. While it could be argued that these are enabling processes, it was considered that they were purposeful in their own right and were therefore a purposeful part of the system, a key element of the core process. Each could generate value in its own right by selling tickets or servicing rail vehicles for other operators. The purpose of the ticket sales process was considered as delivering the optimum mix of passenger loading against ticket revenue. The purpose of train production was to deliver "perfect trains" (a performance standard) to the right station and platform at the right time to fulfil the operational services, as shown in figure 12.4.

These three processes had to be largely self-managing for a number of reasons. The many sets of rail vehicles providing hundreds of timetabled services per day were serviced and maintained at multiple locations along the route. Prospective passengers could purchase tickets from hundreds of locations, including stations, travel agents and online services. Crews could join and leave services at multiple crew depots along the route, and the overall "line of route" covered hundreds of miles in each direction with multiple stopping points for collecting and delivering of passengers. Passengers' secondary requirements for catering, ablutions, newspapers, Internet access and so on could only be fulfilled on the moving rail vehicle. Centralised management was neither desirable nor practical at the operational level. Figure 12.5 shows the core processes with their embedded local management, local homeostats.

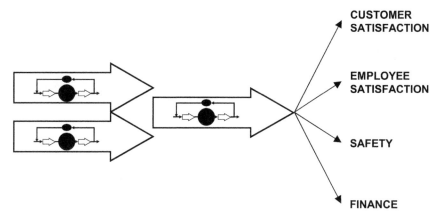

FIGURE 12.5   Core process homeostats

It became very clear that operations could only succeed if both ticket sales and train production succeeded; the dependence was absolute. Any limitation in their performance would immediately inhibit the performance of operations. This demanded a sharp focus on both process capability and the requisite skills and behaviours of the staff and gave meaning and weight to the measurement of performance – all good reasons for not outsourcing the challenge but keeping it within the organisation where it could be managed effectively.

Whilst the organisation as so far designed required significant distributed autonomy if it was to succeed, it was nonetheless evident that a number of enabling processes needed to be carried out on behalf of the whole. Remember: the justification for the existence of any part of the Intelligent Organisation not directly delivering products and services to customers is the extent to which that part enables its continued operation, adaptation and survival.

This was the case with our subject organisation with enabling functions covering information services, regulatory management, financial management, operational human resource management, production planning (the scheduling of maintenance for rail vehicles), stores (supply chain management of all consumables) and control (the real-time management of rail vehicles in traffic).

Figure 12.6 shows the alignment of the enabling functions with the core processes. This required the redesign of these activities to focus on the value they were enabling in the core processes – how what they did contributed to their success and deriving from that the performance standards required for the future. It will not surprise the reader to hear that the simple realignment of the enabling activities around contribution to success and value added provided substantial efficiency and effectiveness gains which translated into reduced headcount and costs. They were doing more with less. Of equal importance is that the oval (figure 12.6) containing all those enabling services represents their integration in a form which relies on appropriate flows of information (the black line arrows). It is setting not an alternative view of a power hierarchy but rather an order of precedence in operational

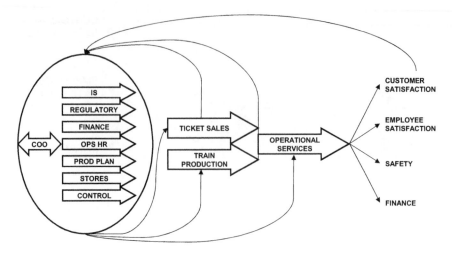

FIGURE 12.6 Managing the present

decision-making, driven by the output requirements which "pull" other decisions through the system. The value-enabling processes are not "more important" than the core value-generating processes even if the people that carry them out are sitting on nice chairs in the head office rather than in the service office on a rail vehicle. They are all of equal importance as failure in any one aspect means failure for the whole.

The first orientation of the enabling processes was the provision of the information, materials, people, resources and so on needed by the value-generating processes in order for them to function. The second orientation, looking towards those processes, was to feed back information from them to enable delivery of improvement in the next cycle both to their own process and to the core process, in effect answering two questions:

- How effective are we? (How well are *we* enabling *them?*)
- How efficient are we? (How well are *we* delivering *our* process?)

The third orientation was towards creating the future. Structurally this is represented in figure 12.7, which represents at the left-hand side the model environment and MoS that is essential to self-awareness in context.

A major consideration in this aspect of the design was to explore the question of when the future starts. This is worthy of a short diversion from the current case study for a little extra thinking.

We have referred before to the "problematic future" because some things about the future are embedded in the present, while other things are unknown and perhaps unknowable. The problematic future contains all of those things which are either known about, likely or, in some circumstances, inevitable given the current position. Each of those things will have a level of probability, from absolute

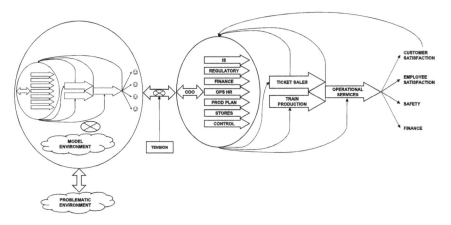

FIGURE 12.7 Creating the future

certainty to likely to possible. The problematic future is concerned with exploring the unknown and reducing the unknowable. In "managing the present" the organisation needs to be able to address all those things which are in the "known" future, to have the capability to adapt and change and either control those things or, more commonly, seek to influence them in a manner which provides a positive outcome (one which is supportive of the objectives). In creating the future, the Intelligent Organisation needs to assess the opportunities and threats arising in its environment to consider its strengths and weaknesses in relation to them and propose choices about its direction. Quite often these possible choices are inconsistent with the current direction, and it is this which generates the tension between the two. "Managing the present" is busy adapting the organisation to the (relatively) short term, the "current future" whilst "creating the future" is generating choices about the "future future". Resolution of the debate is generated by reference to the purpose of the whole organisation and its aspiration for survival. Choices are made by the human actors applying their values in the context of the mission (figure 12.8).

Let's return to the case study: the franchise agreement determined much about its current future (force majeure notwithstanding). That is, in the absence of a major catastrophe the objectives, performance expectations, expected revenues and a whole host of other more detailed aspects were known for the duration of the franchise. These were mainly concerned with "doing more with less", achieving the various outcomes while using fewer resources. It was also the case, and seems to still be so, that the timetabling arrangements – especially given the level of interaction with other operators, the shared facilities (stations, platforms, tracks) and the scheduling of track maintenance – were such that, at the level of "operational services", the future was fairly certain for eighteen months to two years ahead and well understood to the end of the franchise. The "current future" for the whole operational organisation, then, had a time horizon of around two years. This was then taken as the "breakpoint" for process operations and control – anything with

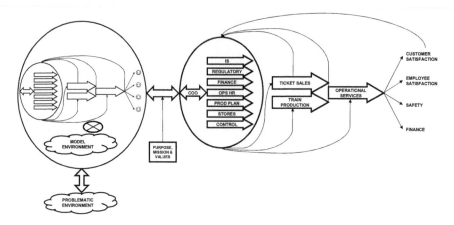

FIGURE 12.8 Resolving tension

less than a two-year delivery time was treated as within the scope of "managing the present", anything beyond that as "creating the future".

A second quick diversion is desirable here as there is a critical element to be addressed. The requirement within the Intelligent Organisation for local auton-omy dictates that all three elements of the "trialogue" must happen within every homeostat. So, whilst the operational organisation is looking at one particular time horizon, the subunits and processes within it are likely to be looking at a much shorter one, and, whilst constrained by the shared "mission and values", they must be managing a present and creating a future for themselves. That, at the level of the individual worker, may mean a "creating the future" time horizon of as little as the next cycle of the process or the next iteration of the task. A shift manager may have a time horizon of the end of the shift whilst a production manager might be planning for the next few weeks and a factory manager planning for a quarter or a year. The planning horizon varies with the position within the overall organisa-tion of the particular function. Look again at figure 7.1 in chapter 7, "Managing Autonomy".

The work so far had delivered a whole new way of thinking about the organi-sation. It served to create a structure in which it was possible to view the original "operational services" as a viable entity in its own right, a business served by the higher order organisation and charged with delivering the particular set of franchise requirements.

That being the case it was then relatively straightforward to add in to the structure one or more additional franchises (figure 12.9). These could take advan-tage of the established enabling structure of the whole organisation whilst rep-licating the service delivery structure of the original franchise. By thoughtful design, the Intelligent Organisation offered a "plug-and-play" solution to the issue of merger or acquisition, minimising the disruption and risk to the whole from the performance of one part whilst at the same time providing significant benefits from integration.

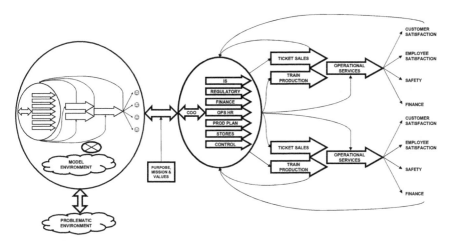

FIGURE 12.9   Integrated businesses

In terms of business impact the redesigned structure enabled a substantial step reduction in the number of managers employed in the business. It delivered savings of several million pounds per annum whilst eliminating a number of other activities which were not adding value, thereby generating further savings. Meanwhile revenue, driven principally by growth in GDP (an environmental effect) was increasing. For those enabling activities which were continued, it became possible for the first time to measure the value of their contribution to the success of the whole and hold individuals to account for their performance. As just one example, it was determined through analysis that the law of diminishing returns was applicable to the marketing activity of the organisation and that a substantial, around 30%, reduction in marketing spend would have no discernible negative impact on either ticket sales or brand awareness. Duly implemented, this proved to be the case.

Information for performance management

The train operator was, at the outset, managed through traditional, functional reporting with all of the limitations already explored. Given the multiple interacting processes and the need for "creating the future" within each one, there was a requirement for a redesign of the information system to support performance management. Most critically, there was a need to ensure that there was organisational closure. Closure is achieved by consistency between purpose, creating the future and managing the present being pulled through operations by the four objectives. It was believed that this informational and organisational closure could be delivered through measurement of performance against outcomes, with the results being fed back to the overall organisation.

After we considered how the process structure fitted together, it was right that the information architecture reflected the organisational architecture. As you read this, it is also important to separate the structure of the information flow from the specific data that flows through that structure, that data being potentially highly variable. This is an important distinction, as it enables great simplification of the information systems. As you read the description, keep referring to figure 12.10 and follow the logic of the relationships.

The organisation now understood the outcomes it needed to fulfil to continue in existence (figure 12.10). The specific measures for each are not important at this point; what is important is that they defined the requirements for train planning. The outcomes defined what services were to be offered and to what standard. These in turn defined what timetable was required and enabled the negotiation of track access agreements (TAA). The TAA are constrained by the existence of competing services for the same permanent way. We can see here the first interdependency appears. The outcome of the negotiation of the TAA defined the capacity (the number of services and passengers) of the business and therefore what could be offered compared to those which were initially desired. In this case the modifying action was to balance the services requested against those made available. The result of that negotiation acted as a constraint on the resulting performance of the business. It limited income because it determined how many services could be offered, at what times and the number of seats. It also determined the level of customer satisfaction that could be achieved, as it was not possible to run all the services that the customers had asked for.

The TAA had the effect of determining what timetables were required, which, in turn, defined the process requirements of the train depots to meet the service requirements and to work within the safety regulations:

- How many vehicles were needed;
- What mix of locomotives and carriages were needed;
- What level of maintenance needed to be provided in which locations;
- What the timing should be.

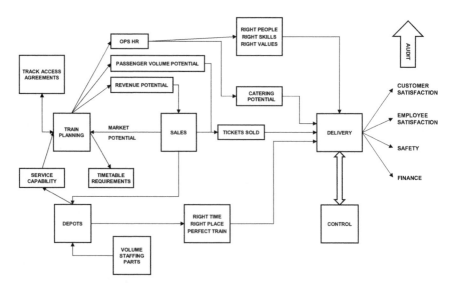

FIGURE 12.10 Delivering the outcomes

Each rail vehicle is subject to periodic examination and maintenance which depends on its duty cycle and that is determined by the TAA and the timetable for the particular vehicle. The TAA also determined the potential volume of ticket sales by route, timetabled service and class. That information looped back to inform ticket pricing, revenue potential and capacity management. Altogether that aligned the business objectives with overall capability; it became possible to understand "the future we are currently in", at least for the life of the TAA and its consequences. Directly arising from that "known" future the HR function could quantify with sufficient accuracy the numbers of staff by role, grade and location needed to run the services. They could then focus on fulfilling their obligations by providing the right people with the right skills and the right values. These were also informed by the understanding of the desired outcomes of customer satisfaction and employee satisfaction that started the process. Meanwhile those responsible for the depots processes had the information to develop their staffing and scheduling arrangements and to develop the parts management and supply chain processes needed to underpin their operation, and they could do so with reasonable certainty for the life of the franchise. Performance standards were also established to ensure the production of "perfect trains" and their provision to the right place at the right time.

Ticket sales, staffing and vehicles could now all be brought back together. They could be synchronised with the timetable requirements to deliver services to standards set in accordance with the initial objectives for the business. Performance could be managed both in real time (control) and through audit-generating feedback about how well the four objectives were being met.

With an understanding of the contribution of each process to the success of the whole and the determination (through the logical flow of the organisation backwards from the customer) of performance expectations and standards, then the measurement and evaluation of performance became straightforward. Managers responsible for each process could both modify their own processes (remember – standards, skills, behaviours, process, task and procedure) to better fulfil their objectives whilst cascading appropriate performance measures to the task level. Enabling management, responsible for the whole organisation, could observe its performance against the objectives and, using their understanding of the process dependencies within the organisation, determine what modifying decisions for improvement were possible.

This was enabled by the redesign of the information system to ensure that the right information was in the right place at the right time and in the right format to enable it to take place. The whole was presented through a series of linked potentiometers (figure 12.11). For each of these,

- capability was limited by the constraints of those processes it depended upon,
- efficiency was measured in terms of the efficiency with which it used its internal resources to deliver those outcomes, and
- effectiveness was measured by the extent to which it met its own customer outcomes.

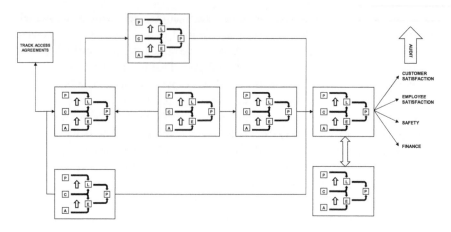

FIGURE 12.11 Linked potentiometers

Specifically, expressed in ratios and working only with the customer satisfaction measure (figure 12.12):

- Assume Customer Satisfaction "demand" is 1;
- Delivery, sales and train planning potential are also therefore 1 because they are set (pulled) by customer demand;
- Train planning (after negotiating track access agreements) only has a capability of 0.9, because its capability has been constrained in the negotiations;
- That result (a productivity of 0.78) therefore constrains the capability of HR ops and depots to 0.78, because they can be no more capable than their predecessor processes;
- Control inherits a capability of 0.77, the productivity of depots, while delivery inherits a capability of 0.71, the minimum productivity of its two inputs (HR ops and depots). Again they cannot perform better than a predecessor process.

Processes which could be acted upon (within the constraint of the train plan) are listed below.

- Sales: potential is constrained by customer demand, so it is not available for action. Sales activity could be acted upon to increase actual sales to match capability.
- HR ops: while potential could be addressed, there would be no benefit whereas its actual performance is falling short of capability, and that would deliver benefit to delivery and therefore customer satisfaction.
- Depots: again there is no benefit to be obtained from increasing potential, but action to increase actual performance would generate benefit for delivery and therefore the customer satisfaction outcome.
- Control: again action could be taken to increase the actual performance of control to get it closer to capability.

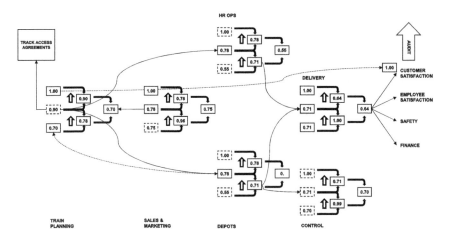

FIGURE 12.12   Measuring performance

In terms of improvement the interesting outcome is that an "improvement" to an internal process that does not lead to an improved outcome for the customer (more reliable trains, lower cost, faster journey times) adds no value to the whole.

If, then: it all depends

The solution revealed in the foregoing pages was not, of course, the only possibility, but it was the one that best fitted the organisation to the achievement of its objectives whilst being consistent with the underpinning thinking and theory of organisations. A number of alternative designs were developed and discussed, but none fitted the situation so well nor answered all of the questions so adequately.

Just in case you are thinking "ahh, but that has set it all in stone; it is just deterministic central planning that is bound to fail", (or words to that effect) then stop and read again. The whole structure and all of its information flows are dependent on the objectives, which, in this particular case, are given to the organisation, and everything flows from their interpretation. They tell us what is important about this particular railway, in the particular set of circumstances that pertained at the time and in the then prevailing political, social and economic context. If the franchisor (the government in this case) decided that, say that safety was less important than moving as many people as possible as fast as possible or that financial performance was unimportant then a different solution might apply but probably not at the overall process level. The structure would probably be the same. What would be different would be the performance measurement, the content of process control, the balance of effort (less focus on "ticket sales", more focus on capacity management). There is a level at which, reflecting Joan Woodward (1965), the process structure can be optimal, there can be a "best" shape for the organisation – and that is rarely a pure hierarchical, siloed form.

Summary

This chapter has provided an overview of the application of the potentiometer as a device for enabling the management of performance. Of particular importance is the ability to use it as a unifying framework through which disparate aspects of the performance of the organisation can both be presented in a uniform language and be compared. Coupled to that it has shown how the performance of interdependent elements, brought to life through the information system, can be reviewed and used to apply improvement effort to the right part of the organisation at the right time.

13

THE INTELLIGENT NATION

Introduction

In the preceding chapters we have discussed the need for a new model of organisation. In this chapter we look at the implications of that new model when applied to the nation state.

To refresh, the Intelligent Organisation is rooted in a synthesis of behaviour, process and information in a structured set of processes which generate and enable value, maximise individual autonomy and, through a shared sense of purpose, nurture the identity (shared values and beliefs) of the organisation. The Intelligent Organisation sustains itself in a changing environment by co-evolving with it, while self-adaptation is inherent in its organisational relationships and logic. It is designed and managed to be survival worthy. If that is essential for normal organisations, how much more necessary is it for a nation?

The state of the nation?

Nations, typically, are oriented around functional departments of education, health, defence and so on. Cottam [webref 13] shows how this bureaucratic organisation (Beckford, 2017) of the state based on rational-legal authority (Weber, 1924; Pugh & Hickson, 1989) can get in the way of both efficiency (productivity of all resources) and effectiveness (achievement of intended outcomes).

We shall not linger in this chapter on the detail of delivery processes; they are dealt with in the chapter on public services. My concern here is to consider how to arrange the distributed governance of a nation so that both that governance and the nation are sustainable! This is not a new concern, Sampson (1993), discussing the United Kingdom (UK), noted that "the gap between government and governed looms wider than ever" and cited Disraeli, who 100 years previously said that "centralisation is the death blow of public freedom". Sampson goes on to remark on the emerging "democratic deficit" in the then European Community, now the European Union. If in the intervening years that situation has not been addressed *and* the problem is not unique to the UK, then perhaps the centralisation of power has continued. Beer (1993) and Beckford (1994) both explored the mechanism, risks and implications of this tendency. More recently, Allan writing in *The Spectator* (webref 14) in 2016, primarily critiquing politics in Australia, said: "The disconnect between the voters and the political class is as large as any time I can remember". He goes on to say:

> "Part of the problem, in my view, is that the politicians seem not to believe that anything is more important than their ministerial limousines and the extra fat superannuation they get. Nothing is worth resigning over. No principle matters enough to fight for and try to win over the unconvinced".

That perhaps says more about Allan's views on the nature of politicians than on the political process itself and is clearly not true of every politician. Nonetheless it might cause us to ask in whose interest any particular nation is being run and any particular decision taken. In the UK in 2018, the BBC (webref 15) reports Heidi Allen, MP, as saying:

> "I just can't help myself. If I see a mess I want to get involved and that's just how I am and it seemed to me my country was economically and socially in a mess and I needed to help".

While Tonia Antoniazzi, MP, said: I'm cross about my own situation and then seeing other people struggle has really made me want to get involved with politics. And Baroness Benjamin commented: "You can do a lot if you really feel committed and you're passionate about making a difference". Each of these politicians is setting out to change something, some aspect of the life of the nation, and with that desire to change something arises the risk that the change belongs to the politician, not the people. Hence, we have a potential tension; while the model of Intelligent Organisation depends on the appropriate autonomy of the individual, politicians want to change things for them – and politics would be utterly pointless were that not the case. In addition, there will be further tension arising from the gap between the problems and their solutions as defined by millions of different citizens. If politicians do not align with at least a significant minority of voters then one set of tensions arise, but if the collective, national or local, elected body does not represent the majority view, however marginal, then a further disconnect arises between electors and elected. The tensions arising in both these cases must be resolved.

We have then to address two issues: one is how to organise a state, and the other is how to maintain the autonomy of the citizen through alignment, i.e. a sense of shared identity between the people and the politicians. This application of the ideas of Intelligent Organisation to the nation state is underpinned by this critique:

- power (authority for decision) does seem to have centralised in many nations, leading to an apparently increasing democratic deficit, to the emergence of views labelled as extremist in some countries and to tensions between the governors and the governed;

- the nation state is commonly essentially organised around vertical hierarchies of control in functional units (the departments of state) rather than citizen-oriented processes;
- the realised as opposed to intended focus of these departments is often on internal compliance (following the process) rather than meeting customer needs (achieving the outcome);
- enabling activities are often constrained by underinvestment and disrupted by the electoral cycles (at various levels of consideration);
- while information and its value are critical to sustainability, history (at least for the UK) suggests that (at least some) governments don't handle information, systems and technology change well;
- some decisions and actions may be motivated by self-interest of elected individuals rather than the needs of the nation.

Adoption of the ideas of Intelligent Organisation will challenge the existing hierarchical and "power of position" decision structures of government administration. It will require political leadership to address the fundamental problem of understanding what the government organisation is for – that is, the purpose, mission and function of government. We shall deal first with the question of autonomy.

Autonomy: democracy, legitimacy and authority

If the first duty of government is the defence of the realm then that must include the defence of the citizen from the interventions and predations of the state. "Defence of the realm", I am asserting in this context, is about the ability of the nation to sustain itself and its population, not a statement of military might. Equally, minimising the intrusion of the state in the life of the individual is not a statement of political belief but of organisational theory. Our principle of maximum appropriate autonomy determines that the state must intervene in people's lives no more than is essential. Equally, unless each individual chooses to relinquish some of their personal freedom for the benefit of others, then the whole system of the state becomes unsustainable. Altruistic self-interest is *not* a contradiction but must rest on choice.

Alignment of the elements of the system (and the indivisible element of any human system is the individual) arises from ensuring that the individual has as much freedom as possible while maintaining the cohesion of the whole. Individual freedom (the conventional word for autonomy), while inevitably at least partly a function of privilege class, race, economic status, education and so on, is not, in a democratic state, a possession of the government to be doled out to citizens in approved quantities but a possession of each individual to be relinquished to government in the minimal quantities necessary to enable social cohesion – and only then reluctantly.

States differ from other forms of organisation because of the various ways in which they are formed and how they derive their authority. In a parliamentary democracy (HM Government, 2011) with a constitutional sovereign such as the United Kingdom (UK), the government (and hence the administrative mechanisms of nationhood and governance) can usefully be thought of as an emergent property of the expressed will of the people. A parliamentary democracy with a constitutional monarch differs from a republic, where the state is often legally constituted as an entity in its own right. In the UK we are the state, and the state is us; this resolves the question of citizen autonomy because everything done by the state is done with our consent. We must remember, though, that elected UK Members of Parliament are governor citizens, representatives of their community, not delegates. The freedom of the MP is to follow their beliefs and their conscience. The freedom of the people is to choose a different governor citizen at the next opportunity.

Democracy, however imperfect, is, in a human system, the key to shared identity. Argument and debate, honestly, rigorously and robustly conducted, delivers the "best" outcome. Participation is essential to legitimising that outcome – because there will (nearly) always be a minority, an individual or group who disagree with whatever decision has been made. Informed by a different perspective and set of beliefs, they may within the structure argue for something different. That is their right, but that right cannot legitimately trump the will of the majority, however ill-informed, ignorant or misguided the others may think they are. To do so would challenge the legitimacy of the democracy, undermine the shared identity and risk the viability of the whole. Genuine participation enables "closure" between the led and the leaders, viability rests in that organisational closure, and the legitimacy of a government underwrites its authority. To quote Beer (1981): "If the government is the people the revolution of government starts with you". While history suggests that any nation with a system of government which, by whatever means, ignores, suppresses or overrides the needs and desires of the population will not be sustainable in the long term, and the principles of Intelligent Organisation help us to understand why. Simply the cost of maintaining such a system outweighs the benefit. Democracy, while undoubtedly inefficient and "the worst form of government except all those other forms that have been tried from time to time" (Churchill, 2008), delivers the lowest overall societal cost with the greatest overall societal benefit.

In a democracy, organisational closure, the alignment of governors and governed, arises through an electoral process. The legitimacy of government and, in consequence the viability of the state, rests in the extent to which the electorate creates the government and the government reflects its electorate.

A state of viability

It seems appropriate at this point to loop back to our starting point: the idea that the first duty of government is defence of the realm. In a globalised economy the notion of "defence" must include not just the traditional military and civil defence of the physical borders but also the defence of its society and economy and include the digital economy which, in both its good and evil aspects, is generating supranational effects. Whilst it may be overstating the case, to corrupt von Clausewitz (1832), to suggest that economic competition is the "continuation of war by other means", there can be little doubt that there is as much a significant effort required to build and sustain the economic well-being of any nation as there is for organisations within that nation to sustain themselves. A sustainable economy must have access to the knowledge, skills, monetary capital and materials necessary to support the population, whether those things are inherent to the nation or achieved through multipartite arrangements. For example, the UK electricity supply depends on interconnectors with other countries; gas and food are imported. I suggest there is a minimum level of internal capacity and capability in all these dimensions for the sustainability of every nation, and falling below that level threatens its survival as an independent entity. Preserving that minimum capability may mean sustaining through subsidy some activities and industries which are thought critical to the well-being of the nation.

Modern states may be thought of as existing along two continua. The first is an economic continuum from socialistic to capitalistic. The second a societal continuum from authoritarian to libertarian. Each state can be mapped to those axes so that we can see how every state fits one of four very broad classifications:

- capitalistic – authoritarian
- capitalistic – libertarian
- socialistic – authoritarian
- socialistic – libertarian

Few states, if any, can be considered viable (in Beer's definition, capable of adaptation and survival) if they are at the extremes of any of the dimensions, though some are perhaps a lot closer than others. Observers of global politics might note that the nations nearer the extremes also appear the least stable and the most challenged economically and in terms of their fit to the environment.

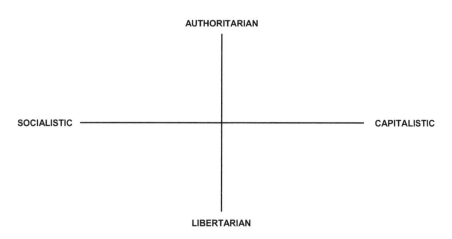

FIGURE 13.1   Dimensions of economy and freedom

In *World in Torment*, Beer (1993) argued that all states, regardless of the economic model, end in a totalitarian position (beyond the authoritarian position that I have noted). That situation arises because some countries simply do not have a democratic political structure, and those which do are subject to a negentropic (Beckford, 1994) process of democratic decay. In that process more power is progressively drawn to and exercised from the centre and increasingly limits discretion for the individual, especially where individual voters do not exercise their rights. Reaching back to the Magna Carta of 1215, hard-won freedoms should not be lightly given up, because they are rarely if ever restored! In the words of Canadian songwriter Bruce Cockburn, "the trouble with normal is it always gets worse". Once a limit, a standard, a restriction on freedom has been enshrined in law or in the discretionary orders possible under enabling legislation (e.g. The Health and Safety at Work Act, 1974), whatever the justification, it becomes very difficult to overcome because every derestriction is perceived and presented as an increase in risk. Similarly, freedoms and equality of treatments achieved in much more recent years – of association, of religious expression, of equality between those of different ethnicity, sexuality, disability and religion – need to be actively defended and built upon; the freedom of individuals to simply be themselves must be preserved. In the digital world of the "Internet of Things", with fifth-generation connectivity and ubiquitous personal cameras and closed-circuit TV cameras, we need to work hard to preserve freedom from the surveillance made possible by those technologies. We must be determined in avoiding an inadvertent drift to a surveillance society with all of the potential for inhibiting the liberty of the individual which that may entail. It is equally no good to attempt to establish an extreme libertarian position. That is no more sustainable than the alternative; the complete absence of rules guarantees not freedom but ultimately an oppression based on brute force equivalent to a totalitarian position, simply with a notionally different form of governance.

The Intelligent Nation, one which is to be sustainable in the long term, must find a point of balance along each dimension where it is viable. That point of balance may well be different for each, being a function of the people (education, skill, capability), of economic, social and democratic maturity and of its relationships with its neighbours. As with all other forms of organisation that position is continually shifting, and active participation by voters in the democratic process should be the key to sustaining that balance.

If intelligent nationhood, a state of viability, is to be guaranteed, then that intelligence and viability must be embedded in the structures of government and of the public services that we create, and that can be best understood if we think about the principles that need to underpin it:

- Power belongs to the individual citizen and is expressed through a democratic process which is fixed in principle but not in method;
- Through that process the individual, not the state, is supreme;
- Decisions must be taken as close to the citizen as possible (the principle of subsidiarity applies to the individual);

- The task of the state is to enable the lives of its citizens, and all money spent doing so arises from the individual citizen;
- State-provided services must be focused on the delivery of desired outcomes and must be designed backwards from the citizen requiring multi-skilled, multitasking teams;
- An appropriate equilibrium must be achieved that balances efficiency and effectiveness with the desire for autonomy;
- Only those things which can only be provided at a national level should be provided at a national level; everything else (the greater part) should be provided locally.

Here, of course, it is essential to recognise that there are more than just two levels of consideration, that separation is to establish a distinction. In truth our freedoms are distributed through a complex set of nested relationships. Commonly, though not exclusively, and working through a geographically oriented sociopolitical hierarchy,

- an individual belongs to a family (however that family may be constituted);
- a family resides in a community (a street, a block of flats);
- a community is part of a village, town, city;
- a city is part of a shire county, a member of a unitary authority or metropolitan area;
- a county, unitary authority or metropolitan area is a member of a state, principality, administrative region;
- a state is a member of an international community of some lesser or greater formality.

The challenge in managing autonomy is to sustain the freedom of the individual whilst also enabling the existence of community at a variety of embedded levels. A freedom restricted by one level acts on all of the lower levels, and therein lies great challenge.

In summary an intelligent nation must continually strive to

- balance
    - the competing demands of a capitalistic economy (because generating a surplus is critical to growth)
- with
    - socialistic public services (because the demands and complexity of a modern nation will always mean that there are vulnerable people that we have an individual and collective duty to support and protect)
- and to balance
    - a libertarian mindset (that enshrines the freedom of the individual to get it wrong on their own terms)

- with

  - an authoritarian understanding (that enshrines the ability of the state to prevent one individual from causing harm to others).

The point of balance will be particular to each nation and will always be dynamic.

Preserving local engagement

Structurally our design must make a distinction between those services and functions that are most appropriately delivered at a relatively local level and those which can only be delivered at the level of the whole nation. This is critical to achieve both efficiency (productivity) and effectiveness (societal benefit), and, of course, there will be trade-offs and compromises – the solution must work in practice not just in theory. The trade-offs and compromises emerge through the political process while the execution of policy is conducted by officers, at all levels of administrative government.

The implication of what is being described is that we must consider what the "whole" should look like. Following the principle of ensuring appropriate autonomy, we must embrace fully the idea of subsidiarity. Subsidiarity means that social and political issues should be dealt with at the most immediate (or local) level that is consistent with their resolution and reflects the organizing principle that matters ought to be handled by the smallest, lowest or least centralized competent authority.

If decisions are to be taken "as close to the citizens as possible" (Sampson, 1993), that can actually mean two things. First, it means decentralising the provision (especially the delivery) of a whole range of public services to the most local level. Second, it means the shortest possible distance (the lowest number of steps) between the electorate and the elected. In the second respect the "first past the post" system in the UK delivers a near-direct link between the citizens and the elected members of local, unitary shire authorities and the House of Commons. That link is corrupted by two things; first is the system of "parties" which can inhibit electoral opportunity for independents but, more importantly, may insert a "party policy" between the citizen and the elected member, whose personal values and beliefs may be overwhelmed by loyalty to the party. The second corruption occurs where officials (public servants nationally and locally) are charged with executing the policies of the relevant authority and, by virtue of the power invested in them, may distort, intentionally or not, the wishes of the electorate as passed into policy and legislation by the relevant body by applying their professional viewpoint, which may not correspond with the public view.

The potential distortion can, in particular, link back to the decentralisation of provision. Charged with delivering "value for money", the relevant bodies seek to lower their costs, and hence we see the outsourcing of some provision – for example, the creation of executive agencies and the closure (usually in the interests of "efficiency") of local facilities which are instead offered at some physical distance from the citizen. The challenge with this is that while the direct "cash" cost to the functional provider might fall, the indirect cost imposed on the service user will often increase. The total societal cost of provision goes up. Examples of this are easy to find. In the 1960s the efficiency of the railways was supposedly increased by a process of closing local branch lines and directing putative passengers to larger stations in larger locations. Because of this cutting off of the passenger supply along the tributaries to the main flow, the cost to the railway may (or may not) have decreased; more likely roughly the same cost was spread over a smaller number of passengers and services. Meanwhile the cost to the individual passenger increased (either in cash or time or perhaps both) because they now had to travel further by other means of transport in order to catch a train – many of them perhaps not bothering. Beer (1979) described this process as a "machine for eating the railway". The same effect can be seen in healthcare with the ongoing consolidation of certain services into specialist centres, usually in larger centres of population, but equally usually at some distance from the patients. The money saved by the service provider is expended by the service user in cash, time and, perhaps, a worse health outcome. A cost displaced to someone else's budget is not a cost reduced; the total cost to society increases.

The defence to this centralising process is normally expressed in terms of the increased expertise to be offered by specialist centres. There is undoubtedly some merit in that argument for some services and some specialities, but it does not offer a universal truth or a single best answer. Those of a questioning mindset might wonder whether that is more about the convenience and position of the relevant experts. Somehow it seems a "specialist service" always requires a more senior staff with a higher cost; meanwhile the service user may suffer. Similar examples to these can be found in everything from waste and refuse management to education and infrastructure maintenance. Displacing costs to others disguises rather than solves a cost problem.

Offender management: not gaining the benefits

There are, at the time I am writing, seven National Probation Service (NPS) regions in England and Wales, soon to be ten. The NPS currently supervises 107,000 offenders. A further 126,000 offenders are supervised by Community Rehabilitation Companies (CRCs).

In 2014 the government reordered the structure and constitution of probation services. Prior to the changes, probation services were organised through 43 geographical areas across England and Wales. The changes saw the creation of a single civil service NPS for England and Wales spread over 11 regions, with responsibility for the assessment of offenders and recommendations of sentencing options, together with the management of offenders who pose a greater risk to the public. Offenders who pose a lesser risk to the public are then transferred to be managed by one of several Community Rehabilitation Companies. These are contracted, private companies covering 21 package areas across England and Wales – an outsourcing of part of offender management services, with a complex contract and performance management regime.

The intention was to improve innovation and effectiveness in offender management to reduce reoffending.

When CRCs were created, the government were aware that the CRCs would have internal pressures to manage improperly the offenders who do not comply with their orders. An inherent tension was created for the CRCs between reporting offenders who breach their orders to promote the reduction of reoffending on the one hand and reducing income through poorer performance arising from fewer completion of those orders on the other. Their commercial nature also created a climate of mistrust with other public sector elements of the criminal justice system. The judiciary in particular were not provided with information about the services provided by CRCs and were reluctant to create a working relationship with them because of their commercial nature. This meant that over time, the judiciary became gradually less aware of community sentence options available to them. This has meant there has been decreasing trust in CRCs on the part of the judiciary.

Because of the competitive commercial nature of performance information, CRCs were not allowed access to NPS information systems. Given that all offenders are first assessed by the NPS before being passed to a CRC, and that they hold old records of offenders' performance on previous orders, this makes it harder for CRCs to manage effectively the offenders allocated to them. Also, in most areas, CRCs were prevented from being based in NPS accommodation in order to promote the separation of identities and to prevent an incumbent contract holder from gaining a competitive advantage. This has prevented both organisations from realising the benefits of co-location.

While costs may have been reduced – a notional gain in efficiency – effectiveness has undoubtedly fallen. In 2019 the whole failing system is under review.

It is reasonable to say that, with increases in knowledge, professional expertise and both the capital and operating costs of some equipment, universally local provision might be inappropriate. The task of the public servant as service provider must be to strive to achieve the most sustainable balance point, taking account not just of the direct costs and benefits to the particular service but also of the costs and benefits delivered to society at large as experienced by the individual and the natural environment. This brings us back to the idea of the "competent authority" as a way of resolving the problem. In this respect the delivery of services that do not require a physical presence (i.e. administrative services) is open to the possibility of a digital transformation. Changes in information provision and the underlying technologies are rendering services which are centrally enabled and locally, even individually, provided. These extend to the taxation system (inevitably I suppose!), to obtaining and renewing some personal documents and to making claims and receiving benefits in respect of some aspects of the welfare system.

Service provision in the Intelligent Nation must be designed backwards to deliver desired outcomes to and for its citizens. We must redesign the provision backwards from the citizen and the societal outcome and recognise where a service can be virtual and individually delivered, where it must be delivered locally and where it can only be delivered nationally. This may mean challenging the current departments of state and the structures and processes of delivery and realigning them around the new model.

A useful example here is to think about the challenge of policing in contemporary society. The accountability of the police forces and the deterrent effect of the visibility of police officers demands a local presence and engagement. In a society enjoying policing by consent, such as the UK, that local connection is critical to acceptance. However, when we consider the current and emerging nature of crime and criminal behaviour, we can see increasingly that while the crime may well be experienced locally – the criminal is acting at a distance (e.g. cybercrime, online fraud, pornography) – or be controlled at a distance (distribution of illegal narcotics where the leaders and owners of the process are significantly distanced and hidden from the very local distributor). While policing a locality may enable the prevention or detention of the local distributor, it is unlikely to have the capability or resources to identify or arrest the ringleaders. Hence, we need both local and national policing. It can be argued in the UK that the structure (43 police and crime commissioners, each controlling a force) is inadequate to the task. Here we need to really address the challenge. In order to be effective in their primary task of preventing crime, local forces need to relinquish some of their activities to specialist units at a national (even international) level with dedicated skills and capability – but when they do, local accountability may be lost. This can be addressed through a mechanism in which investigation and detection are carried out nationally while arrest and detention are carried out locally, but, to be efficient as well as effective, that requires a change which enables a national police force to exist in its own right (to carry out only those specialist policing activities) rather than inefficient duplication of effort through "task forces" and "alliances". The individual forces must, reluctantly, give up some of their control to the national interest if policing is to be effective in a world of cybercrime or cyber-enabled crime. This is not something to be added to the existing approach but something that replaces some parts of it.

V8: polis and the new data challenge

The Aristotelian notion of a city-nation state or polis suggests that any society requires some form of policing, and this has often been achieved through ideas of enforcement. These have given rise to many forms of criminal justice – inquisitorial, adversarial and restorative – which have altered and rationalised technology, religion and industry as changes have occurred in society.

Presently in the UK the polis is itself regulated by many different bodies: the Inspectorate of Constabulary (and now Fire and Rescue Service), Investigatory Powers Commissioner, Biometrics, Forensic Science Regulator and the Information Commissioner, to name just a few.

Increasing reliance on networked data systems is generating unprecedented demands upon policing. Examples include cyber-enabled crime (victims and perpetrators both using computers) from online abuse and fraud to cyber-dependent (computer-to-computer) related attacks. These can deny online services, disable infrastructure or "steal" data for nefarious purposes such as blackmail or economic advancement. Away from cybercrime, nearly all crimes and many non-crime incidents leave what is regarded as a digital footprint. In all of these cases the ability to capture, acquire analyse, retain and disclose data are key. Such data may be on devices held on public service and commercial networks and be retained within or outside of the UK. Countering terrorism and organised crime are additional categories of demand where more sophisticated networked threats exist internationally. The ability to deploy collaborative effort on threat-related data is essential to keeping citizens safe and regulating criminal justice.

The operating context is complicated by the very nature of data on networks. The V8 model is a framework for considering these data challenges. It deals with the "what?" rather than the "so what now?".

V8: signs and symptoms

The V8 model, a framework for thinking about intelligent policing in a digital crime environment, can be used to assess the nature and extent of a particular disruptive digital event or application of technology. The current state of development is qualitative and descriptive rather than quantitative; however, a matrix-based approach could help to map such disruptions over time.

- *Volume: proliferation with some data now also ephemeral;*
- *Velocity: dramatic acceleration, 5G with quantum-like latency and perhaps more than 66 times faster than 4G;*
- *Variety: data types altering and expanding;*
- *Validity: data more challenging to ensure as being "true" rather than probabilistic, with provenance and continuity being both intelligence and evidential challenges;*
- *Veracity: spoofing of identifiers, people, websites and artificial intelligence applications;*
- *Vectors: threats morphing and adapting constantly and rapidly;*
- *Vulnerabilities: defining and calibrating networked vulnerabilities are increasingly challenging;*
- *Virtualisation: data stored in many cloudy and obscure jurisdictions, "farmed" through software defined networks, will change the whole approach to the delivery of data, processing and threats.*

How might some of these symptoms be recognised in the real world? Consider recent examples of policing trying to prosecute rape. Two reported cases [(webref 16)] have collapsed over the inadequate analysis and disclosure of Short Message System (text) and social media messages between alleged victims, suspects and witnesses. The volumes of data involved have been a contributory factor in these cases, and this is widely reported as a problem for both policing and prosecutors, and in both cases there were potential miscarriages of justice. The Criminal Procedures and Investigations Act 1994 requires officers to conduct "all reasonable enquiries" relating to an investigation. There may be tens of thousands of lines of data on a modern handset, and being able to discriminate between that which is of material interest and that which is unused can be complicated. It may relate to specific witness statements or comments made by the alleger or accused. The misinterpretation of just one message or comment can turn a case. Reviewing these messages could literally take weeks, and then there is the issue of all of the other digital sources which may be relevant to that case; vehicle telematics, communications data, traces from "Internet of Things" (IoT) devices. Murders have been successfully prosecuted just from single device forensics of smart devices.

Complex and organised crime is most often a product of human networked behaviours. Each actor or node in that network will have a digital profile and often use technology as part of delivering a network effect or criminal outcome. They may also act within other criminal networks and certainly their own social networks – for example,

- *movement of illegal commodities,*
- *people trafficking activities and*
- *use of violence.*

The widely reported "county lines" phenomenon does not involve sophisticated organised criminality but nevertheless preys upon the vulnerable and uses network behaviours to ply their trade ^(webref 17). Faced with the challenges of a data and networks and the need to adapt rapidly, can credible and flexible systems be developed within the present structures and systems of policing?

Present Governance of Policing

Local policing functions are delivered within geographic boundaries. In England and Wales these often align to local government administrative areas, and each chief constable is held to account by either a city mayor or a policing and crime commissioner, both being elected roles. The Police Service of Northern Ireland reports to the devolved administration, and Scotland has recently created a single national police service reporting along similar lines. The National Crime Agency is accountable to the Home Secretary and provides a range of specialist services and some enforcement capability. Counterterrorism is delivered through a network approach and is headed by an assistant commissioner in the Metropolitan Police. There are regional organised crime units such as Zephyr ^(webref 18) which act as a coordination hub proving specialist services to local forces. The National Police Chiefs' Council, which is a collective rather than a legal entity, provides a basis for policy and practice coordination. There is the College of Policing for England and Wales and a separate Scottish Policing College. Partnerships exist with local government and central government agencies, and, excluding the devolved administrations, the Home Office has a legislative policy and funding role. There is a plethora of collaborations between forces and outsourced service contracts to commercial providers. There are some national networks and information systems, but local forces often provide information communications technology internally. There is limited used of cloud storage and only a few systems which might be considered as *national tools. Legislation* (webref19) *promotes "localism" of policing services. Prosecutions take place under English and Welsh law, Scottish and Northern Irish procedures.*

In terms of responding to challenges of digital disruption, the fundamental questions appear to be cybernetic ones:

- *Are these arrangements able to provide viable management systems at recursive strategic, tactical and operational levels which can withstand the challenges of significant data disruption?*
- *Can the present approach deal with threats and develop opportunities in an environment of constant and accelerating change to meet challenges such as the law of requisite variety?*

The final consideration is about future posture and readiness rather than simple and reactive response to the demands of the present. This requires the development of systems for capability development and innovation. A capability can be defined in many ways, but all capabilities are a function of people, processes and technology within a network.

Future Efficacy

The Police Transformation Fund (webref 20) *was created by the Home Office, and this funds the Digital Policing Portfolio which appears to be based upon an NPCC strategy called "Vision 2025". This states:*

"By 2025 digital policing will make it easier and more consistent for the public to make digital contact, improve our use of digital intelligence and evidence and ensure we can transfer all material in a digital format to the criminal justice system".

Three separate programmes were established to deliver

- *digital public contact,*
- *digital investigation and intelligence and*
- *a digital interface with the criminal justice system.*

The efficacy of this vision and the corresponding programmes has yet to be discerned. The strategy appears to be predicated upon the capability of the present structures to be able to work at the speed and scale and deal with the complexity of the global networked data environment. These traditional organisations are unlikely to be able to respond to the demands while retaining their machine age, bureaucratic forms of organisation.

Arguably the V8 model can be used to assess rapid and complex perturbations in a networked society, amplifying demands on policing which it does not always have the capacity or capabilities to attenuate and therefore provide effective policing. Data-driven threats which are manifest parts of a networked society need equally agile and effective polis capabilities which are networked and can respond effectively.

It is in this disrupted context that UK policing must meet the many demands of a postmodern industrial democracy which may now be embarking on some of the most significant social-technological changes seen for decades, with 5G networks, expansion of the "Internet of Things", cyber-physical systems, artificial intelligence, smart cities and many other networked technologies. How might the polis respond? At the core of this entire scenario lies the challenge to develop a "network of networks" and blend local and non-local capabilities: an intelligent police service for an intelligent nation.

Achieving and sustaining an appropriate balance of central and local control in such circumstances presents a significant challenge to those in political and executive office – but it must be addressed. The solution may rest in that notion of subsidiarity, a recognition of where "competence" exists, but perhaps the national level should do only those things that *can only* be done at the national level? Everything else should be left, granted as much autonomy as is consistent with systemic cohesion.

No island is an island

When we consider the nation state with the systemic mindset essential to the idea of Intelligent Organisation, we must recognise that every nation is, to some degree, engaged in relationships with many others. These relationships may be close or distant across a range of aspects such as trade, freedom of movement, defence, health and the will to embrace culture, religion, political systems and so on. Any nation that seeks to isolate itself from such relationships must have sufficient resources and capability to at least sustain its population and defend its borders, and in attempting to do so, may well exist in a state of some tension with its neighbours, perhaps threatening, perhaps feeling threatened.

The principles of Intelligent Organisation demand that the Intelligent Nation exists in a state of mutual co-operation with other nations, a peaceful coexistence in which each nation can benefit from its relationship with others while not being threatened. This is a difficult status to manage in a world of global economic competition, and hence a number of arrangements and accords exist to assist. The World Trade Organisation, The European Free Trade Area, The Asia-Pacific Trade Agreement, The North America Free Trade Agreement were all created to facilitate international trade. The globalisation of economic activity extends to goods, services and utilities.

These principles and mutually beneficial arrangements are challenged when nations seek to, in effect, trade their sovereignty. If, in seeking to work more closely together, they seek to bind each other in ways which limit their independent nationhood or when political power (remember the citizen is supreme) is ceded to a supranational organisation, then there may be a threat to their viability. This arises perhaps because the distance between the led and the leaders may become so great that the connection is lost. It may arise from a lack of shared identity or economic disparity which is only able to be bridged by a transfer of wealth through a social contract unsupported by the electorate. Human history is littered with examples of empires, the bringing together of nations through the use of military power, and all have ultimately failed. If each nation is to survive and thrive while working in collaboration with its neighbours, then all must find a way to do so, not by the application of might nor the limitation of democracy and reductions in freedom but by recognising and respecting the sovereignty of each other, working collaboratively where they can and respecting their decisions and boundaries. Intelligent nations can no more exist in isolation than they can exist when absorbed into the machinations of other states or supranational organisations.

Summary

The purpose of this chapter has been to begin an exploration of how the principles of Intelligent Organisation work out when applied to the challenges of the nation. It has not set out to change or revolutionise the world, nor can it claim to be complete. The principal learning that perhaps can be taken is that the principles can be applied, that such application might mean a significant shift in power and authority from the centre to the parts, not inconsistent with the devolution of some powers in the UK over recent years. It is perhaps incumbent on the powerful to relinquish some of that power, to cede control back to the individual, and incumbent on all citizens to exercise their democratic rights, perhaps to see those rights as obligations to be fulfilled for their own sake and that of their fellow citizens.

14

THE INTELLIGENT ORGANISATION AND PUBLIC SERVICES

Introduction

Having considered the principles of Intelligent Organisation when applied to the notions of national governance, we can now consider how those principles apply to the delivery of public services. Brief case studies are included looking at energy, transport and healthcare.

There are four key factors that distinguish public service from private sector organisations in general. First is that public service organisations do not enjoy the same degree of self-determination, autonomy, as those in the private sector. Their purpose is given to them by government, which also largely controls their funding. Second, the focus of activity often appears to be on output (compliance to process) not outcome (customers whose needs or requirements have been met). Third, with their maturity, size and the complexity of the rules they need to observe (e.g. tax law and benefits law), a lot of organisational inertia has to be overcome to deliver substantial change. Even the youngest government services such as healthcare and education are now long established while diplomacy and defence go back hundreds of years. Meanwhile both extrinsic and intrinsic public servant incentive systems and behaviours are typically geared towards administrative compliance and stability rather than innovation or leadership. Finally, such organisations are either information driven or information enabled, sometimes both, while government (at least in the UK) has a long history of less-than-successful IT projects!

Purpose, effectiveness and efficiency

If we are to observe the principles of the Intelligent Nation in thinking about redesigning public sector organisations, we should then consider these aspects:

- There must be real clarity about the purpose of publicly funded activity.
- There must be real accountability for its value.

- Services must be demand led and outcome oriented.
- Services must be delivered through structures which reflect the idea of subsidiarity, (closeness of decision-making to the citizen) blending those which are subject to

  - national policy and national delivery,
  - national policy and a mix of national and local delivery,
  - national policy and local delivery,
  - local policy and local delivery.

- The extent to which any service might be provided virtually must be fully understood.
- The understanding of the cost-benefit case for considering centralisation must be systemic, embracing service users, service providers, the social and physical environment.

In respect of this latter point it will be useful to follow the work of Taguchi (1987) in considering the product or service from the perspective of "the cost imparted to society". It is sensible to see how that could also embrace the benefit imparted to society and the difference between cost and benefit calculated! There is significant work going on in and on behalf of governments in this regard, considering in particular the idea of a "social return on investment" [webref 21].

When clarity of purpose is absent, examination of any budget leads to a cost-reduction focus considering either marginal activity (what can we stop doing?) or "big ticket" items. Emphasis will be on reducing the operating budget, and, because the biggest budget numbers in any service-oriented organisation are staff costs, that usually translates into reductions in headcount. That in turn either limits the number of the population whose needs can be met, reduces the share of activity that each customer receives or, sometimes, displaces cost to another service – something that has already been warned about. Such phenomena continue to be reported in the press internationally while, in the UK GPs protesting at levels of funding and reducing the service provided locally to patients have displaced those patients to A & E departments. The GPs' waiting times are thereby "managed"; their costs are reduced. Meanwhile the A & E waiting times and costs are increased, and the patient suffers. The costs have not been reduced, just displaced. The "head office" demand for reduced spending may or may not be met, but the service fails to the extent that its purpose is not fulfilled. Government, regardless of political persuasion, usually provides additional funding rather than addressing the problem.

In many cases, services were given purpose many years ago, and government has tweaked and changed, adapted and adopted but not fundamentally rethought provision. Traditional practices, ways of working and bureaucratic hierarchies built around the original purpose, intentionally or not, inhibit changes that would not only reduce costs and/or improve performance but are desired by the citizen customers of the service and many of the staff. Meanwhile, some of the purposes may need to be altered to more adequately meet the needs of a changed society and to take advantage of the potential (particularly of digital technologies) now available. Attempts are being made in the UK to do this at scale, particularly in the health sector, which is pursuing digital transformation.

There is, in many countries, pressure for "public sector reform", usually translated as "doing more for less". Good government recognises that its legitimacy depends on a democratic process and that the ability of the government to provide services is a function of the willingness of the electors to fund them. Consistent with the maximisation of the autonomy of the citizen is the obligation on the part of government to recognise that it should spend on goods and services *and* on its own internal administration no more than is necessary for the fulfilment of the mandate against which it has been elected. An intelligent government would recognise that it must demonstrate to electors that it is increasing efficiency and therefore value for money each year and, perhaps, reducing taxation. While some states are wholly or partly funded by extraordinary means (taxation on gambling in some, oil and gas revenue in others), the greater part of state spending and investment in most countries is derived through taxation of individual and corporate earnings (income taxes) and on spending (consumption taxes). As most states only spend money directly derived from their citizens, continuing in governance over the medium to long term depends both on economic well-being (a major winner of votes) and on the government seeming to respond (or not) to the broader wishes of the people and, at some level, being able to demonstrate value for money. There is of course scope for debate about the range and extent to which any level of government should provide services to and on behalf of its population of citizens as a whole. Though that is not the purpose here, interested readers might reflect on the four dimensions of ideology outlined in the previous chapter and explore the implications of different positions. There can be little doubt, though, that public services (whether national or local) should consider themselves under an obligation to manage those services to provide the maximum benefit to citizens (customer outcome) at the lowest cost. However, like any organisation, the state must over time spend less than it receives in order to be financially viable.

Sparking a thought

Attending a multi-country summit on electric infrastructure security, I was struck by the extent to which the pursuit of short-run efficiency distorts the way we think about performance in our utilities. It is not just electricity – particularly with the levels of interconnection and interdependence that now pervades the whole. We need to consider performance of utilities by the extent to which they meet the (evolving) needs of the society they exist to serve. In the UK many of those utilities are now privately owned and operated, some by international organisations. Others are still provided by the state through arms-length organisations (e.g. the railway infrastructure operator Network Rail and the Highways Agency). Regardless of the ownership model adopted, the purpose of the utility from the perspective of the citizen or business (as customer) is the provision of the service, and, because it is a utility, that needs to be achieved at the lowest cost consistent with sustaining service provision. We need to consider performance in utilities by the extent to which they meet the (evolving) needs of the society they exist to serve, not just the surpluses or subsidies required.

Public sector organisations have different survival criteria to those in the private sector. First, while funding levels vary over time and budgets may be over- or underspent, they do not cease trading or retain a surplus, they are not motivated to perform by profit, and they are constrained to perform within budget. Second, if they overspend or underdeliver they do not generally lapse into administration but are rescued by one means or another by being merged or absorbed. The particular delivery organisation may fail, but the service is still required, commonly the bulk of the staff are secure in their posts. Although individual senior employees may be removed from office, the organisations themselves are invulnerable to the ultimate failure of bankruptcy, they do not have to "adapt to survive". The inevitable sense of security will impact the thinking and behaviour of those employed in the particular service. Overcoming this inertia may be one of the reasons many governments globally have chosen to outsource some services as, regardless of performance (or indeed budgets), they are persistent and protected, although "rationing" of some services does occur. Third, they have (at least) two distinct and discrete "customers" to serve, the public (who receive the services) and the government (which funds them through taxation). The price of their protections is that they do not enjoy power of self-determination (autonomy) equivalent to the private sector. They cannot choose to "grow the business" to the same extent, nor can they decide that the resources which they receive would be more productively employed in pursuing different goals; they operate to fulfil the tasks allotted to them. They are protected but constrained, functioning on decision cycles largely dictated by elections and budgets. Those private and third-sector organisations to which public services are contracted (whether executive agencies, community interest companies, public service mutuals or a range of "outsourcers") do not have the same protections. While some must be managed to recover their own costs (through fee or licence income), many others, even those with primarily social objectives, may also have a profit motivation.

Whilst independent organisations are, ultimately, governed by their shareholders (or trustees if a charity), represented by their board, every public sector organisation is subject to a sociopolitical level of governance. The government, whether national or local and by virtue of its mandate, determines organisational purpose and performance expectations. Public sector organisations often have very broadly drawn purposes, making it difficult either to know what constitutes good performance or, indeed, how much of a particular service is "enough" – regardless of the political drivers. While governments are criticised for attempting to set standards and targets for various services, as we have discovered in the rest of the book, these are essential to process delivery and control but are meaningless in the absence of a clear purpose. It is fulfilment of purpose that is the measure of success.

Drucker (1986) writes of the need for public services of all sorts to be entrepreneurial, to innovate, but recognises that they can only do so when they have a clear sense of purpose; that is, when innovation and entrepreneurialism are expressed in terms of the outcome to be achieved. Clarity of purpose enables all of the other criteria of the Intelligent Organisation to be addressed:

- Who are the customers?
- What are the outcomes they expect?
- What do the processes need to be to achieve those outcomes?
- What behaviours and values are appropriate?
- How much is "enough"?
- How can we manage, adapt, develop the organisation?

In the absence of clearly defined purpose, effectiveness cannot be addressed, and the question of efficiency is an irrelevance. In that case, then, we cannot reasonably expect public sector organisations, or the people employed in them, to deliver the outcomes we want. We cannot have what we have not defined.

Organising public services: subsidiarity

There are, of course, two aspects to our consideration of "organisation". One is to look at how an intelligent nation balances central and local policy and delivery, the other how it becomes customer focused and comes to provide a differentiated service to each individual.

The balance of central and local delivery needs to draw on the categories identified at the beginning of the chapter, with the decisions resting on the meaning of "competence", i.e. the legal authority to act. More simply, other than those competences which any particular country may lend to its international relationships, while some things may need to be reserved to be only done nationally, other things should be done locally unless they cannot be achieved on that basis.

So, if competence is national for some things, how do we work out what "cannot be achieved" locally, how do we allocate authority, and how do we delegate responsibility for action in a manner consistent with our principles? As soon as we start to pursue a clean, rational approach it starts to fail. A nation and its structures are messy, untidy, inevitably more nuanced than any binary distinction can deal with.

We can consider a nation (figure 14.1) as emerging from a set of ten interdependent infrastructural sectors in which five primary sectors (energy, transport, water, ICT and waste) support five secondary sectors (healthcare, defence, education, commerce and civil administration). The emergent property of these interacting enabling activities is society. The whole system taken together both enables and generates value; society reflects the sense of identity. In any substantial situation it is clear that it will not be practicable for these sectors to be fulfilled on a centralised, national-only basis. There will need to be at least geographical divisions, possibly variations in overall provision related to population density, economic well-being and a range of other criteria. The system is circular and not easily open to

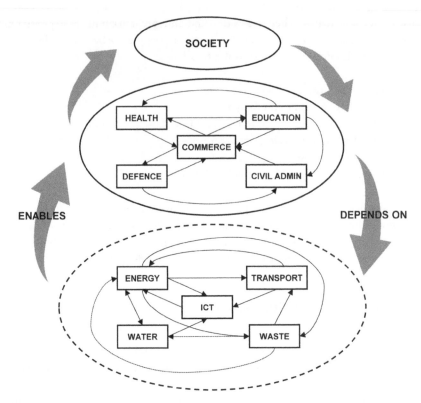

FIGURE 14.1 National interdependencies

Source: Adapted from Webref 22

disentangling! Nonetheless we must try if we are to deliver an intelligent nation. Let's look at the case of UK Railway, a subset of the transport sector.

Managing the railway

Since 2011 substantial work has been undertaken in considering how UK Railway can be adapted to the possibility of climate change. Studies have been commissioned domestically by Network Rail and the Rail Safety and Standards Board and latterly internationally by Union Internationale des Chemins de fer (webref 23) *to consider how that might be achieved. One of the realisations emerging from that work is how control and authority for action are distributed throughout the railway.*

UK Railway, like many railways, is the responsibility of central government, which both owns and largely funds it. The infrastructure operator with ownership and respon-sibility for the assets, Network Rail, is centrally funded but in an arms-length relation-ship to government, while rail vehicles are mainly owned by finance houses and leased to train operating companies (TOCs). Meanwhile, Network Rail outsources significant elements of its maintenance activities to third party providers.

The funding of UK Railway comes in three major parts. Part one is ticket revenue, paid by passengers to the TOCs. Second is arrangements between the TOCs and local or regional authorities in relation to fare subsidies. Third is funding provided by central government to Network Rail to pay for maintenance and upgrading of the infrastructure against a pre-planned schedule of works. A complexifying factor in these arrangements is that in order to provide some surety of funding, UK Railway is funded in "control periods". Control periods are five-year blocks of funding allocated against a planned schedule of maintenance and upgrades. The train operating companies have franchise periods of varying lengths, a franchise being a licence to operate services in a geographic sector. Franchise periods do not align with control periods nor to the various cycles of local, unitary or county and national elections. The political and financial environment in which rail executives seek to make decisions is, at least, difficult!

Whether this set of arrangements is most appropriate is perhaps a debate for another chapter. In this one it helps us to explore the balance of central and local control and its implications. While the whole system is nationally owned and offers a nationwide service, it is broken down into principally geographically based franchises for service purposes and to "lines of route" for engineering purposes. Any one service may use more than one line of route; any one line of route may be used by more than one service.

Inevitably any decision to be made by one party is either enabled or constrained, or sometimes both, by the decisions being made by other parties. Each element of the railway is contained in a recursive (because the decision structures based on the trialogue are invariant) set of embedments with decisions nested inside each other. Figure 14.2 shows how immediate-term, "local/specific" decisions ("this piece of track needs repairing now", or "this train can leave now") are constrained by higher order "operational" and short-term decisions (say, a budget period).

While operational decisions are constraining or enabling local/specific decisions, they are in turn enabled or constrained by strategic decisions which are affected the same way by sociopolitical decisions.

While local/specific decisions are concerned with the immediate activity (fix this problem, and keep the trains running), operational decisions are concerned with implementing higher order decisions already made (we will run this timetable using these vehicles). Strategic decisions are concerned with a longer view but, as seen above, are constrained to a control period. Meanwhile the sociopolitical decisions:

- *Should we have a railway?*
- *How much should we fund it?*
- *Could it be nationalised?*
- *Could it be fully privatised?*

These decisions are both the preserve of national government and constrained by the electoral cycle.

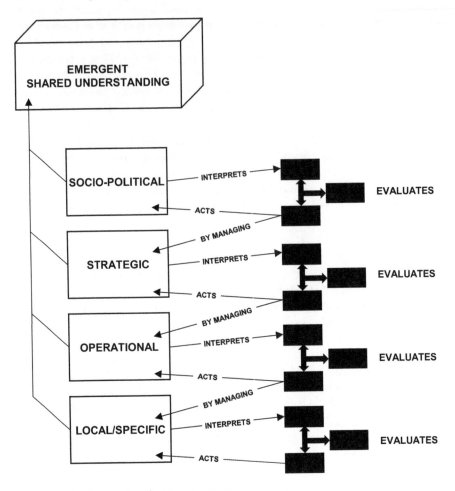

FIGURE 14.2 A recursive decision structure

The conversation between central government (sociopolitical) and UK Railway (the collection of bodies constituting the strategic level in this model) can only be imagined, but it will essentially be this (and I simplify):

- *Socio-Political: Here is some money, we want this much railway;*
- *Strategic: If you want this much railway, we need that amount of money. For some money you can only have a lesser amount of railway.*

A dialogue, a negotiation, will ensue, out of which will emerge a plan and a funding arrangement which ultimately will enable a certain amount of railway to be provided. Those decisions will constrain or enable the whole railway and its performance not just for 5 years but for the whole life of the impact of the decisions.

When we considered the rail infrastructure just from an asset management perspective, it was realised that many rail assets have a 30-year refresh life with a total life

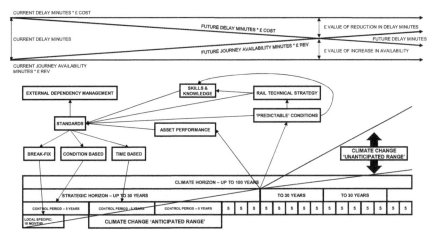

FIGURE 14.3   Asset management framework

in excess of 60 years. Figure 14.3 shows how the decision cycles of the railway need to reflect those time periods if it is to be sustainable. The three asset management approaches – time-based, condition-based and break-fix – all of which are appropriate for different types and classes of asset, need to deal with decision horizons of up to 30 years and yet are constrained within a structural model itself constrained to a 5-year view.

While this study is describing the railway, much the same considerations can be applied to other sectors, and, while the time frames may be different, the mechanisms of constraint no doubt apply. The positive element that comes from this is the element of technical control that emerges and the assurance that the whole railway is maintained in a consistent manner; the negative element is the financial cost of operating in such a bureaucratic manner, the human cost to those working in the system who are (or feel) unable to exploit their abilities and, last but not least, the limitations that a producer-focused organisation imposes on its customer.

Organising public services: customer focus

The overall design of state services is, in general, functional and producer led, so we must turn now to the second challenge, a shift to customer orientation. This demands different thinking about the delivery of public services. The historic convention is to regard the service as the more or less bureaucratic discharge of an obligation to the public in which the task is demonstrably carried out. The Intelligent Organisation convention is that the desired outcome be achieved.

We can all recount tales, either from our own experience or reported in the press and media, of traps, systems in which circularity of logic prevents the desired outcome; for example, an individual cannot register for benefits without a permanent address but cannot obtain a permanent address without benefits; an individual on a low income cannot afford to earn more because the consequent loss in benefits outweighs the increased earnings; an individual is so busy dealing with the demands of various agencies that they have no time to pursue employment. All of these traps are absurd, unintended consequences of a functionally arranged system focused on internal accountability. Any citizen, a customer of the public sector, is likely to have multiple interactions with the functionally organised state. If "the customer outcome" should be the focus of the organisation, then we need to organise things from the customers' perspective, and functional, internally oriented organisations cannot do that.

Most of us interact with the state quite extensively. We pay our taxes, send our children to school, have our bins emptied, receive healthcare and eventually collect our pensions. The system mainly works but is "customer inefficient": we have to deal with multiple agencies and multiple ways of working, a plethora of forms and systems each holding some portion of the entire story. It could, should, be better.

If everyone fitted a standard pattern, perhaps we could deliver significant improvements whilst working within the established structures. However, and this will always be the case, there are a wide range of individuals and families with a wide range of needs. While the majority may place little demand on the various systems, a relatively small proportion of the whole population needs support and engagement from a wide variety of services, often in parallel, to cope with the demands and complexities of contemporary life. Those who are fortunate should not fool themselves into thinking that coping is simple.

The provision of services to this latter few requires careful consideration. Their needs are likely to be complex, and they will be in continuing contact with multiple arms of the state – healthcare, social services, adult services, children's services, police, welfare. The conventional way of dealing with these individuals and families has been through multi-agency working, that is, the "pushing" of individual services through a combined and agreed strategy but with continuing individual service engagement (i.e. the overall approach is agreed but the parts are delivered separately). While this may deliver some benefit, it is both costly and inefficient to manage "internally" through the functionally arranged delivery organisations. It absorbs resources in both direct and indirect (management) activity. It is possible, if not probable, that the cost outweighs the benefit when the "cost" to the customer, whose life is still peppered with multiple visits from multiple agencies, is taken into account. Remember, we must comprehend and work with the total system effect which includes the cost and benefit to both provider and consumer!

Overall, this coordinated approach should be some degrees better than an uncoordinated one, but it is customer inefficient. Designed from the perspective of the provider, not the consumer, it may have an element of self-protection for those providers built in to it – "we all worked together and did our best".

Perhaps it is time to really challenge what the process and organisations should look like. If we design the service delivery backwards from the customer to deal with the full range of demands, we would be sure to develop a single "touchpoint".

That is a point at which the state as provider connects with the customer as consumer and which acts as the focus for all of their interactions. That means that customer "demand" would pull through the system those services and interactions needed (and, yes, some people will always need support to identify when they require help). The internal processes, decision systems and hierarchies would exist only to enable the continuing interaction, not to "manage" or "control" it – and certainly not to "ration" the service or add it to the "postcode lottery". The key to "better" for the majority of clients perhaps rests in three dimensions:

- Processes aligned to deliver the customer outcomes – efficiently for both parties;
- Effective capture and use of information – about the customer, the process and its control;
- Adoption of an organisational form in which process improvement, expressed in terms of customer outcome and fulfilment of purpose, is embedded.

Perhaps we should fracture and disrupt the current functional design, cluster services in ways more suited to the 21st century and capitalise on the potential of contemporary technology to integrate services. Some of this is being attempted in the UK with the slow shift to a system called "Universal Credit" which integrates a number of financial benefits; that, however, only addresses the financial dimension. A more thoughtful solution would perhaps be to integrate primary healthcare with primary social care at the very local level and connect the provision of financial benefits (whether benefits payments, local authority taxes or state taxes) to the needs of the individual adult and dependents: a single point of contact assessing all of the needs and facilitating provision of support services which not only address the immediate issue but also assist the individual towards achieving a greater level of independence.

Organising public services: performance

Much reform, in both the private and public sectors, fails because it attempts to overlay process on a functional structure rather than to replace it. The upshot is that cost is added and effectiveness is reduced because more of the resources of the organisation are devoted to managing itself. Our desire should be that state organisations are (or become) intelligent organisations. If levied taxes, in all forms, fund value-enabling activities at national and local levels, then each and every such organisation should seek to fulfil its purpose at the lowest possible cost. The "savings" can be applied to value-generating activity, and that means, as with any organisation, to sustainably do more with less. While the absolute costs of provision of state services may increase as a function of population, they should be managed in a manner that continually seeks to meet the desired customer outcome while lowering the cost per transaction.

We have already established that very large organisations are difficult, if not impossible, to communicate through and with. Functional hierarchies and centralisation of control compound the problem, yet that is how many state organisations are arranged. Long-established institutional structures also mean that such organisations are often unconsciously profligate – that is, rooted in Weberian bureaucracy, legitimate "rational-legal" authority (Pugh & Hickson, 1989). They have no mechanism by which they can be conscious of waste. Waste, or inefficiency, is embedded in the interfaces between long-established procedures in such a manner as to be invisible. Managed essentially the way they have been managed for 100 years or more, they are bureaucratic (in the pejorative sense), fragmented, siloed and might be considered as "suprahumanly autopoietic" (Robb, 1989), beyond human control. Their costs, embedded in the inefficiency of historic structures, cannot even be meaningfully identified let alone reduced. This is, of course, not a new phenomenon; for the history buffs, take a look at the diaries of Samuel Pepys (Latham & Williams, 1978).

Whilst there has been much change in recent years that change has essentially been delivered within the established model of organisation. It is likely, therefore, that if or when the pressure for change is relieved or if there is a change of political will then the "system", paradigm unchallenged, will revert to its previous state; that is, the organisation will revert to the pursuit of its own ends (pathological autopoiesis), and as a result the costs will grow and services will deteriorate. Unless we act to change the underlying process, the system behaviour will reassert itself.

The public sector is not alone in exporting process inefficiency to its customers. Supermarkets and other retailers use "self-scan" tills ostensibly as a means of reducing queuing with the beneficial effect (for them) of outsourcing the cost of labour to the customer. They have not reduced waste in the system or its overall cost; they have simply displaced some elements of it to the customer. Online retailers, in some cases, offer "low-cost" delivery by providing collection points in local shops or other areas. Again, they have not reduced the cost; they have displaced it so that it is now borne by the customer in terms of time. Perhaps the salvation for public services would be achieved by them being managed as intelligent organisations instead of being major employers of good staff let down by a bad system they are powerless to change.

Information systems

It is always comical when, following some failure or another (it matters not what; the list is endless), a Minister of the State is reported in the press, usually apologising and pronouncing that "lessons will be learned". Well, guess what? They won't. Lessons often cannot be learned, or where they might be learned they cannot be implemented. The institutional structures and the information systems (or lack of them) get in the way. If the information systems are not designed to enable and support learning (by both individuals and the organisation), and the system of incentives acts to keep things the same, then the only sure bet is that another very similar failure will happen in the future.

Nothing here should suggest that public sector organisations have not attempted to change. There are examples of successful investment in information systems which have delivered significant gains. Though it probably pains any UK taxpayer to say so, the changes in HMRC (tax collection) systems over recent years have indeed made the process of paying our taxes much simpler and more transparent even if not entirely painless. So, it can be done.

However, this short list of examples and their financial scale demonstrates the point being made here:

- C-Nomis (National Offender Management Information System), budget £234m, spend £700m, abandoned;
- NHS National IT Programme, budget £2.3bn, spend £12.4bn, dismantled;
- National Identity Card Scheme, estimated cost £5.4bn, scrapped on repeal of act of parliament.

I could go on, but I won't.

We appear always to be trying to solve process and information problems with technology solutions. That is bound to fail. If we are to revolutionise public services, then as information-hungry, information-driven organisations we need to get the basic things right. I do believe that effective investment in information is the best way to transform public services in any country. But "effective" is the key. If the investments are to be effective, then we cannot make them, or make them work, without understanding

- the needs and wants of the citizens that the services address;
- the purpose of the particular public service, the outcomes required;
- the decisions that need to be made *and* the information required to make them;
- the processes, tasks, procedures, skills and behaviours that are required to fulfil the purpose;
- the data structure necessary to underpin decisions, processes, tasks and procedures;
- the mapping of the informational and organisational architectures;
- how to separate the information structure (which, like the organisation, is semi-fixed) from the variable data that flow through it.

We cannot do that within the existing, centralising, functional structures. We must change the system. This next vignette shows us what happens when we do.

University College London Hospital (UCLH): Digital Transformation

UCLH has embarked on a digital transformation that will enable it to deliver substantial efficiency and productivity gains while demonstrating increasingly effective use of its funding. UCLH is adopting a data-driven bed management and resource allocation methodology that aim to increase throughput, reduce delays and cancellations and improve utilisation of all resources, whether human or material. A project to deliver both a Coordination Centre Programme and an electronic health records system (EHRS) was launched (after extensive preparation) in October 2017 to stimulate this change.

The diagnosis of the prior situation was that operational management of care delivery rested on outdated systems involving manual data capture and transmission and whiteboards in a variety of locations across the very large, multisite, campus. The unreformed approach to operational management meant there was no live or real-time understanding of the status of the hospital as a whole, let alone its numerous wards and specialist units. This inhibited effective decision-making, including resource allocation, case escalation and prioritisation, with a negative impact on patients, their relatives and supporters and both clinical and non-clinical staff. The impact was felt on patient flow, clinical outcomes and, of course, delays of various sorts.

UCLH embarked on an organisation-wide transformation programme to ensure the efficient delivery of the best patient care possible. The two elements of the programme were the following:

- *Coordination Centre: to assess and improve core operational processes;*
- *EHRS: to bring care and clinical information together and enable research and education.*

The vision is to remove operational frustrations and ensure that the hospital delivers excellent care all of the time. There were three elements to the scope:

- *A standardising of relevant processes in conjunction with an operational management system to optimise patient flow;*
- *A real-time locating system focused on tracking of assets and patients through theatres and other areas of clinical procedure;*
- *A physical coordination centre with hospital-wide visibility of operational flows to enable optimisation of bed deployment as well as improved demand and capacity planning.*

Key improvement areas were aimed at delivering greater visibility, better informing daily clinical decisions, auto-discharge of patients, auto-despatch of porters and bed cleaners, real-time tracking of assets and enhanced reporting and decision-making. It was expected that from this project UCLH would be able to develop more effective data analytics and predictive tools and could adopt the idea of "dashboards" to ensure consistent, near real-time deployment of information.

Immediate post Launch

As with any major change, particularly in a very traditional organisation, there were a number of challenges post launch. The technical side, notwithstanding some relatively minor niggles with the technology, went well. More challenging was the change in process, not because of resistance – quite the opposite. However, with such a large, distributed and diverse population of staff working a variety of shift patterns, it was always going to be a significant task to develop consistency in the interpretation of the new processes. Early dashboards shared at meetings showed how those differences in interpretation were affecting performance, and significant additional effort was put into achieving consistency through further training and support.

A particular example was the use of "Ready to Move", (a concept developed by TeleTracking), a signifier to be triggered on the system when a patient's status was meeting that condition, for example for transport to a different unit. The expectation was that the trigger point meant what was said. However, some staff on some units were triggering when the patient was "nearly" ready to move. Investigation highlighted that this was caused partly by different interpretations of the training, partly because "everybody knows there will be a delay", so some staff were factoring that delay in to their timing. It did not, of course, take long for other staff to recognise this trait and modify their response time accordingly ("x is never ready when they say they are – no rush") with the consequence risk of compounded delays. The data revealed when a "Ready to Move" input was followed shortly afterwards by a "Job Delayed" input, enabling identification of emerging problem areas where further or refresh training was required.

The project team rapidly got to grips with this, with targeted training, reminding relevant people of the process and the need for adherence to it, and gradually over time damping down the variances. This is one of those processes that will require constant monitoring and refresh training. As in any organisation, there is a risk of process decay as staff move on and new staff are appointed. Without continuing reinforcement of the process, lack of understanding of how the whole system works will allow errors in use to creep back in.

The project team have delivered significant benefits to UCLH through their use of the data now being provided by the systems. Data has subsequently been used to underpin the development of improvements in working practice, changes in shift patterns for some colleagues to align staff availability more closely to demand, and to demonstrate, using statistical process control charts, that processes are under control and to highlight scope for improvement. With a process "under control" the scope for improvement rests in change to that process since other causes of error or variation have been reduced or eliminated. One challenge the team needed to address was to ensure that aggregation of data was not arithmetically masking error. This risk occurs when reporting as "in control" at the whole-hospital or whole-unit level, a process might be "out of control" at a lower embedded level – but the "signal" from that becomes "noise" at the higher level of aggregation.

In human terms, when someone asks "how are you?" the tendency is to report "I'm fine, thank you" rather than reporting the toothache or ingrowing toenail that, while locally painful, is insufficient in impact to constitute "not fine" at the level of the whole body!

One characteristic of the system as built has been that its reporting is, essentially, functional rather than processual. That has left the project team and managers across the Trust with the non-trivial task of building what, for Intelligent Organisation, we call "models of self" to allow them to more fully comprehend processes which depend on multiple functions. While building such a model would be non-trivial from a time perspective, it would make excellent use of the available data. It would enable UCLH to more fully visualise where, when and why delays occur, where capacity is being realised and where it is being strained, leading to potential for full optimisation. However successful, there is always scope for further improvement, and the task of a GPF (the role of the author at UCLH is as Guide-Philosopher-Friend) is to push harder and demand more of the system than it is so far giving.

These are, from early post-implementation of the systems, reports of how the changes were experienced were being received:

- *"Fantastic improvement in bed cleaning times";*
- *"Phones are definitely ringing less, we have more time for patient care";*
- *"Seeing the information helps us see what we need in real time and avoid duplication";*
- *"Reports are helping us identify the one thing stopping a patient from being discharged".*

These qualitative reports are supported by quantitative improvements in bed occupancy, bed turnaround times, reduced delays. These figures really do speak for themselves:

- *Time from Emergency Department "Decision to Admit" to "Patient Transfer" reduced from an average of 3 hours 32 minutes in December 2017 to 2 hours 8 minutes in December 2018 – a reduction of 48%;*
- *The number of delayed discharges from the Intensive Therapy Unit to wards from December 2017 to December 2018 – a reduction of 30%;*
- *Bed idle time (from patient leaving to next patient occupying it) down from around 4 hours 50 minutes to under 2 hours 30 minutes – a reduction of 48%;*
- *Bed cleaner response time down from 85 minutes to 58 minutes over 12 months – a reduction of 31%.*

The digital transformation is gathering pace at UCLH.

Public sector: revolution

It may be that public sector organisations are trapped in "managing the present" because there is no mechanism, internal to them, through which they can "create the future" because those decisions are reserved to others. Good people are doing their best despite the system rather than because of it. There is substantial pressure, driven by "austerity measures" (or their local equivalent) to "do more with less", and that translates most often into reducing the number of hierarchical levels, consolidation of small units into larger ones, outsourcing of some elements and reduced numbers of staff working harder to produce the same outputs. Some of this change might be reasonable, much of it might not.

When

- a chief constable announces that his force will be bankrupt in three years;
- a local authority reduces the frequency of bin emptying;
- an ambulance service, sanctioned by government, reclassifies types of emergency so that it achieves targets;
- a railway decrees that a train is "on time" as long as it is no more than ten minutes late; or
- a health authority "rations" one treatment and records a surplus on another,

then something is wrong: the attention of the organisation is focused on itself, not its customers. The system reports better performance while the service gets worse.

Effective change requires a customer-oriented, structural, processual, informational and behavioural revolution. We must learn to do the right thing right, not the wrong thing better.

What is needed to drive public sector transformation is not an improved version of "what is" but a coherent vision of "what could be". Managers and leaders must not continue to be imprisoned in an inadequate MoS that simply delivers budget cuts (compliance to procedure) but must be liberated into thinking about what is possible, about realising the potential of the organisation in terms that meet the outcomes for customers.

We might expect clear leadership from government ministers, but perhaps this can only meaningfully be given at the level of policy. They are, after all, not often technical experts in the area of governance for which they have responsibility. We should not, cannot, expect them then to provide technical leadership. Hence, in the absence of a guiding mind from government, the leaders of the various organisations must develop that vision of what could be, propose it as the way forward and then make it happen. This will require government to liberate these organisational leaders to become active co-creators of the future rather than passive administrators. While ministers may hold the power of decision, they can only make choices about "what" between the options that they are presented with by their party or by policy advisers. The "how" is in the gift of the public administration, and that is where the opportunity for change resides. Government must decide, with the electorate, whether to provide a particular service and how much of it there will be. Public servants can determine how and how well it is done.

Public services are always, at the organisational level, value enabling. They are there to let the rest of the country function – its commerce, utilities, enterprise and so on. Internally, though, they are split like any other organisation. They have elements which are value generating, that deliver current services to current customers to meet current outcomes. Some are focused on value enabling, supporting the provision of current services, developing future services and products, preparing things for tomorrow and enabling national adaptation to changes in the world. Whole functions of government must be reorganised to reflect this, and it may be that, when we are considering this, the functional split of public services needs to be challenged. There might be more effective ways of organising public service to be both more effective and more efficient. In the UK the consolidation of HM Inland Revenue and HM Customs into HM Revenue and Customs appears to have delivered such benefits. Work is going on to integrate some aspects of health and social care provision at both national and local levels, to deliver digital transformations in healthcare, in systems of taxation. Perhaps there is scope for more?

Summary

This chapter has looked briefly at some particular challenges faced by public sector organisations, considering in particular their freedom to act, their clarity (and breadth) of purpose, their structures and the ways in which information is, and could be, used. The potential for change has been highlighted, and it remains substantial.

It is difficult, in the abstract, to say how much might be gained in performance, but experience suggests that, simply by eradicating duplication of data capture and enhancing information provision, a change of the order of 20% could be achieved in most organisations. That benefit would be amplified by reductions in delays; information being more readily available, then decisions could be made more quickly. Savings would start to arise across the system in consequence. Seddon (2005, 2008) frequently refers to "waste" in the public sector and provides examples. His case studies are well worth reading, rooted as they are in a systemic approach to reform. He gives this example (2005): "The estimated he and his staff spent only 40% of their time organizing services for drug users – the rest of their time was consumed by producing paper plans and reports for Whitehall". Some public services are "pure" information processers (e.g. pensions, social security), others use information to drive processes (e.g. clinical decision-making), but *all* must become intelligent organisations. They must examine the interaction of their structures, processes, behaviours and information, challenge established practices and synthesise a whole new way of being. That is how they will, sustainably, do more with less.

15

THE INDIVIDUAL AS INTELLIGENT ORGANISATION

Introduction

The principles of Intelligent Organisation apply as much to each of us as individuals as they do to organisations fitting a more conventional definition. The previous two chapters have discussed how the state might be organised to better support the individual, maintain the legitimacy of government and deliver efficient, effective public services. It is clear that all of us will need that support at some stage in our lives, some more than others (Hills, 2015), but surely, as much as it is an obligation for the state to be sustainable, so it is our obligation to ourselves and each other to be as self-reliant, as sustainable, as we can be. That way we minimise the need for support or intervention by the state or other actors and ensure that our resources, provided to the state through taxation, are available to support those who really need them.

Career and "job-for-life" certainties seemingly once offered by major employers were perhaps a reality for a generation or two but are increasingly rare and, in the contemporary environment, unrealistic for both employer and employee. Because of the emerging "gig" economy of temporary, casual, often part-time work enabled by latest technologies, continuing growth in the number of small enterprises, uncertainty of continuity of employment and the pursuit of "work-life balance" suggest that we should all consider ourselves as organisations, individual intelligent organisations. We must just as much invest in our physical, mental and social well-being as in our economic well-being. To enable individual sustainability, we must generate and enable value for ourselves, be self-organising, deliver outputs, achieve outcomes, manage our information, balance our resources and, importantly, do that in the context of work, family, friends and other relationships, the networks that support and enable our lives. We must create our own futures and, through all of that, nurture our identity, the set of values and beliefs that define us and our relationship with the world.

It's Tuesday – I must be Kate

It is common for us to grant equivalence to processes and roles (one role = one job), especially in a functional hierarchy. However, the intelligent individual will occupy more than one role (both in and out of work environments) and often several more. While the physical "self" is indivisible, most of us occupy multiple roles in different parts of our networks.

One day, as my wife was leaving the house to go to work, I asked her what she was up to that day. She stopped, thought for a while and said: "It's Tuesday – I must be Kate."

She understood that people fulfil roles and those roles often differ from day to day. That day she would be fulfilling another's teaching duties. While we are each indivisible, we each carry out multiple roles, typically as employees, partners, parents, children. We need to think about how we organise our "selves" in order to fulfil those roles – minimising tension, maximising effectiveness. We need to be able to see ourselves as organisations.

If we, the individuals who constitute our organisations are not adaptive, not learning, then we inhibit the ability of the organisation to adapt. That may offer some relatively short-term benefit to us, perhaps, by preserving a role or way of working that suits our needs. However, in a rapidly changing technological environment, particularly one in which the growth of "smart" things is coupled to mass data collection and rapid rudimentary developments in artificial intelligence, some skills and knowledge will no longer be required from individuals. We can ultimately be made redundant by these changes (Kaplan, 2015), or we can learn, adapt and use them as opportunities.

Managing my "self": value generation

I imagine readers may have located themselves in the model of the Intelligent Organisation like this:

I am an employee: what is my process, what are the tasks and procedures, and who is my manager?

Or

I am a manager: what process do I manage, what output am I trying to achieve, and what are my inputs?

However, each of us both carries out our processes, tasks and procedures *and* is to some significant degree self-managing. We are each both worker and manager. The requirements, activities and skills may be different for each part, but all must be done. We have to be multi-competent (skilled and knowledgeable). It is not enough just to know how to do our job; we must also be able to deal with money, relationships, systems and plans or strategies and imbue it all with a sense of our purpose.

Most writers would here present a case study of a mythical individual, but all readers would recognise that it was really about the author. Here, I don't pretend. It makes me uncomfortable to write, yet perhaps it will make you think.

At the beginning of the book we discussed the idea of the "model of self", the need for an organisation to constitute a representation of itself so that it can be "self-aware", so that it can observe itself in relation to its environment. The same is true for each of us as individuals: we must be self-aware and understand the impact of what we do (or don't do) on ourselves and on each other. Picking up from the previous section, we must recognise that, unless you are a hermit – in which case it is not likely that you are reading this – each of us exists at the centre of an individual network (figure 15.1), one which includes our future self (selves) and is symbiotic, bringing benefits and obligations, rights and responsibilities.

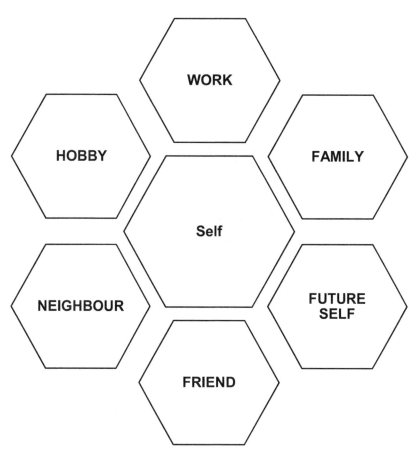

FIGURE 15.1   Self at the centre of the network

There is only one physiological me, a "self" that eats, sleeps, drinks and ages but I fulfil a number of roles in parallel. I have several selves; I am contemporaneously (and sometimes simultaneously)

- husband and father,
- researcher and scientist,
- consultant and educator,
- volunteer.

Each of these value-generating instances of my self represents one way in which I am my self, processes through which my "purpose" is fulfilled. It is through these activities that I express my identity to the world and that the world engages with me (it is my environment). This is all represented in figure 15.2.

Some of these processes are more obviously economic work than others, but they cannot be separated from the aggregate, indivisible me and I must balance my

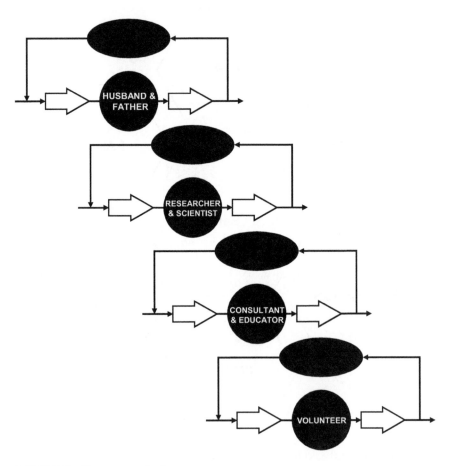

FIGURE 15.2 Processes and roles

time and energy (my principal resources) across them. Each has benefits, obligations, a desired outcome. Each has inputs, outputs, process, structure, decisions; each requires skills and behaviours; each generates and uses information to enable me to self-regulate. While the value-generating self of "husband and father" draws most heavily on emotion, behaviours and skills, my "consultant and educator" self relies most heavily on process, structure, analysis and synthesis. "Researcher and scientist" demands analysis and synthesis with a strong process element and draws on a different blend of skills and behaviours. "Volunteer" calls on the whole range of skills and behaviours but is modified to suit the particular circumstances of working with other volunteers. Skills and behaviours are an infrastructure, an underpinning set of capabilities, available to be drawn on as required by each "self". They are transferable between roles, each is common to the other selves and blended according to the needs of the relationships in that role, each requiring that multiple competencies be brought to bear, requiring self-awareness, my inner senior management.

For each self I must

- focus on the desired outcome;
- understand how the intended process output enables that;
- provide the necessary inputs;
- observe the output of the process and modify the inputs to improve my performance – to be a "better" self, a reflective cycle of learning and adaptation.

Being self-managing, I must also hold myself to account by considering

- whether I achieved the outcome expected by "customer" – whether that be my wife, children, client, research community, stakeholder – and
- whether I need to change my skills, processes, standards, behaviours to improve myself.

It is critically important that I apply corrective action to the right self and that I do not apply the wrong skill to any particular process. When my wife is telling me about something happening for one of her "selves", it is perhaps unhelpful for me to explain to her how she could go about resolving it (my consultant self) when what she wants is to be listened to (my husband self). Think about this in relation to your partner, your children, your boss, and your colleagues.

I need to balance my resources across my four "selves". I must both manage each individual process *and* manage the management of them so that intended outcomes are achieved and that effort and outputs are balanced to meet the needs of all of my stakeholders: my wife, children, clients, students, collaborators. That necessitates a higher order control loop (figure 15.3), (meta)self-management, a "senior management", a logically higher order decision-making function capable of comprehending and balancing the competing demands of each self with the others and with the needs and opportunities of the network that supports me.

I am, then, like most people, quite a complex self, living what Handy (1985) called a "portfolio" life. In order to remain in a state of relative equanimity, I must

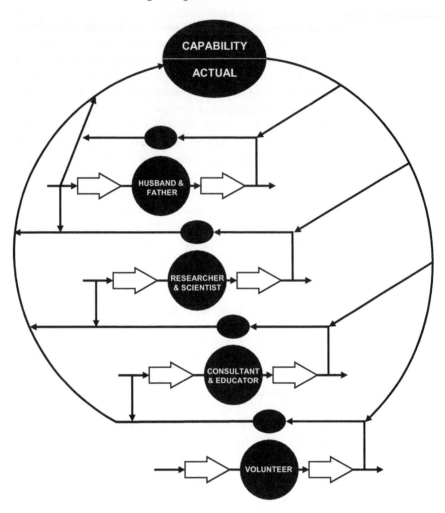

FIGURE 15.3 Managing my selves

balance the demands and priorities of each role against the others. I must consider the ways in which process, skill and data need to be blended to allow each to happen, and I must consider how to manage my knowledge. How do the things I experience and learn about in one of my roles inform both that role and others?

The value-generating selves deal only with the things I do already, their existence says nothing of other things I might do tomorrow. How do I adapt to changes in my self, my relationships and my environment?

Before you move to the next section, you could usefully spend some time thinking about your own life in this way:

- What roles do you fulfil (in work and out of it)?
- What processes are you responsible for conducting and managing?
- How do you balance your time and effort across those roles and processes?

- How do you hold yourself to account?
- How do you adapt and learn?

It may be that in considering those questions you find sources of tension in your life which could be resolved through this understanding. Draw your model of self using the conventions in figure 15.3 and make a note of your various environments.

Managing my "self": value enabling

Value-generating activity must be complemented with value-enabling activity: the maintenance and development of the underpinning infrastructure of behaviours, skills, knowledge and beliefs and the making of choices about the future.

Our current "selves" are subject to opportunity and threat, to changes in the environment and to changes in us (our mental, physical and economic well-being) and to our hopes and aspirations. Many of those things that look stable and certain may be impermanent, transient and changeable, regardless of whether we want them to be! While we don't have to grow up (the psychological maturity of adulthood often evidenced through improved impulse control), we do grow older. Our lives change: young people who were dependent on us become independent, or they depend on others, or perhaps we come to depend on them. In work the processes and tasks we carry out are challenged by changes in working practices, in technology, in market demand. Most of us cannot guarantee a future employment market for our skills – and the more narrowly drawn the skill set, the greater the challenge.

The value-enabling challenge is to think about the future, to consider the threats and opportunities in our individual environments and to consider what changes may be necessary, or desirable, to continue to fulfil our individual purposes. That requires the development of a model of the model of self (MoMoS), an understanding of "who I am". Self-aware, we need to become aware of our environment, the people, organisations and circumstances which influence us and which we influence. Through that we can comprehend the choices available to us – choices which may include ending one or more roles, adding one or more roles or selecting a different environment in which to operate. Comparison of where we are with where we aspire to be helps to determine what changes are necessary or desirable.

There is a big distinction between "necessary" and "desirable". "Necessary" is a response to any threats to the continuation of my current selves. "Desirable" is a response to opportunities and unfulfilled aspirations. It could demand the realignment of "what I do" with "what I wish to do". The outcome is to develop a strategy which leads to a better "self", one which is more closely aligned to "the person I want to be". In simple terms it would perhaps make "me" more content. There is a debate in the psychology literature about the extent to which we can really understand our selves, given that we all have what Wilson (2002) calls an "adaptive unconscious", an inner self that we cannot access. However, our concern here is with the things that we do, the ways we express ourselves to the world, and these are, or can be, a matter of conscious choice, whatever the underlying "story of me" that we tell ourselves to justify them.

Back to my personal case.

While my autonomy is willingly constrained by membership of the higher order organisation (my family) and the choices made with its members, my operational selves (how I express myself to the world) are largely a function of the choices I make, not fate nor the dictates of any other person. I recognise that I am fortunate in being able to say that. My choices then can be informed by the things that I value. Value, for any individual, needs to consider both intrinsic and extrinsic factors. Intrinsic factors are those, such as the sense of self-worth, that arise from being true to one's self. Extrinsic reward means being valued for who we are, not simply for what we do, and having a sense of belonging, esteem, prestige and, of course, earnings.

Given finite resources, I must operationally balance my energy across my four "selves" as long as they exist. Strategically, I can make choices about them. I could change or rebalance the investment of resources around "researcher and scientist", "consultant and educator" or "volunteer". The role of husband and father is subject to change in the way it is articulated over time (Handy, 1989). Like any relationship, my relationships with my wife and children must be invested in if they are to be sustained.

The operational environments of my four selves are relatively discrete, but they have some overlaps either of clients, relationships, services, skills, geography. However, when it comes to considering the whole self and the problematic future, they come together in a single place. This is partly because of the overlap but mainly because opportunities or threats in one implies potential for change which necessarily has implications for the others; remember that resources are finite. Taking a systemic approach, if I shift the boundary or limits of one articulation, changing the time or energy required for its fulfilment, to some extent I will take something from the others. Somehow we must continually rebalance resources across all activities in order to retain our state of allostasis, dynamic stability.

While it would be too grand to suggest that every individual has anything as formal as a "strategy", there is a need to pursue personal growth, psychological rather than physiological. For me, I want to be a "smarter" business not a bigger business (or indeed a bigger person). No individual can remain static. "Business as usual" means, at the very least, continuing adaptation to the changing circumstances of the environment. That requires, however informally, self-reflection following the same essential pattern of enquiry as any other organisation.

We all perhaps dream about possible alternative futures. Indeed, Maltz (2001) argues that we must visualise the future we want and then we will change our actions in order to achieve it. He may have a point. The challenge for each of us is to understand how we should adapt our "posture" in relation to our world. Where there is tension between these things, that tension is resolved by reference to our identity, the sense of "self" and choices about those things which we value most, which include time, energy, money, but perhaps most fundamentally are about relationships and contentment. In considering the idea of entrepreneurship (Beckford,

1993), I wrote of a decision cycle for each individual considering their future which, adapted here, looked at the following.

- Mission: the purpose each seeks to fulfil;
- Objectives: the attributes of knowledge and skill needed by the individual;
- Environment: the context and the opportunity;
- Self-assessment: consideration of personal and network capability and reach;
- Self-determination: understanding the risks and challenges and discovering the tools to address them.

We require information, however imperfect, and it will be imperfect, about the future environment(s) in which our operations will be carried out. These are the networks of professional relationships, the changing needs and desire of family and so on. Each of those networks of relationships needs to be authentically invested in, managed and farmed for long-term sustainability – otherwise they will decay. Meanwhile we must distinguish between those relationships which reward investment (increase contentment in one way or another) and those which simply drain energy; we can then make informed choices about them. Wrapped around all of these are the political, technological, social and economic factors that influence each of them.

We require information about our "selves". What desires and ambitions can be fulfilled through the network of relationships? What skills and knowledge can be used (or need to be acquired) in order to maintain mutual value exchange? What is the capability to provide value to each? What is the capacity that might be available to each one – and how does that balance against the possible demand? This covers our "HR" function – skills, knowledge and behaviour.

In a perfect world there are perhaps more opportunities than there is capacity. The decisions then become about allocation of scarce resources to most rewarding opportunities whilst effectively countering any threats and balancing opportunity against desire and intent. The overall process is outlined in figure 15.4.

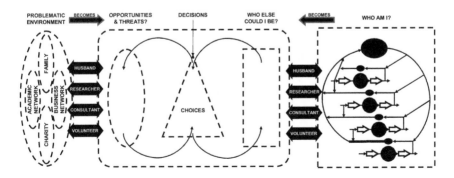

FIGURE 15.4   Enabling value for the individual

Development and maintenance of authentic relationships require investment of time over time with significant fluctuations in both workload and cash flow. As any self-employed individual or small business will confirm, there is a tendency towards famine and feast. There is either too much to do and a struggle to deliver it or not enough to do with consequently poor cash flow. Each of us must manage our finances to ensure that there is sufficient funding to support current costs and investment in the development of existing and new relationships. Funding is a key enabler of both current and future activity. Any attempt to shorten the "new business" development cycle risks moving from an authentic relationship based on mutual trust and respect to one which is purely transactional with possible short-term benefits but a high risk of long-term loss. In a commercial world addicted to the lowest cost for each transaction, a business model built on establishing authentic relationships based on integrity, trust and a shared comprehension of value may appear heretical, but for sustainability of all parties, it is essential.

The thinking equally applies to each of us seeking personal sustainability, whether we are self-employed or employed. We each must keep adapting to survive; the question is whether with each year passing we gain new and different experience, which perhaps implies making new mistakes, or whether we simply repeat the experience of the past.

It is not enough, of course, to have authentic relationships and enough working capital to survive. We must determine what work we will do and, if appropriate, with which organisations. Choices here depend upon both a rich understanding of the self in terms of skills, knowledge and competencies and the set of preferences that support their effective application.

The opportunities I seek in my problematic environment and the relationships in which I am investing time, energy and money must contain challenges and problems amenable to my skills and knowledge. I must find individuals and organisations which share my essential values and are willing to hire those skills to apply to suitable problems.

So much is common sense.

Again, before moving to the next section, give some thought to these questions:

- Where are you in relation to your goals and objectives?
- Where do you aspire to be and why?
- What opportunities are there?
- What constraints are there?
- What risks do you face?
- In order to fulfil your purpose what could you change about your

  - roles?
  - goals?
  - objectives?
  - skills?
  - behaviours?

Draw on figure 15.4 to assemble a picture of your options and choices.

Managing my "self": autonomy

The application of the decision model is to my "professional" selves rather than the personal as these are the ones which require management. It is part of the legal definition of "self-employment" in the UK that the individual enters a "contract for services" in which the client specifies the output required but the contractor specifies the means and methods and, often, provides the tools. There can be, then, no particular "process" specified by the client and there is a lot of autonomy for the individual.

To attempt to operate as a consultant and have no process at all would smack of "dilettantism" (Weber, 1924), and so over many years a generic consulting process rooted in cybernetic thinking and called "VSMethod"[(webref 24)] has been evolved and made public. This provides the minimum necessary framework to conduct projects but, being generic, draws heavily on a range of skills and knowledge about clients, processes, skills, behaviours and performance.

The star (figure 15.4) represents my perception of my position for each element. Looking at the business model, my activity is low volume, high value. I am perhaps involved in delivering between three and five projects at any one time (although there should be another three or so in development at the same time to ensure continuity of work and income). Turning to the "process progression" element, I have selected a position between generic (the use of VSMethod) and customised. It is reasonable to say that all the projects I undertake are rooted in the same essential methodology, but each is customised to the particular needs and circumstances of the client.

Consistent with that, on the skills progression continuum I have classified myself as a seasoned professional. Justification for that is in two underpinning sets of information. The first is about formal training and qualifications: these are sufficient to justify "professional". The second set of information is about "seasoning". This is not a function of age but of experience and exposure. Here I can evidence experience with a wide range of clients, a range of different industries, private, public and third-sector organisations, international experience and, very importantly, a progression of engagement from small local projects to large national and international projects over a long period of time. These can be regarded as sufficient to justify "seasoned".

Risk I have rated as low probability, low consequence (although close to the border on both). No work I undertake carries with it more than minimal risk of injury or death to me or others. Advice and guidance that I give is not insubstantial to the clients and can have significant business impact on finance, people and systems, so it is non-trivial.

Finally, I have considered alignment of personal, organisational and professional interest, and here I am lucky. I am in a position where I can actively seek to manage and sustain a position where the tensions between these three things are resolved, and I am able to act in a manner which maintains that position, but only over time. At any particular time I may be leaning more towards one than the others.

While "no man is an island", I need to sustain a position in which my processes, skills and behaviours generate results and outputs that are of value to my various

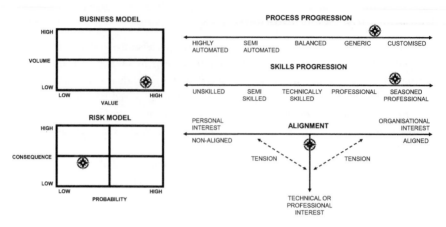

FIGURE 15.5 Autonomy

clients. I am in a position where a high level of autonomy seems appropriate and justified. To maintain that position, I must ensure that my generic process remains appropriate and fit for purpose – a question that will be visited in the final chapter. The focus of my attention in enabling value must be on the development of the skills and knowledge I bring to bear on the challenges faced by my clients. To be content I need to maintain the alignment between my personal, organisational and professional selves.

Using figure 15.5 try to establish a picture of your state of autonomy. Think about where you are aligned and think about why you are in those positions. Which ones might you want to change and why?

Managing my "self": identity

I am sure it will come as no surprise that the combination of value-generating with value-enabling activity brings us to Dudley's trialogue (Dudley, 2000). The activity of nurturing identity is, for the individual, a process of discerning what is important to them, their values and beliefs and of testing whether they are acting in accordance with them. Acting in a manner consistent with your espoused identity (that is, being true to yourself) dissolves tension between the present and the future. There is a whole catalogue of literature to help with this from religious sources to self-help manuals, calling in at the already mentioned psychology literature along the way. I will not seek to guide you here but refer you to that literature.

Summary

This chapter has attempted to articulate the idea of the intelligent individual, one capable of adaptation and change. To avoid embarrassing others it has drawn extensively on the way I see and interpret myself in my world. I could, of course, be completely wrong about myself, especially if we are, as Wilson (2002) suggests, "strangers to ourselves".

In writing this, I hope that you will take the time to give some thought to yourself here, a little appropriate selfishness. To try and illuminate our world in a different way, to see it from a different perspective, can often lead us to find a new way ahead.

16

DISSOLVING THE CHALLENGE

Introduction

Creating an intelligent organisation is not about achieving a finite end but about creating a set of structural, informational and behavioural conditions which enable the continual evolution of the organisation in concert with its environment and its current and future customers. Intelligent Organisation emerges when individuals are free to do the right thing for the customer, the organisation and themselves. The thinking may be considered idealistic in places, it is distinctly non-conformist, even heretical (even if it now looks like common sense now that you have read this far), so if you decide to pursue it, don't expect to be popular or be given an easy time!

Realising this idealised way of thinking about how we should manage organisations may be challenging but we must try, because trying will get us closer to where I and, I hope, you think we should be. We should be synthesising behaviours and process through the use of information to achieve organisational purposes, satisfy customers, maximise productivity and minimise waste! As has been shown throughout the book, the potential for both social and economic gains is substantial.

I aim in this chapter to offer an outline of ideas for applying the thinking to any particular organisation. Please take notes, use the models and diagrams as inspiration (hold to the principles and conventions) and, of course, read again the chapters as you go – they are presented in the way they are to make it easier for you to use. The intention is to stimulate your thinking. It will not lead you to an easy answer or a prescription but to a more useful way of thinking about your organisation and how it might be better. That will be the measure of usefulness of the model.

You

The transformation of an entire organisation is not something to be undertaken lightly. The task if not led by the "C-suite", (chief executive, chief transformation officer, chief information officer) needs at the very least the positive engagement of the executive and non-executive leaders of the organisation. If you are not in one of those leadership positions, then you need to be directly and closely engaged with them, and their sponsorship of the process must be visible to all. There is no doubt that implementing the principles of Intelligent Organisation is a leadership role and challenge. You can, of course, lead change in parts of an organisation from less senior positions – and you should seek to do so – but you will be constrained by lack of autonomy (see chapters 7 and 8)!

It may be worth at this point briefly revisiting the "model of self" I suggested you draw up in chapter 15. Consider yourself as an intelligent organisation and reflect on whether the person you think you are and the person you need to be to address this challenge are aligned. Do you have

- the technical skills?
- the knowledge?
- the authority (whether explicit or implicit)?
- the skills of communication in persuasion and attraction?
- the support and resources you need or access to them?

Can you articulate the opportunity or threat in the environment of the organisation to others sufficiently well to draw their support? Most importantly, does the outcome matter enough to you that you can find the courage and persistence?

The GPF

You, me, none of us will be able to address this undertaking alone. Aside from the support needed internally, you will need to be able to thoughtfully draw on external expertise. This is partly to enrich and challenge your analysis and review of the current situation, partly to bring in specialist expertise where the organisation does not already retain the skills or knowledge necessary. Critically, in leading the process you will need a confidante, someone with whom worries and fears can be shared, a sounding board with whom ideas and thoughts can be explored. That person must also have a strong grasp of the principles of the model, and they must be able to help you in testing progress against the ideal state and limiting the drift back to tradition.

Stafford Beer suggested that the role of the consultant in this regard is a triple of guide, philosopher, friend (GPF), and that is both well phrased and appropriate. The guide helps to interpret and translate the map and instructions, offering insight and suggestions on the next steps. The philosopher comprehends the thinking that underpins both the model and the need for change in the organisation and assists in translating the thoughts into practical actions. The friend offers support and challenge, probably in equal measure, probably whether they are wanted or not! When the process gets tough – and overcoming the inertia of the status quo, the entrenched positions, does get tough – the friend is essential to the process.

What the GPF must not do, cannot do, is undertake the process for you. If the transition to Intelligent Organisation is going to succeed, the ideas must be owned, disseminated, shared, the difficult decisions supported internally, the work of change undertaken by those who do the work of the organisation. This transition cannot be handed over to consultants to "analyse, recommend and implement" some changes: that will simply fail. It would fail to respect the principles of the model by simply imposing a different set of constraints on the staff. It would also fail because once the pressure to change is relieved (and it always is) the organisation would revert to its previous behaviours. Pemberton (2014) describes the relationship between a smoker and a cigarette as abusive, one in which the smoker "loves" the cigarette while knowing it is bad for them. They need to recognise this abuse in order to stop smoking. We might regard "we've always done it like that" and "the way we do things around here" as, if not the abuser of our organisations, at least its addiction. It is always, in the short term, easier, cheaper, quicker to do what we have always done. Everybody knows how, and no investment is needed in training, in equipment, in management; the job can unthinkingly be done. In the medium- and long-term we are then overtaken by others who innovate, develop new ways of thinking, doing and being that which offer advantages to customers, staff, costs and value and who render us redundant. The task of your GPF is to help, support and guide but never to own the change for you.

The organisation

One executive working alone will not, of course, suffice to see through change on the scale envisaged. No one person can have such reach, such influence within the organisation, so they must recruit supporters.

Shared knowledge, common understanding, a different way of thinking disseminated throughout the organisation changes that situation. Once the gaps and potential are understood and accepted, then many of the challenges of intelligent organisation are dissolved. Collective understanding is a large part of any solution. Achieving that understanding necessitates authentic inclusion of relevant people throughout the organisation as the dialogue evolves. It is vitally important, even if the process commences with individual discussion as it usually does, to rapidly move to an inclusive dialogue. These parties must include "those 'involved' (client, decision taker, designer) and those 'affected' but not involved (witnesses)" (Flood and Jackson, (1991) on Ulrich (1983). This inclusive dialogue matters for three reasons. First, in order for the Intelligent Organisation to be survival worthy, the people who create its "collective consciousness" (Durkheim, 1893) through their interactions need to share its purpose and values. What better way is there to ensure this than to include the people in defining them? This does not mean the abandonment of the organisational goals and ideals, nor an abdication of leadership; rather, it requires that leaders who wish to be effective must persuade and encourage others to share their position.

This is at heart pragmatic. People aligned with the purpose and values are likely to be more strongly motivated towards the desired outcome. Unaligned people, first given the opportunity to appreciate the values and purpose may then exercise their autonomy to join in or not, possibly seeking work elsewhere. Unaligned people remaining within the organisation and either actively or passively resisting its future will be damaging to themselves and their host: "Passive resistance is the most potent weapon ever wielded by man" (Tucker, 1887). The second reason is even more pragmatic. The people who populate the organisation know far more about what customer outcomes are required and how to deliver them than those from outside or their own managers. Engaging them in the process of design just makes sense.

The third reason is again pragmatic. Working towards the idea of Intelligent Organisation is not one process but two, nested inside each other. The first process is that of becoming an intelligent organisation, acquiring the behaviours, skills, processes. The second, and this is where the leadership and GPF are crucial, is in developing reflective cycles so that the people and the organisation acquire the ability to continually develop themselves.

There is a paradox in all this. The principles of Intelligent Organisation require both clarity of leadership and adherence to the ideals of the model because without them it will not work. At the same time the model requires that the autonomy of individuals be as great as possible so each person must choose to support the ideas, or not. This paradox is resolved by the limiting factor of autonomy being "consistent with cohesion of the whole". If an individual chooses not to support the organisation and the chosen course is legitimate (i.e. the authority of the leadership is itself legitimate), then the individual must be free to choose not to be there!

Developing a shared view can draw on a number of approaches; the systems literature in particular incorporate several inclusive methodologies (Beckford, 2017). Here we can also draw on the methodologies developed in the application of the ideas of Intelligent Organisation (webref 25, webref 26). The latter is concerned with the development of a shared understanding between the participants in a conversation. A consultant, a GPF, a friend or mentor works with you – the leader of the Intelligent Organisation transformation – to articulate your understanding of the situation, what is called in figure 16.1 the "client model of problem". This process rests on questions filtered and

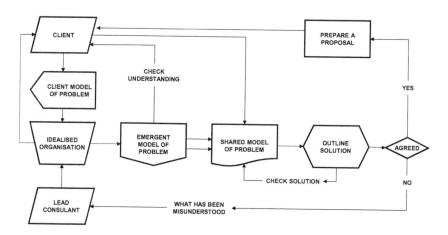

FIGURE 16.1   Developing a shared model

inspired by the GPF's understanding of Intelligent Organisation, from which a model of the problem situation starts to emerge. Through iteration, a reflective cycle, the conversation converges on a shared model, a common understanding of the problem, challenge or opportunity. The conversation constitutes a homeostat, a learning device enabling progress. Once the shared model is achieved, it becomes possible to contemplate options and choices for change and to develop proposals for a way forward. If a shared model is not achieved, then further iterations can be useful though sometimes (I am speaking as a GPF) the divergence of opinion about the model or the solution can be too great. That is a good point to walk away – for both parties!

Diagnosis: seven key questions

Once a first agreement has been reached about the problem and possible alternatives, then a proper diagnostic process can be commenced. Represented in the form of a homeostat (figure 16.2) the desired outcomes are

- a change in the state of your collective knowledge about the organisation below.
- a consideration of its condition compared to the ideal of the Intelligent Organisation;
- a comprehension of its capability (people, process, behaviour, systems) to fulfil its espoused purpose.

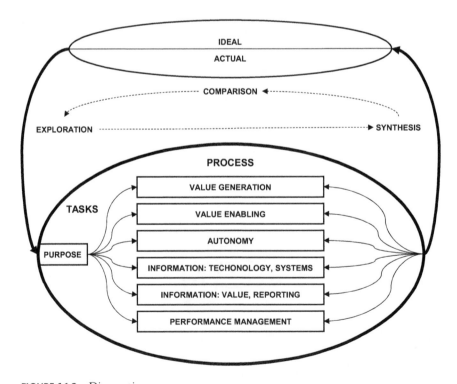

FIGURE 16.2 Diagnostic process

An essential but simple cycle sits at the centre of the figure and is described as:

* Exploration: collecting data about the organisation;
* Synthesis: coalescing that data into an overall understanding;
* Comparison: comparing that with the principles of the Intelligent Organisation.

We pursue coalescence through synthesis, the integration of elements and their interactions from which something new emerges, in this case the emergent understanding of your chosen organisation as intelligent (or not!). Wrapped around the outside of that simple cycle is the fuller process of study which embraces all of the key aspects of the Intelligent Organisation. Each of the headings in the model provides us with a line of enquiry.

What is the purpose of this organisation?

A definition of "purpose" must be developed through an understanding of customers' needs, engagement of the workforce and agreement with the leadership. In the absence of a clear purpose, then, demand will always be infinite and the resources inadequate. Even in the case of what the marketing department would characterise as a "distress purchase", such as the payment of taxes or petrol for a car, defining the desired customer outcome (and including the customer in the process of definition) is critical. A statement of purpose is not a mission statement or a vision. It is a straightforward, operational, measurable definition. For example, if we look at the railway purely as a railway then we might consider the purpose to be "to move people and goods to and from locations on the system" Beckford & Dora, 2013 [webref 27]. This definition codifies the aim, determines who/what the customer is (people and goods) and limits the range (locations on the system). So, our measure of effectiveness would be concerned with the success of the rail journey, and our measure of efficiency would be the minimisation of the resources used:

maximum benefit to travellers at the lowest cost.

Definitions of "effectiveness" and "efficiency" are measurable against that statement of purpose.

Beer (1985) argued that "the purpose of the system is what it does", so in making our diagnosis we need to identify the impacts that the organisation has on its customers and its environment as well as recognising the intent of those who purport to own or manage the system. There is often a gap between the actual outcome and the intent, and that provides the first opportunity for change.

Now you can look at the organisation itself. Is there a clear sense of purpose? Can people articulate to you the reasons the organisation exists? The need or opportunity it seeks to fulfil (beyond the constraint of profit, surplus or budget)?

It is helpful in diagnosis to think about it from the customers' perspective because that helps to broaden organisational thinking. We need to be concerned not with what the organisation does but with what its customer values. For example, an oil company may define itself in terms of its products, very and deliberately simply, of petrol and diesel, and in doing so lock its future into its past. If on the other hand it defines itself in terms of its customers' needs, it could conceive of itself as "a provider of energy" because "energy" is the need that is fulfilled: the specific mechanism by which the energy is provided is not in the long term important. In making that choice, the oil company shows a greater understanding of its customer and, at the same time, opens itself up to new ways of fulfilling that need in the future – for example, in a low-carbon, renewable-energy-based economy.

What are the value-generating processes?

Value-generating processes are the sequences of activities undertaken by the organisation that meet the needs and expectations of its customers. You need to understand what the customer values and ensure that your processes meet their expectations.

Typical value-generating processes include sales, manufacturing or assembly, service or customer support. As you pursue this thinking, try sketching the high level processes and use them to visualise how things fit together (or don't!). Some examples:

- A paper mill had a simple process running backwards from new paper through conversion and production to raw materials;
- A motor dealership does two things that deliver customer outcomes – sell cars and service cars;
- A police force perhaps has two processes – prevention of harm and crime and the detection and arrest of criminals.

The paper mill has a continuous interdependent production process; it just makes paper. The motor dealership operates two processes (sales and service) which are distinct from each other, though they will certainly share some customers. The processes operate on independent time cycles and, perhaps, locations. The police force example is interesting because the better they are at the first, the less they will have to do of the second. If we compare the functional organisation of a police force with these two suggested processes, I wonder if they would align. Similar considerations would apply to fire and rescue, health and social care and any other services where preventative activity is possible.

Your organisation may be distributed (for example, a retailer) addressing the same customer need in multiple locations (branches, shops, countries). The value-generating process should, in principle, be the same everywhere (think fast food) and recur in each location. So you must consider how the organisation reflects (or should reflect) in its structure the distribution of its customers by geography, market, customer or product.

It will be useful here to refer back to the case studies and see how the subject organisations are constructed.

You need ultimately to discern not just the processes themselves but whether things are organised such that people involved have the information, skills, knowledge and authority to both manage current performance and locally adapt it to its future. If any of these elements are absent or weak, then the process will be failing in one or more ways or the higher order management will be compensating by intervening more than should be necessary.

Process definition and diagnosis sprint

One of the key ways of engendering direct support and buy-in to the value-generating *processes is to engage people by having them execute the change in the process from problem definition and diagnosis to implementation.*

Working with James Robbins, then a CIO in the energy sector, we needed to develop a deeper understanding of the core processes of the organisation to reduce the impact of material quality issues. The core process ended with the production of electricity but began at multiple locations in several countries with a process cycle time measured in weeks.

However, the material was difficult to manage and could become dangerous through degradation on its journey. The client was experiencing huge amounts of waste, inefficiency of fuel and HSE fines as a result of a new "greener" process – taking the equivalent of over 3m cars off the road. Prior to using design thinking and systems thinking, their cross-functional international team had failed to resolve the processing. Using data science and systems thinking, a solution was found within 5 days – as described below and implemented shortly after. It enabled the company to reduce average cycle times from 60 days to sub 40 through a range of innovative experiments which reduced degradation and improved efficiency.

An international squad was formed and brought together in London and included people from every stage of the company supply chain supported by sprint facilitators from Market Gravity, data scientists from Oracle, senior management from the company and myself as GPF to James. Over 5 days we collectively

- *mapped the overall process and analysed associated data,*
- *identified 11 opportunities for improvement,*
- *made 24 "bets" to explore,*
- *created 6 experiments to action and*
- *built action plans.*

The process mapping and data analytics phases of the sprint highlighted how important a sound grasp of the data to be used in decision-making can be. A number of areas of previous confusion were resolved through this.

The sprint generated a real change in understanding and ownership of the process, its challenges and opportunities. It delivered potential savings of £1m per annum from possible improvements, created capacity for further change and changed thinking. None of these things are ever perfect; the limits to autonomy were discovered, and the need for real "political" alignment behind the potential transformation was emphasised.

The sprint process proved a powerful way of rapidly developing understanding of the value-generating process.

A useful question to ask is at which level which "process decisions" can be brought together. A clue here: if it is at director or head of function level or, worse, CEO level, then the organisation is not oriented towards its customer but towards itself. Think then about what that tells you of decision-making and autonomy. If routine decisions are being made high up the organisational tree then autonomy is necessarily limited at lower levels. Does that suggest something about the directors? Are they all people with enormous brains and infinite capacity for work? If not, then they are probably being overworked if not overwhelmed. Decision power may be too remote from the value-generating process. Consider what impact that may be having on the customers.

Now that we have established a structural overview of the value-generating processes, a whole range of systems methods and conventional tools and techniques can be brought to bear on the deeper analysis when required. Most typically these can be applied by the people in the organisation (perhaps with some guidance), rather than being wielded by consultants or other external aides. It is important that the organisation and its people own the outcomes of this work.

What are the value-enabling processes?

Value-enabling processes face in two directions. In one direction they face into the organisation providing services and support to the value-generating processes. In the other they face out into the environment of the organisation exploring the emerging opportunities, risks and challenges to be faced. Their overall task is to propose to the organisation actions, changes and activities that will nurture and protect it, that will sustain its future.

Typical value-enabling processes include human resources, finance, information services, technology, systems, procurement, property, quality, health and safety and so on. They are often clustered (IT and procurement with finance, for example) and are most usually managed functionally rather than in an integrated manner.

Human resources can be thought of in this way:

Facing in: recruitment, remuneration, training, industrial relations
Facing out: HR strategy, organisation development

Finance can be considered this way:

Facing in: bookkeeping, payroll, management accounting, cash management
Facing out: statutory accounting, strategic financing, treasury

While the processes may be separate it is almost inevitable that many individuals running those processes will face different ways at different times. One of the hardest things to do is to comprehend and work with the different decisions that facing in two directions implies. The logic is unjammed when we take account of time – what are the decisions that we must take *now* in the light of the current situation, and what do we need to do differently in order to prepare for the future? If we were a motor manufacturer we might, for example, continue to sustain skills in the development and maintenance of internal combustion engines whilst simultaneously beginning to develop skills in electric propulsion technology. In finance we would be simultaneously tightly managing current profitability whilst investing in several emerging products, technologies or markets, knowing that at least some of the investment will be wasted.

The logic of the value-enabling processes is the same as that of the value-generating processes: identify the customer (in this case the value-generating processes) and consider whether the outcome achieved supports them appropriately. If not, then there is a fundamental problem. You need to consider all aspects of the value-enabling process, including the understanding of the desired outcome, the process design itself (is it capable of delivering the outcome?), the skills, knowledge and behaviours of the relevant workforce and the information provision. Any one of those elements being misaligned or inappropriate compromises the performance of the whole.

There are some processes which can be interpreted either as value generating or value enabling. A good example of this can be found in the supply chain, e.g. the provision of materials into a manufacturing flow. The determination of where to place them rests on a couple of criteria. The first is to consider the extent to which the supply chain is integrated (organisationally and informationally) to the value-generating process flow itself. If the organisation is operating a "just-in-time" fully integrated model, then most benefit will be obtained from treating the supply chain as part of the value-generating activity. If on the other hand the flows are disaggregated (i.e. there is a need for a storage or warehousing phase, or the process demand on the supply chain is stochastic or random), then most benefit might be obtained from dealing with them separately. The second is to consider whether the enabling process is, at least in principle, capable of independent existence, i.e. it could be provided by another completely separate organisation. Here we might think about plant maintenance as an example. While the plant itself must be maintained in order for the value-generating process to be sustained, there are genuine choices to be made about whether that maintenance is undertaken within the value-generating suite of activities or within value-enabling. What matters most is that you are aware of the consequences of the decision that you make in this regard.

So, we need to find out whether future-oriented work is being undertaken in a systematic, ordered and thoughtful manner which is offering new opportunities for the future or, if it happens at all, if it is mainly reactive to adverse events either in the wider environment or the organisation itself. It is useful at this point to unearth some of the myths and stories that pervade the atmosphere of every organisation; these tell us much about "the way things are done around here"!

Ultimately the investigation of possible alternative futures needs to be brought in to the strategic dialogue. Taking the information so far discovered about both value-generating and value-enabling activity, you can create your own version of the "model of model of self" – the simulation environment where the options and possibilities can be explored. That exploration is conditioned by the identity of the organisation, the values and beliefs that underpin its decision-making. Where there is tension, and there should be tension, it can be addressed through reference to identity in the conversation called the "trialogue".

How is the trialogue constituted?

The trialogue brings together information from the "outward-looking" enabling process and the "inward-looking" enabling process into a conversation in which decisions can be made about things to do in the future. Is that being done with a sense of integration of the "whole system", or are partial or functional decisions being made which optimise one element while damaging another? Typically the value-generating processes constitute the greater part of the organisation, the bigger budgets and the dominant voices. The challenge with this is that it draws the conversation mainly towards the short term, a better version of now rather than any more substantial rethink.

You need to establish what, if any, mechanisms exist for these conversations to happen and how the implications of one with another are understood and resolved. In a perfect world, you will find yourself in an ongoing and coherent conversation about the whole future as the basis of all decision-making. More likely you will see functionally oriented business cases presented to boards and/or executive teams in which proposals compete for time and money (winners and losers) rather than complement for enhanced effectiveness. Lots of analysis will have been done but no synthesis.

If the trialogue is not in existence, then you need to determine how strategic decisions are being made.

Arrow XL: the hackathon

Joining Arrow XL, James Robbins was charged with the task to "transform the organisation, its systems, its processes, its IT, its profitability". The company has a long history peppered with changes of ownership and underinvestment in the processes and systems essential to reducing costs and increasing performance in the digital age.

After the initial investigatory activity, it was clear that a substantial shift was needed in the way that the organisation undertook its work and, because the organisation had been so closed off to innovation, that it needed to be inspired by insights from the wider world. It was not that the people were not capable, but simply that their exposure to innovation and challenge was very limited.

Rather than pursuing a typical consulting engagement route, James decided to really open matters up and run a data hackathon. A team comprised of a pair of facilitators, James, key executives from Arrow and myself as GPF to the whole was established, and a hackathon event designed. A prize was offered for the best insight that could be gained in a two-day time period – comprising both cash and the opportunity to partner with Arrow in addressing the problem.

Invitations were sent to organisations and individuals, and the whole event was promoted on social media. Meanwhile a large historic data set was extracted, cleaned up, anonymised and made available on a dedicated server ready for analysis.

Six teams entered the event: one traditional Big Four accounting firm, two young tech start-ups, a university research team, a team of process and data scientists and one individual cybernetician. Most were on site for the event, but the university worked remotely, and one of the start-ups was using a remote team in Russia. They were given insight to the challenge, access to the data, access to the key executives who run the business and the delivery drivers and warehouse staff, all of whom were available throughout the time.

At the end of the second day each team presented its insights and findings both to the Arrow team and to each other. A number of really useful insights to the problems of process, performance management, routing, depot and warehouse location, information management and distribution were brought to the table. Subsequently three of the organisations are now working with Arrow XL. Most importantly the process, which engaged people from across the Arrow XL organisation, not only opened up their eyes to what they could be doing but, critically, demonstrated that they were themselves valuable; they were (and are) significant contributors to solving the problem. The insights were valuable; the sense of engagement for staff invaluable.

The common responses to these questions are that the only point at which the whole organisation comes together as a coherent whole is in the board meeting. The tensions are not then actively managed, and measurement of performance is about short-term financial results having little, if anything, to do with long-term sustainability.

How is autonomy sustained?

It is important to understand whether autonomy is being managed or if there is just an embedded, historically driven "scheme of delegation" which acts as its proxy. A scheme of delegation is important, but it also has to be meaningful.

This needs to be considered in the context of the decision points in the structure: do they align with the processes? Are they consistent with the needs? Do they cause delays? Are too many requests for permission being passed up and down the command chain, or, alternatively, is too much local action being taken either despite the rules or in the absence of any? Or is there a bit of both? That is surprisingly common. The "rules" don't work, so people work round them or through them! It is important to comprehend *why* this is happening!

It is rare to find in any organisation that a deliberate and conscious decision has been made about levels of autonomy other than in relation to delegation of financial decision-making (and it is common to find with finance that the cash sums are small). It is worth investigating the extent to which this has been thought about and to determine the real scope of autonomy and whether that is understood.

Practical autonomy and invisible outcome

In one organisation I considered, a particular individual had signing authority for cash disbursements up to £500 – a reasonable but modest sum which allowed for local purchases of essential material supplies. However, his practical autonomy, the real difference he could make to the organisation, rested in his ability to decide other things. In the particular instance, as a Health and Safety Manager, he was responsible for determining the frequency of refresh training for a number of key processes (manual handling, working at heights, safe methods of working) in an organisation where process failure could easily kill. In reviewing this he had determined, without reference to anyone else, that the frequency of refresh training should be doubled, i.e. that each individual should attend a half-day workshop on each topic twice per annum instead of once. The implication of that was a doubling of the amount of training to be provided, doubling of the backfill required to ensure that work was completed and a commensurate increase in overtime working to compensate. The "cash cost" of the decision was around £250k per annum, some 500 times his signing authority for expenditure. I cannot say whether his judgement was right or wrong; I can say that his decision was made without any assessment of the financial consequences (or any other organisational consequences, e.g. disrupted shift patterns) of the proposed change and without reference to the legal and regulatory requirements with which his particular organisation was bound to comply.

This is but one of many instances where autonomy may be inappropriately used. However, it is far more common to find that it is unnecessarily constrained. Consider using the framework for autonomy provided in chapter 7 as the basis of assessing this aspect.

How is information provided? Technology and systems

The next area for consideration is the information systems and technology, that is, the software applications, the hardware and the networks. You need to determine first whether these are consistent with the orientation of the organisation; functionally oriented organisations usually have functionally oriented IT! Integration is commonly achieved through a "business warehouse" or "business intelligence" application, and more frequently it is done by individuals using spreadsheets. It is important to grasp how this is done and understand the following:

- What are the consequences for workload?
- What are the consequences for cost?
- What are the consequences for data and decision integrity?

In one recent case we determined that the finance function was too large and had been driven by the inadequacy of information systems. Making sense of the data demanded a lot of time and cost a lot of money and added no value!

You should also at this point take a look at the technology and hardware:

- Does it appear to be consistent with the needs of the users?
- Do people complain about their various devices?
- Is speed of response of the systems commensurate with the needs of the business?
- Is hardware compatible with processes?
- Does it get in the way, leading to workarounds?
- Does it make things simple?

A good source of information is to enquire about recent information system and technology projects in the organisation. How did they go? Do people have better information as a result of them and therefore find it easier to do their jobs, or are they simply following the old process on a new machine? What you are trying to understand is what information benefit is being achieved from the investments! Information provision is the point of the systems and the hardware.

A further test is that of data integrity:

- Does every application that uses a particular data set share it, or are there multiple versions of the truth?
- Are there multiple applications dedicated to carrying out similar activities (or separate aspects of the same activity)?
- How is the data brought together?
- Are there different ways of measuring or characterising something depending on who is using it and for what purpose?
- If there are, do those differences make sense?
- Is each complete and accurate in its own right, or are there evident weaknesses?
- How is information provided and brought together in a coherent manner to inform decisions?

The answers to these questions will tell you a lot about the size of the challenge you are dealing with and the scope of the change project that will be needed. The nearer to "one version of the truth" the organisation shows itself to be, the smaller the problem!

Is information valued: is reporting meaningful?

This is a critical area. Given that information, the way it is captured, stored, utilised, generates the potential opportunity for becoming an intelligent organisation, you need to consider whether the information systems are fully aligned and integrated to the organisational processes. Or do they sit alongside them, useful but not fully embedded? Ask about the last two or three information system projects: were they technically biased, organisationally biased or informationally biased? I asked a group of master's students about the most recent information systems projects in their nine separate organisations. Every one of them had delivered a "technology" improvement, but none had delivered any information benefit.

Given the answers to those first questions, explore how information is valued by your organisation:

- Does it recognise information as having value in its own right?
- Is there an understanding or appreciation of the value of the information?
- Does it explicitly make an issue of exploiting the value of its information?
- Does it account for value realisation in any change or improvement projects?

Ask someone to demonstrate information value and show how it has been or is being realised.

Now you can consider the outputs of the system – and here you should avoid being sucked into particular parts or technology or applications. A helpful starting point is to gain sight of the last set of management reports. Are you presented with a neat set of management accounts, perhaps accompanied by output reports from each function (HR, safety, operations, sales, production) or a set of information which is customer process oriented and integrated, dealing with all aspects of the process and addressing the customer outcomes? Are customers represented as a "nuisance" or the whole reason the organisation exists?

If you found a functionally oriented organisation chart, it is highly likely you will get functionally oriented reports. Ask how the reports are compiled. Are they produced in a single operation from a single source, or are they formulated in free-form documents in which the data has, in effect, become unstructured because it is embedded in the storytelling?

The evidence builds, it demonstrates a consistent picture.

Performance management

Finally, although you probably know the answer by now because you have seen the reports, have a look at how performance is being managed. Is it aggregated into an overall view of process performance or presented in separate, functionally oriented and essentially financial reports? Is it backward looking and reactive or forward looking and pre-emptive? Review the agendas and minutes for management meetings. What was the focus of concern? Was it explanation of the past or preparation for the future? If both, where was the balance of attention? How was information about past performance used to help think about and understand performance in the future?

A common finding is that decisions are, primarily, made using only the financial data, and it is that for which individuals are held to account. However, as has been suggested earlier in the book, financial outcomes are a consequence of other activities, so it is important to find out how those other activities are included in the dialogue. It is not uncommon to find that they are not.

Recursion

All of the work you have undertaken so far has been about the whole of the organisation or, perhaps, the whole of the relevant part of the organisation. You have a diagnosis at that level.

One of the great economies of the Intelligent Organisation is that the same set of questions can be asked about any particular higher or lower order unit. These questions enable you to consider things at any organisational level.

Prognosis: the future you are currently in

While that is necessarily a quick romp through the exploration, your version should be much richer in data than mine! The exploration element of the diagnosis is roughly complete at this point. Enough can be known through the questions asked (and all the others that will fall out of asking them) to be able to offer a prognosis of the future of the organisation. I cannot speak for your particular example, but in all those I have looked at, there has always been a substantial gap between where they are and where they could be – and that gap has always contained more than enough value to compensate for the cost of closing it.

It is usually most helpful as you complete the first iteration to line up your thoughts around a few themes. In each case adopt a position *and* have reasons:

- Is the business orientated to itself or its customer?
- Is it managed functionally or through its processes?
- Is the language used internally or externally focused?
- Is information provision considered in terms of its cost or its value?
- Is information functionally segregated or integrated with processes?
- Is control centralised or distributed?
- What is the focus of management? Is it biased towards fixing the past or creating the future?

Some of your views will be subjective, but much will be evidenced by the things you have found out on the way through.

Compare your findings with the idealised Intelligent Organisation in all its aspects and reflect on the gap (if any!). You have enough information to determine whether or not the organisation responds to those principles, and if it doesn't you have a good initial idea of the opportunity. Essentially, and I am being deliberately extreme, you should be able to make one of two statements:

> This is an organisation whose people and processes are customer oriented; it understands and exploits the value of integrated information and uses it to distribute control. It has a healthy balance of managing the present and creating the future, and tensions are resolved through a strong sense of identity.
>
> Insert your evidence here. . . .

Or

> This is an organisation whose people and functions are internally oriented; it regards information provision as a cost and seeks to minimise it to the detriment of effective decision-making with those decisions mainly made remotely from the customer. It is focused on the identification and rectification of past mistakes and as a consequence is prone to being overtaken by events.
>
> Insert your evidence here. . . .

Most organisations will, of course, have elements of both. As you build the evidence base to support the assertion, it is OK to modify the overall thinking!

By understanding the dynamics of the situation as you perceive it and in the light of your knowledge of what could be, you should now be able to make a number of useful, evidence-based assertions about the future of the organisation.

The future you are currently in is a projection or extrapolation of the current performance set in the context of the changing environment. Assertions, sometimes entertaining, sometimes disturbing, can be made about the likely result of the organisation either not changing at all or carrying on down a particular path. There is always a point sometime in the near future when it will go bankrupt, when the key staff will all retire, when critical systems will or may become unavailable, when the market will shift irretrievably or a competitor or new threat can be expected to emerge. The ability to make that assertion in the light of grounded information about the current position is usually enough to grasp attention!

How would it be if. . .

Before you proceed to share your thoughts and findings with a colleague (or two) it is probably worth at least beginning to think about the future. It is one thing to be able to offer a critique of the current situation; it is another matter again to offer a way forward and receive more positive responses from your colleagues. Nobody likes to be told they are doing a bad job. Most will enjoy a vivid picture of a better future.

Rooted in the critique you have just created, you can develop an initial vision of the future. Think about what success would look like and make that vivid: bring it to life with examples of things that would happen and of things that would no longer happen. Understand and express how it would address identified deficiencies and create new opportunities, and, very importantly, begin to develop an idea of the financial consequences of the things that you think should change. But remember that there are consequences, products of change in other aspects of the organisation. The finances cannot be delivered without the process, behavioural, structural and informational changes that enable them.

Think also about how you will engage people. How will you share your concerns and explore theirs? How will you validate your work so far, and how will you challenge "the way we do things round here" and develop a robust business case for change? What do you believe will (or should) be the hard and soft benefits, and how will they be achieved?

For me, the opportunity for most organisations is immense, but so is the challenge!

Conclusion

These same questions drive each iteration of the engagement methodology. They are the key substance of the events and can be asked at every organisational level (whole organisation, process, task, procedure) and with every level of employee. So, whether we are considering the whole organisation, one process, factory or unit, or looking at an individual part or single employee, we have a language and process for diagnosis.

As you progress through the cycles of investigation, the detail underpinning each element should become clearer. However, it is important to realise in undertaking this process of enquiry that simply by asking the questions we have influenced the organisation.

Summary

I like to imagine an organisation existing in a state of Zen-like calm. Reality will be that the co-evolution of the organisational environment and the organisation itself must be dynamic and that those of us charged with managing must learn to deal with that dynamism. We are not, though, victims of circumstance. By taking responsibility for leadership, by understanding and holding to the purpose of the organisation, by active management to anticipate, provoke and guide the response to external changes, we can evolve towards Intelligent Organisation.

REFERENCES

Ackoff, R.L., (1981) *Creating the Corporate Future*, Wiley, New York, NY.

Alpaydin, E., (2016) *Machine Learning*, Massachusetts Institute of Technology Press, Cambridge, MA.

Ansoff, I., (1987) *Corporate Strategy*, Revised Edition, Penguin, London.

Ashby, W.R., (1952) *Design for a Brain*, Chapman Hall, London.

Beckford, J., (1993a) *The Viable System Model: A More Adequate Tool for Practising Management*, Ph.D. Thesis, University of Hull.

Beckford, J., (1993b) A process for the entrepreneurial decision? *Entrepreneurship, Innovation and Change*, Vol. 2, No. 2, Plenum, New York, NY.

Beckford, J., (1994) Entropy and entrepreneurship: The centralisation of capital as a barrier to innovatory behaviour, *Entrepreneurship, Innovation and Change*, Vol. 3, No. 1, Plenum, New York, NY.

Beckford, J., (2017) *Quality*, 4th Edition, Routledge, London.

Beer, S., (1959) *Cybernetics and Management*, Wiley, Chichester.

Beer, S., (1966) *Decision and Control*, Wiley, Chichester.

Beer, S., (1974) *Designing Freedom*, Wiley, Chichester.

Beer, S., (1979) *The Heart of Enterprise*, Wiley, Chichester.

Beer, S., (1981) *Brain of the Firm*, Wiley, Chichester.

Beer, S., (1985) *Diagnosing the System for Organisations*, Wiley, Chichester.

Beer, S., (1993) *World in Torment: A Time Whose Idea Must Come*, Presidential Address to the Triennial Conference of the World Organisation of Systems and Cybernetics, New Delhi, India.

Bender, R. & Ward, K., (2008) *Corporate Financial Strategy*, 3rd Edition, Elsevier Butterworth-Heinemann, Oxford.

Beynon-Davies, P., (2013) *Business Information Systems*, Palgrave MacMillan, London.

Borges, J.L., (1962) *The Library of Babel in Labyrinths*, Trans. D.A. Yates & J.E. Irby, New Directions, New York, NY.

Brynjolfsson, E. & McAfee, A., (2014) *The Second Machine Age*, Norton & Company, New York, NY.

Canal and River Trust, (2018) *Annual Report and Accounts 2017/18*, Canal and River Trust.

Carr, N., (2003) IT doesn't matter, *Harvard Business Review*, Vol. 81, No. 5, 2003, pp. 41–49.

Checkland, P.B., (1981) *Systems Thinking, Systems Practice*, Wiley, Chichester.

Churchill, W., (2008) *Churchill by Himself*, Ed. R. Langworth, Ebury Press, London.

Clausewitz, C. von, (1832) *On War* [Von Krieg], Indexed Edition, Eds. M. Howard & P. Paret, Princeton University Press, Princeton, NJ, 1984, p. 87.

Clemson, B., (1984) *Cybernetics: A New Management Tool*, Abacus Press, Kent.

Conant, R.C. & Ashby, W.R., (1970) Every good regulator of a system must be a model of that system, *International Journal of Systems Science*, Vol. 1, No. 2, pp. 89–97.

Council for Science and Technology, (2009) *A National Infrastructure for the 21st Century*.

Dennis, P., (2007) *Lean Production Simplified*, Productivity Press, New York, NY.

Drucker, P., (1969) *The Age of Discontinuity*, Oxford, UK: Butterworth Heinemann.

Drucker, P., (1986) *Innovation and Entrepreneurship*, Pan Books, London.

Dudley, P., (2000) *Quality Management or Management Quality? An Adaptive Model of Organisation as the Basis of Organisational Learning and Quality Provision*, Ph.D. Thesis, The University of Hull.

Durkheim, E., (1893) *Division of Labour in Society*, Trans. W.D. Halls, Free Press, New York, NY, 1997.

Einstein, A., (1946) Atomic Education Urged by Einstein, *The New York Times*, May.

Eliot, T.S., (1934) *The Rock*, Faber & Faber, London.

Fayol, H., (1916) *General and Industrial Management*, Ed. S.R.L. Dunod, Paris, Trans. C. Storrs, Pitman, London, 1949.

Feigenbaum, A.V., (1986) *Total Quality Control*, McGraw-Hill, New York, NY.

Flood, R.L. & Jackson, M., (1991) *Creative Problem Solving*, Wiley, Chichester.

Goldacre, B., (2013) *Bad Pharma*, Fourth Estate, Harper Collins, London.

Goodwin, P. & Wright, G., (2004) *Decision Analysis for Management Judgement*, Wiley, Chichester.

Goulding, F. & Shaughnessy, H., (2017) *Flow*, Flow Academy, London.

Greengard, S., (2015) *The Internet of Things*, Massachusetts Institute of Technology Press, Cambridge, MA.

Hammer, M. & Champy, J., (1993) *Reengineering the Corporation*, Nicholas Brealey, London.

Handy, C., (1985) *The Future of Work*, Blackwell, Oxford.

Handy, C., (1989) *The Age of Unreason*, Century Hutchinson, London.

Harper, W.M. & Lim, H.C., (1982) *Operational Research*, Pitman, London.

Herzberg, F., Mauser, B. & Synderman, B.B., (1959) *The Motivation to Work*, 2nd Edition, Wiley, New York, NY.

Hills, J., (2015) *Good Times, Bad Times*, Policy Press, Bristol.

Hislop, D., (2013) *Knowledge Management in Organizations: A Critical Introduction*, Oxford University Press, Oxford.

HM Government, (2011) *The Cabinet Manual*, Crown Copyright, London.

HM Treasury, (2015) Valuing infrastructure spend: Supplementary guidance to the Green Book. https://assets.publishing.service.gov.uk/government/uploads/system/uploads/attach ment_data/file/417822/PU1798_Valuing_Infrastructure_Spend_-_lastest_draft.pdf!

Huff, D., (1991) *How to Lie with Statistics*, Penguin, London.

Hutber, P., (1973) City Editor, Hutber's Law, *Sunday Telegraph*.

Jackson, T.W., (2015) *The Connected Jungle and The Digital Tree*, Inaugural Lecture, Loughborough University, Loughborough, Leicestershire.

Johnson, G. & Scholes, K., (2007) *Exploring Corporate Strategy*, Prentice-Hall, Harlow.

Joseph Rowntree Reform Trust, (2009) *Daily Telegraph*, March.

Kahnemann, D., (2011) *Thinking, Fast and Slow*, Penguin, New York, NY.

Kaplan, J., (2015) *Humans Need Not Apply*, Yale University Press, New Haven, CT.

Kaplan, R.S. & Norton, D.P., (1992) The balanced scorecard: Measures that drive performance, *Harvard Business Review*, January-February, pp. 71–79.

Knott, G., (1991) *Financial Management*, Macmillan, London.

Kotler, P. & Armstrong, G., (2013) *Principles of Marketing*, 15th Edition, Pearson, London.

Latham, R. & Williams, M., (1978) *The Illustrated Pepys*, University of California Press, Oakland, CA.

Lewin, K., (1947) Frontiers in group dynamics, in D. Cartwright (Ed.), *Field Theory in Social Science*, Social Science Paperbacks, London.

Lindsay, A.D., (Trans.) (1906) *Plato, The Republic*, Everyman, London.

Lorenzo, O., et al., (2011) *The Long Conversation*, Palgrave Macmillan, London.

Lynn, M., (2015) Taking Over the World? Tech Giants Blowing Billions, *Daily Telegraph*, Business Section, London, 20th February.

MacCormick, J., (2012) *9 Algorithms That Changed the Future*, Princeton University Press, Princeton, NJ.

Malik, O., (2008) *The Grown-Ups' Book of Risk*, New Insight Press, Malmesbury, Wiltshire.

Maltz, M., (2001) *The New Psycho-Cybernetics*, Prentice-Hall, New York, NY.

Maslow, A., (1970) *Motivation and Personality*, 2nd Edition, Harper & Row, New York, NY.

Maturana, H.R. & Varela, F.J., (1987) *The Tree of Knowledge*, Shambhala, Boston, MA.

Mayo, E., (1949) *The Social Problems of an Industrial Civilisation*, Routledge & Kegan Paul, London.

Mazzucato, M., (2018) *The Entrepreneurial State*, Penguin, London.

McGregor, D., (1960) Theory X and theory Y, in D.S. Pugh (Ed.), *Organization Theory, Selected Readings*, 3rd Edition, Penguin, London, 1990.

Mill, J.S., (1974) *On Liberty*, Pelican, London.

Mischel, W., (2014) *The Marshmallow Test*, Bantam Press, Random House, London.

Moore, G.E., (1965) Cramming more components onto integrated circuits, *Electronics*, Vol. 38, No. 8, pp. 114–117.

Moore, P., (1986) *Basic Operational Research*, 3rd Edition, Pitman, London.

Murphy Paul, A., (2005) *The Cult of Personality Testing*, Free Press, Simon & Schuster, New York, NY.

News, (2014) *Times Higher Education*, No. 2181, p. 10, 4th December.

Oakland, J.S., (2003) *Total Quality Management*, Butterworth-Heinemann, Oxford.

Oakland, J.S., (2019) *Statistical Process Control*, 7th Edition, Routledge, London.

Ohno, T., (1988) *Toyota Production System*, Productivity Press, New York, NY.

Pagnamenta, R., (2018) Are Emails Destined to Go the Way of Telegrams, Faxes and Pagers? *The Telegraph*, p. 2, London, 6th December.

Pemberton, M., (2014) *Stop Smoking with CBT*, Vermillion, London.

Peters, S., (2012) *The Chimp Paradox*, Vermilion, Random House, London.

Peters, T. & Waterman, R., (1982) *In Search of Excellence*, Harper Collins, New York, NY.

Pitchford, D., (1984) *Footloose*, Paramount Studios.

Porter, M., (1980) *Competitive Strategy*, Free Press, Macmillan, New York, NY.

Pugh, D.S. & Hickson, D.J., (1989) *Writers on Organisations*, Penguin, London.

Reichheld, F. & Markey, R., (2011) The ultimate question 2.0, Harvard Business School Publishing.

Robb, F., (1989) Cybernetics and suprahuman autopoietic systems, *Systems Practice*, Vol. 2, No. 1, Plenum, New York, NY.

Sampson, A., (1993) *The Essential Anatomy of Britain*, Coronet, London.

Schein, E., (1988) *Organisational Psychology*, Prentice-Hall, Hillsdale, NJ.

Schwab, K., (2017) *The Fourth Industrial Revolution*, World Economic Forum, Geneva, Switzerland.

Seddon, J., (2005) *Freedom from Command and Control*, Productivity Press, New York, NY.

Seddon, J., (2008) *Systems Thinking in the Public Sector*, Triarchy Press, Axminster, Devon.

Senge, P., (1993) *The Fifth Discipline*, Century Business, London.

Shingo, S., (1987) *The Sayings of Shigeo Shingo*, Trans. A.P. Dillon, Productivity Press, New York, NY.

Silver, N., (2012) *The Signal and the Noise*, Penguin, London.

Slack, N., et al., (1995) *Operations Management*, Pitman, London.

Smith, A., (1776) *The Wealth of Nations*, Everyman Edition, Random Century, London, 1991.

Taguchi, G., (1987) *Systems of Experimental Design*, Vols. 1 and 2, Unipub/Kraus International Publications, New York, NY.

Taleb, N., (2010) *The Black Swan*, Penguin, London.

Tapscott, D. & Tapscott, D., (2018) *Blockchain Revolution*, Penguin, London.

Taylor, F., (1911) *The Principles of Scientific Management*, Plimpton Press, Norwood, MA.

Tennent, J. & Friend, G., (2005) *Guide to Business Modelling*, Profile Books, London.

Titcomb, J. & Pagnamenta, R., (2018) Watchdogs Close in on Silicon Valley Giants, *Sunday Telegraph*, Business & Money, London, 16th December.

Torrington, D., Hall, L. & Taylor, S., (2008) *Human Resource Management*, 7th Edition, Pearson, London.

Tucker, B., (1887) The Method of Anarchy, *Liberty*, 18th June.

Tucker, M., (1996) *Successful Process Management in a Week*, Headway, Hodder & Stoughton, London.

Ulrich, W., (1983) *Critical Heuristics of Social Planning*, Haupt Verlag AG, Falkenplatz, Bern.

Vose, D., (1996) *Quantitative Risk Analysis*, Wiley, Chichester.

Warwick, K., (2012) *Artificial Intelligence*, Routledge, London.

Weber, M., (1924) Legitimate authority and bureaucracy, in D.S. Pugh (Ed.), *Organisation Theory, Selected Readings*, 3rd Edition, Penguin, London, 1990.

The Week in Higher Education, (2014) *Times Higher Education*, 14th August.

Weiner, N., (1948) *Cybernetics: Or Control and Communication in the Animal and the Machine*, Massachusetts Institute of Technology, Cambridge, MA.

Weiner, N., (1954) *Cybernetics and Society*, Da Capo Press, Boston, MA.

Wilson, T.D., (2002) *Strangers to Ourselves, Discovering the Adaptive Unconscious*, Harvard College, Cambridge, MA.

Woodward, J., (1965) *Industrial Organization: Theory and Practice*, Oxford University Press, Oxford.

Web References

1   www.bbc.co.uk/news/business-46142025, 9/11/2018

2   https://ico.org.uk/for-organisations/guide-to-the-general-data-protection-regulation-gdpr/, 27/11/2018

3   www.enterpriseappstoday.com/business-intelligence/why-most-business-intelligence-projects-fail-1.html, 27/11/2018

4   www.cfo.com/printable/article.cfm/3006814, 2/4/2015

5   https://publications.parliament.uk/pa/cm201719/cmselect/cmtrans/1163/116304.htm#_idTextAnchor004, 7/12/2018

6   http://orr.gov.uk/__data/assets/pdf_file/0018/39042/inquiry-into-may-2018-timetable-disruption-september-2018-findings.pdf, 7/12/2018

7   www.itv.com/news/2018-07-30/northern-rail-reintroducing-75-of-cancelled-services-after-timetable-chaos/, 7/12/2018

8   http://orr.gov.uk/news-and-media/press-releases/2018/orr-lays-out-timetable-recommendations-to-improve-service-for-passengers/, 7/12/2018

9   https://corporate.walmart.com/our-story/our-business/, 27/12/2018

10   www.microsoft.com/en-us/news/inside_ms.aspx/, 27/12/2018

11   www.jaguarlandrover.com/2016/reports-and-financial-downloads/, 27/12/2018

12   www.merriam-webster.com/dictionary/subsidiarity/, 27/12/2018

13   www.ted.com/talks/hilary_cottam_social_services_are_broken_how_we_can_fix_them#t-909265, 20/12/2018

14   www.spectator.co.uk/2016/07/why-go-into-politics/, 11/1/2019

15   www.bbc.co.uk/news/uk-politics-44539946, 11/1/2019

16   www.telegraph.co.uk/news/2016/04/11/four-students-cleared-of-raping-woman-at-college-ball/

17   www.independent.co.uk/news/uk/crime/modern-slavery-drugs-london-county-lines-gangs-swansea-girl-teenage-jailed-a8303691.html

18   www.swrocu.org.uk/

19   www.legislation.gov.uk/ukpga/2011/13/contents/enacted

20   www.npcc.police.uk/documents/Policing%20Vision.pdf

21   https://ccednet-rcdec.ca/files/ccednet/pdfs/2009-SROI_Guide_2009.pdf, 21/1/2019

22   http://beckfordconsulting.com/wp-content/uploads/2014/05/Reimagining-the-Railway-VF.pdf, 21/1/2019

23   http://beckfordconsulting.com/wp-content/uploads/2018/08/Rail-Adapt-report.pdf, 23/1/2019

24   http://beckfordconsulting.com/wp-content/uploads/2014/03/Introducing-VSMethod.pdf, 2/4/2015

25   http://beckfordconsulting.com/wp-content/uploads/2013/08/Hull060213.pdf, 23/1/2019

26   http://beckfordconsulting.com/Papers/Towards%20a%20Participative%20Methodology%20for%20Viable%20System%20Diagnosis.pdf, 29/1/2019

27   http://beckfordconsulting.com/wp-content/uploads/2014/05/Reimagining-the-Railway-VF.pdf, 1/3/2019

INDEX

Note: page numbers for figures are in *italic* type.

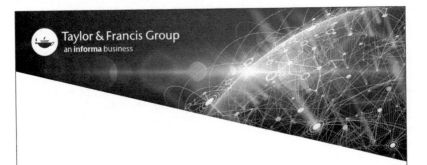